The Learning Perspective

Allan Christensen (ed.)
Søren Keldorff
Erik Laursen
Jens Lind
Ove Mølvadgaard
Kjeld Nielsen
Jan Brødslev Olsen
Søren Voxted

Aalborg University Press

LEO-serien no. 35

The Learning Perspective

Authors:
  Allan Christensen (ed.)
  Søren Keldorff
  Erik Laursen
  Jens Lind
  Ove Mølvadgaard
  Kjeld Nielsen
  Jan Brødslev Olsen
  Søren Voxted

© The authors and Aalborg University Press, 2008

Cover: Watercolour by Gunilla Rosenberg
  Graphical arrangement by Guldbæk Grafisk

LEO-serien no. 35

Lay out: Inge Andersen

Printed by Toptryk Grafisk ApS, 2008

ISBN: 978-87-7307-945-4

Distribution:
Aalborg University Press
Niels Jernes Vej 6B
9220 Aalborg
Denmark
Phone: (+45) 99 40 71 40, Fax: (+45) 96 35 00 76
E-mail: aauf@forlag.aau.dk
www.forlag.aau.dk

All rights reserved. No part of this book may be reprinted or reproduced or utilized in any form or by any electronic, mechanical, or other means, now known or hereafter invented, including photocopying and recording, or in any information storage or retrieval system, without permission in writing from publishers, except for reviews and short excerpts in scholarly publications.

Preface

Over the last ten years, the concept *The Learning Organisation* has attracted a lot of attention. From private companies and social institutions. From universities and institutions of higher education. The background for this attention is well-known; an accelerated rate of change in society makes heavy demands on companies and social institutions to change, continuously and rapidly, which in turn makes them demand the same from their employees and managers. The attention is also evident in the many interesting books treating the concept the learning organisation. The authors of this book wish to be simultaneously loyal and critical in relation to the books treated in the following pages.
Besides a loyal and critical approach, the authors have wished to contribute with a book that takes its starting point in different kind of professional knowledge. The authors' ideal claim has been to illustrate application of the concept *the learning organisation* in relation to different ways to present problems. It has been necessary to make a number of choices and reject some choices in relation to the concept. We do not delude our self into thinking that it is possible to include most of the relevant literature about learning organisations, or that we will able to reach a conclusive evaluation. We will leave that to other authors. The modest goal of this book has been to show the strengths and weaknesses of the concept *the learning organisation* in relation to the overall development of society and organisations, to organisational and individual learning, to labour market, to management, to technological development etc.

Two books on the same topic appeared in Danish some years ago. It is our hope that the content of this book will bring us in dialogue with students and teachers at universities and institutions of higher education in other countries. The chapters have been updated in relation to new literature and new aspects of problems.

The authors would like to thank Inge Andersen for her extensive work in connection with the contributions and layout, Marianne Morell's never failing support in the genesis of this book and Marianne Risberg for a competent and very difficult work with the translation.

On behalf of the authors
Allan Christensen

Contents

Introduction 7

Chapter 1
The Dynamics of Organisational Learning
Significant Theoretical Elements.
by Allan Christensen.. 13

Chapter 2
Images of Learning
- and the Development of Learning Behaviour in Organisations.
by Erik Laursen 47

Chapter 3
Personal Development – for whose sake?
By Jan Brødslev Olsen.. 77

Chapter 4
The"Must" of Sensibility in the Knowledge Society.
On the Psychological Roots of Job Enrichment and the
Learning Organisation.
by Søren Keldorff 89

Chapter 5
The Labor Market and the Learning Organisation.
by Jens Lind 129

Chapter 6
Learning Environment in the Process Industry – Methods
and Results.
by Kjeld Nielsen and Ove Mølvadgaard 153

Chapter 7
Learning Organisations in Practice.
by Søren Voxted.. 187

Chapter 8
 The Institution HOME and the Concept of the Learning Organisation.
 by Allan Christensen..217

Conclusion 249

Authors 251

Introduction

The many books, articles and reports published in the last few years on *the learning organisation* have tended to concentrate either on the theoretical aspects of the concept or vision, or on how to establish a link between on one hand the various concepts and models and, on other, a concrete exemplified part of reality.

In this book we have chosen to let the theoretical and practical aspects of the concept *the learning organisation* take their point of departure in different professional areas' understanding of it. This means that the concept or the vision of the learning organisation is related to a societal level, to an organisational level and to an individual level whenever certain issues are considered within the different professional areas. It is not the intention of this book to cover all theoretical and practical aspects of the concept *the learning organisation*. Our perspective is a more modest one. It is, from different point of departure in different professional areas, to give examples of the ways in which the concept of the learning organisation can be expressed on these areas. The book is to be considered basically as a number of chapters and the authors "standpoint" as a part of a lager picture.

The chapters in this book intend to present the concept *the learning organisation* loyally and at the same time critical. However, the introduction and the conclusion depart from this dual approach. All conceivable, reasonable efforts can be made beforehand to change an organisation, but the really difficult exercise is to handle the issues which are difficult to identify. The most difficult exercise of all is probably to enter unknown areas when an organisation with learning-orientation and an orientation towards change is intent on learning within existing structures and well known areas.

The first chapter of the book "The Dynamics of Organisational learning – Significant Theoretical Elements."
by Allan Christensen.
The chapter deals with the setting for the emergence of the concept the learning organisation.
The chapter aim at uncover the concepts and models as they appear in the texts of three different authors. Finally, the chapter compares the authors' thoughts in relation to how companies and institutions can develop under the concept *the*

learning organisation. In this connection, the possibilities and difficulties for an "unfinished" organisation are outlined. First, the possibilities for establishing development-orientation and utilization of human resources is considered, and second the difficulties of keeping the organisation free from traditional control and administration i.e. from one-sided constructed management tools and from limiting possibilities by steering the course of activities and change into mainly well known areas.

Chapter 2, "Images of Learning – and the Development of learning behaviour in Organisations."
by Erik Laursen.
Chapter 2 takes its point of departure in two assumptions: First that learning is to day the most widespread generally accepted way to describe positive, personal changes in a society like the Danish. Second that the single most important reason for the considerable popularity and penetration enjoyed by the management and change concept *"The learning organisation"* since the nineties is that it manages to formulate a convergence of interests between the management's wish to optimise the organisations ability to change, e.g. through employees flexibility, and the employees wishes to be "the director for their own lives and producer of their own development".
The chapter especial focussed on the relationship between learning behaviour and understanding of learning. Its topics are various approaches to learning as facilitators or inhibitions of learning processes. Especially the form of collegiate learning happening through "structured and planned on-the-job learning". The chapter goes through six widely used "approaches to learning", and discusses the relative success of the different approaches to learning in organisation.

Chapter 3, "Personal development – for whose sake?"
By Jan Brødslev Olsen.
The author discusses the concept of personal development in the context of organisational learning. The concept is used in many different areas from basic training in social work and health care, from business courses and evening classes in psychology and communication, to job training for social security clients. Two main approaches immediately stand out. The first approach is *problem oriented*, dealing with the reparation functions, and it is typical for the public, social sector. The second main approach is *groth oriented*, dealing with development functions, and this approach is typical for the public sector of education, basic education as well as supplementary education, and for the private sector's multifarious businesses of education and consulting services. Personal development in the context of organisational learning will mainly focus

on the growth-oriented approach, but might also involve problem-oriented elements.

Chapter 4, "The "Must" of sensibility in the Knowledge society. On the Psychological Roots of Job Enrichment and the Learning Organisation"
by Søren Keldorff.
The author begins with some reflections on new and older knowledge. Déjà-vu is an expression used when you think you have seen something before. And many of today's popular HRM-hybrids: Job Enrichment and The Learning Organisation. They seem very similar to the themes and utopias of work Psychology which was introduced in a critical manner in the seventies, even though as theories and models they were old-fashioned at that point of time. A hasty conclusion might therefore be "Old wine, new bottles". The whole point of this chapter is the opposite. It wants us to consider the development of work demands as cumulative. True, some of the concepts may be the same. The main difference seems to be that time has caught up with the concepts – in the sense that it is now realisable. In this way, time forms a different horison for the working man: the possibility at long last to become a valid subject of his own working life, try to describe these demands on the individual through the use of the concept "sensitisation" and "sensibility" - to point out a new type of competence, one mobilising reason as well as feelings.

Chapter 5, "The Labour market and the Learning Organisation"
by Jens Lind.
Whether or not to adopt a strategy of a learning organisation management will take account for several factors of significance for the company. One of them being the development on the labour market; and that is what this chapter deals with. Does the labour market act as a facilitating or inhibiting factor in relation to chances of a company developing into the direction of a learning organisation? Conceptually and theoretically, the chapter investigates trends in the labour market connected with application of manpower in a functional flexible way. The chapter will refer to two Danish research projects uncovering the extent to which companies apply functional flexibility.

Chapter 6, "Learning environment in process Industry – Methods and results."
by Kjeld Nielsen and Ove Mølvadgaard.
This chapter presents a newly developed evaluation method and the results of a recently concluded evaluation investigation of a supplementary education program in a process industry. The evaluation method developed was used both to measure traditional effects of courses among participants in two groups

participating in different educational activities and learning courses aimed at qualifying them to operate a new plant construction. The method was also used in an evaluation of learning processes concerning working environments which, during the process, were exposed to great variation in stability and quality. On the background of the evaluation method developed and tested, one of the main conclusions is that stability and quality in the learning environment is created through the participants' active involvement in extensive and open communication between the participants.

Chapter 7, "Learning Organisations in Practice."
by Søren Voxted.
How many companies are learning organisations?
It is the aim of this chapter to answer the question and in addition find out also what characterises learning organisations. This is done by identifying learning organisations through the responses in a survey investigation that including 1.900 companies in construction, building and service.
The investigation shows that less than 10% of the companies comply with the definition used in this chapter to define learning organisations. In spite of this, they have attained good results in many areas, seen in relation to the rest of the trade. They have larger employment growth, their managements states their employees are more motivated and involved, and they cooperate with other companies and institutions to a greater extent. Finally, the investigation points out agreement between a series of theoretical features on learning organisations and practice in the companies identified as learning organisations.

Chapter 8, "The Institution HOME and the concept of the Learning Organisation"
by Allan Christensen.
In many Danish companies and institutions, employees as well as management have taken an interest in the vision or concept *the Learning Organisation*. This is also the case at the institution HOME, which is an institution for the physically and mentally handicapped in the southern part of Jutland. But in this case, the employees' and managers' interest has also included the application of the concept as a pattern for introducing changes aimed at improving the quality of life for the persons living in the institution, improving the institution as a work place, and improving the institution's future change-orientation. This chapter reports on the employees' and managers' efforts in the preparations for and the introduction of the first round of changes under the concept *the learning organisation.*

In this book *"The Learning Perspective"* the authors' different approaches to and understanding of learning, organisational learning and the concept *the learning organisation* are composed in such a way that they supplement and complement each other, reflecting the many-sidedness of the concept and vision of the learning organisation.

Chapter 1

The Dynamics of Organisational Learning - Significant Theoretical Elements

By Allan Christensen

Introduction

The learning organisation is a vision about the development potential of organisations. The vision embraces the most fundamental elements of organisations, which is why it has attracted attention from researchers and actors within organisations and institutions as well.

According to the common conception of model, the learning organisation is not a model for organisational change. On the other hand, the vision of the learning organisation can be seen as a coupling of several models, each and which, and in various combinations, deals with the possibilities of organisations for developing in accordance with the vision mentioned.

Since the early twentieth century, organisation researchers have engaged in a variety of topics related to organisational structures and processes, topics still prevalent in contemporary organisational research.

In effect of important sociological tendencies and related research interests much attention has been directed toward organisational processes. Organisational structures are still central to organisational sociological practice and research, but concurrently with growing demands for the changeability of organisations and institutions, focus has shifted toward organisational processes.

The organisational structure approach to research and practice in companies and institutions looks at norms, rules, routines, competence domains, and decision competence related to the sequence of actions in the organisation, whereas the organisational process approach focuses on the preconditions, planning, and coordination of actions. Nevertheless, the organisational structure is of fundamental import due to its ability to further or impede the development of preconditions, planning, and coordination of organisational processes and the outcome of actions.

The concept of organisational structure is primarily static. It is a fixed template for governing and controlling the way in which the organisation functions. In the organisational context, the concept of process is dynamic. Through organisational processes, i.e., through planning, action, and coordination resources and preconditions result in products or services. The process itself is dynamic, but it also adds dynamics to the organisation by virtue of the need for reconfiguring processes and meeting the demands for flexible processes and process coordination.

The new sociological tendencies indicate a shift in the environment from being stable to being characterised by multiple and rapid changes. For organisations this implies changes in the actors' interpretations. In an environment characterised by stability, the actors are, in general, more certain of their perceptions and interpretations. In an environment characterised by change and instability the foundations of actor interpretations are considerably more uncertain. Especially in the recent decades organisations have spent vast resources on developing positive attitudes toward change among employees and managers. It is in this context that new ways of organising activities and new areas of and procedures for learning have become topical.

Social Development and the Vision of the Learning Organisation

The vision of the learning organisation is about making the organisation oriented toward development and about making available, develops, and utilizes the great knowledge potential among employees, middle-managers, and managers. The backdrop to these attempts is changes in the environment. Virtually no organisations experience their environments as static and simple. Quite the contrary, most organisations experience their environments as threatening exactly because of the dynamics caused by extensive and rapid changes and accelerating complexity.

In recent year, many publications on the social development have discussed the concept of the "Information Society". The transition from industrial society to information society has in many ways been demanding and problematic - and still is. Having not yet completed the transition we are now facing another transition - from the information society to the knowledge society. This change project is conceived as:

> "The information society is actually only a step toward the knowledge society. New knowledge is consumed and diffused much faster than earlier. In effect our knowledge soon becomes obsolete. This has consequences for the competitiveness of organisations and the employability of people. Today knowledge is reduced to 50% in seven years, which makes it difficult for people around 40-45 to survive in the labour market if they only possess basic education." (Lindholm, 1995).

If organisations wish to achieve a reasonable status under these conditions they must be flexible and be able to manoeuvre appropriately in relation to the dynamics and complexity of the environment. Even though financing and budgeting are necessary for most organisations other resources are also important for interaction with the environment.

In the course of developing from the more traditional situation toward what has been termed the learning organisation, less priority is given to economy, financing, and organisational structure as the basis for management. Focus shifts toward the many organisational processes through which resources are gathered, established, and used to improve present and future goal achievement. This only requires a minimum of structure that can function as the core for coordination and integration of the organisational processes mentioned.

The following quotation reflects the process of knowledge production:

> "Knowledge is in the process of changing to become the strategically most importance resource whereas learning becomes the most important process – for the individual, for organisations, and for society. Therefore, society as a whole must re-evaluate how the production of knowledge takes place. This invites to an educational reform of historical dimensions. It will also be necessary to consider best way of using the new information technology to establish and spread knowledge in and among organisations and institutions in society. This assessment is necessary for being able to strengthen industries within which Denmark has international advantages and in order to create new industries that can make Denmark living." (Lindholm, 1995)

Lindholm (1995) also discusses the disadvantages of information technology. According to Lindholm, the development within information technology favours people that possess knowledge and are capable of processing information and knowledge. The development may result in polarisation between a highly educated, knowledge producing elite and a poorly educated group of unskilled and unemployed. Lindholm finds that there is a need for developing a new social strategy that focuses on new ways of training the weakest groups. This is, according to Lindholm, a precondition for utilizing information technology strategy, for long-term economic growth, and for social stability. He is undoubtedly right, but analysing his point in detail falls outside the scope of this chapter.

The Learning Organisation is Rooted in Sociological Tendencies

In the following we shall look at a series of sociological tendencies that has made topical both a strategic and an organisational approach to the process of change. The transformation from industrial society to information and knowledge society is characterised by a series of tendencies that have or may have direct impact on the way in which organisations and institutions function. It is the same tendencies that have made topical preparedness for strategic and organisational change.

The transformation of the industrial society to the information and knowledge society is characterised by the following changes:

Figure 1.1: Effects of the transformation industrial society to the information and knowledge society

---

Information technological development
- important for increasingly larger aspects of work
- growing demands for education
- more user-friendly technologies

Development of knowledge organisations
- growing number of knowledge organisations
- products, services and processes are becoming increasingly knowledge intensive
- the supply of products and services are becoming increasingly knowledge intensive

Educational development
- the scale of training is increasing
- diverse forms of continuous training
- increasing problems of polarisation

Development in management and managerial processes
- shift from emphasis on control to emphasis on flexibility and renewal
- shift from managing managers to supportive managers
- shift from reactive change to proactive change

Development in organisational forms
- shift from hierarchical to flexible forms
- shift from delimited to expansive forms
- shift from emphasis on structure to emphasis on processes

Development in the labor market
- growing emphasis on development of qualifications
- growing emphasis on individualisation and organisational orientation
- growing emphasis on flexibility in and among labor market sectors

Changed focus of market- and exchange orientation
- changed importance of the combination product and market
- growing internationalisation
- growing importance of combinations of public and private sector

---

These changes in social conditions are important for both large and small companies and institutions, for private and public organisations, and for companies and institutions producing goods, commodities, and services. In other words all organisations are effected by the embedded demand for changing in accordance with the social development. This is the major reason for the salient interest in the vision about the learning organisation among practitioners and researchers.

Development Oriented Organisations

In her book *The Change Masters – Corporate Entrepreneurs at Work* Kanter (1983) discusses the adaptability of organisations to extremely variable social and economic conditions. The book focuses on the conditions for and capabilities of organisations for being innovative.

Based on her findings from a study of 100 companies and case studies of ten key companies, Kanter tries to show what characterises innovative and non-innovative companies, respectively. Naturally, numerous factors have contributed to create these differences, but Kanter shows that factors related to human resources, participative approaches, and action plans are of fundamental significance for the innovativeness of companies.

The term innovation is often associated with technology – with new products and new production methods. But companies may produce many innovations that are neither products nor production methods. Such innovations may be important in themselves, or they may directly or indirectly affect existing products and production methods as well as product and productions methods in progress.

Kanter's (1983: 20-21) definition of innovation is broader:

> "Innovation refers to the process of bringing any new, problem solving idea into use. Ideas for reorganising, cutting costs, putting new budgeting systems, improving communication, or assembling products in teams are also innovations. Innovation is the generation, acceptance, and implementation of new ideas, processes, products, and services. It can occur in any part of the corporation, and it can involve creative use as well as original

invention. Application and implementation are central to this definition; it involves the capacity to change or adapt. And there can be many different kinds of innovations, brought about by many different kinds of people: the corporate equivalent of entrepreneurs."

The approach that creates innovation is tied to a particular way of seeing problems – integrative action – which is characterised as:

> "The willingness to move beyond received wisdom, to combine ideas from unconnected sources, to embrace change as an opportunity to test limits. To see problems integrative is to see them as wholes, related to larger wholes, and thus challenging established practices – rather than walling off a piece of experience and preventing it from being touched or affected by any new experience." (Kanter, 1983: 27)

Integrative thinking that results in change occurs more often in companies of integrative culture and structure, i.e., which support seeing problems as "wholes". It is characteristic of this type of organisations that they break up isolated organisational units, create mechanisms for exchange of information and new ideas across organisational boundaries, take into consideration the diversity of perspectives in making decisions, and support coherence and direction of the whole organisation. According to Kanter innovativeness flourishes in team oriented environments. The opposite of integrative thinking is *segmentalism*.

> "...it is concerned with compartmentalising actions, events, and problems and keeping each piece isolated from the others. Segmentalist approaches see problems as narrowly as possible, independently of their context, independently of their connections to any other problems. Companies with segmentalist cultures are likely to have segmented structures: a large number of compartments walled off from one another – department from department, level about from level below, field office from headquarters, labour from management, or men from women." (Kanter, 1983: 28).

Companies characterised by segmentalist thinking have difficulties in being innovative and managing change. Change confuses the clear division of the organisation and much energy is spent on embodying change and confines it to certain departments. Furthermore, this type of organisation strives to allow the existing structure to dominate the process of change isolated.

Control and governance are salient features of the segmentalist type of organisation. Taylor (1911) is the most prominent representative of control and governance. Structure and culture are separated. The same applies to problems and problem solutions. Rules and over-specification govern resources, making experimental operations almost impossible. Kanter's image of the segmentalist organisation is close to Burns and Stalker's (1961) mechanical organisation and Weber's bureaucratic organisation:

> "Segmentalism, then, is what keeps an organisation steady, on course, changing as little as possible, making only minimal adjustments. This style, this mode or organising protects the successful organisation against unnecessary change, ensures that it will repeat what it already "knows". For those activities which should be repeated – the areas of high certainty where routine, habitual action is efficient and desirable – segmentalism works.
> But segmentalism also makes it harder for the organisation to move beyond its existing capacity in order to innovate and improve."
> (Kanter 1983:31)

The message is clear: Organisations that are predominantly segmentalist limit their potential for extensive innovation. Even hard-core innovators are facing almost hopeless conditions. Moreover, such organisations are restricted in the possibilities for utilizing and disseminating embryonic innovations.

Later on we shall return to Kanter's recommendations for developing segmentalist organisations into integrative organisations. Kanter's perception of innovative organisations includes several important elements for developing the learning organisation.

Learning as the Point of Departure for Developing toward the Learning Organisation

Argyris and Schön (1987; 1996) also stress experience as fundamental for new individual learning. However, individuals base their actions on different experiences, both due to the fact that they have different experiences and because they form different systems of beliefs from similar experiences. Argyris and Schön refer to systems of beliefs or patterns of performance as theory-in-use. The concept is based on the authors' book *Theory of Action*. Theories of action are theories or fundamental assumptions underlying individual action. Argyris and Schön term such theories "espoused theories". The given action needs not comply with the theories, but theories that are implicit in the individual's performance are referred to as *theories-in-use*.

The individual may act inconsistently or in conflict with "espoused theories". Being part of a larger organisational context, the individuals' understanding of the structure and patterns of performance may be deficient.

In the case of collective learning, individual "espoused theories" must be brought to harmonise. This requires dialogue and discussion. Harmony cannot be dictated. Organisational learning presupposes both individual and collective learning. It is individuals who act and learn. Simultaneously, the organisation is the framework that either supports or impedes the interplay of individual and organisational learning. According to Argyris and Schön (1987) organisational learning can be single-looped or double-looped. In the former errors are corrected and problems solved within existing sets of norms and values. In effect, the organisation will only change in a reactive sense. In the latter case errors are corrected and problems solved simultaneously with existing norms and values being questioned. The individuals question their total set of "espoused theories". Why do we act in this way? Why do we solve problems in this way? This is the core of organisational learning and development. As Kofoed (1994:76) says:

> "The challenge is that the organisation's theories-in-use are not conflicting with the espoused theories, thus becoming a barrier to understanding the organisation and one's own role, and consequently a barrier to organisational learning and development."

The process of organisational learning includes elements from individual learning, informal collective learning, and formal organisational learning. There are many perceptions of individual learning. We have chosen to start from a model that understands individual learning as cyclic (van Hauen, Strandgaard & Kastberg, 1995). The cycle consists of experience, reflection, thinking, decision and action. The model entails feedback processes. Actions can be followed by experience accumulation and experiences may be subject to reflections in relation to certain actions. Similar feedback processes characterise shifts between the phases of thinking, decision, and action.

Figure 1.2: The organisational learning cycle

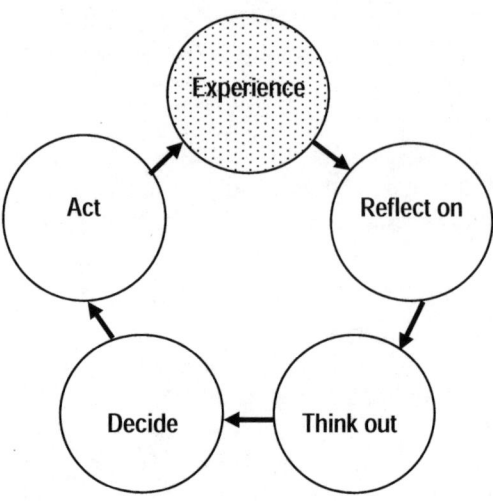

Several other scholars are discussing the same practical aspects of learning processes related to information technology systems.

In relation to external and internal effects and changes it is important to clarify whether the preconditions for reasonable reaction exist. Are organisational learning and development determined by traditional interpretations or by the organisation's way of functioning and its problems?

Concepts and Models of the Learning Organisation

The numerous books and articles on the learning organisation reflect that scholars engaged in the vision of the learning organisation operate with many different definitions of the concept of the learning organisation. Neergaard (1994) summarises the existing definitions.

According to Neergaard (1994) an organisation is a learning organisation if it contains one or several of these elements. The problem is, however, that the authors that Neergaard discusses start from both very narrow and very broad problems in their approach to the visions or juxtapositions of concepts of the learning organisation. Here we will confine ourselves to discuss only a few of the definitions and the models applied by the authors in question. Each of the authors signifies in their definitions and models what they find important for the concept of the learning organisation.

Below we shall discuss in detail how these scholars couple definitions, concepts, and models.

A. The learning company and the multiple possibilities for learning

Pedler, Burgoyne and Boydell (1991:1) define the learning organisation as:

> "A Learning Company is an organisation that facilitates learning of all its members and continuously transforms itself."

This definition emphasises support of all organisational members in learning and of the continuous transformation of the organisation itself. The book is consequential in that the model or juxtaposition of concepts reflects the definition. The authors are using different words for the model or juxtaposition of concepts depending on the organisational approach in focus, but they all comprise eleven dimensions that the authors find characteristic of the development toward the learning organisation. The basic form is the so-called *Blueprint*, which is a juxtaposition of the important factors in the development process. We shall take a closer look at this basic form. The eleven dimensions of the development process of the learning organisation are furthermore presented as similar to a puzzle and termed "the identikit" of the learning organisation. Finally, the dimensions are subsumed under the names of *fishbone*, *fir tree* and *fountain free* each symbolising a specific approach to organisational learning. Figure 1.3 illustrates the basic form *Blueprint* that we will discuss below.

Figure 1.3: Characteristics of the learning organisation ("Blueprint")

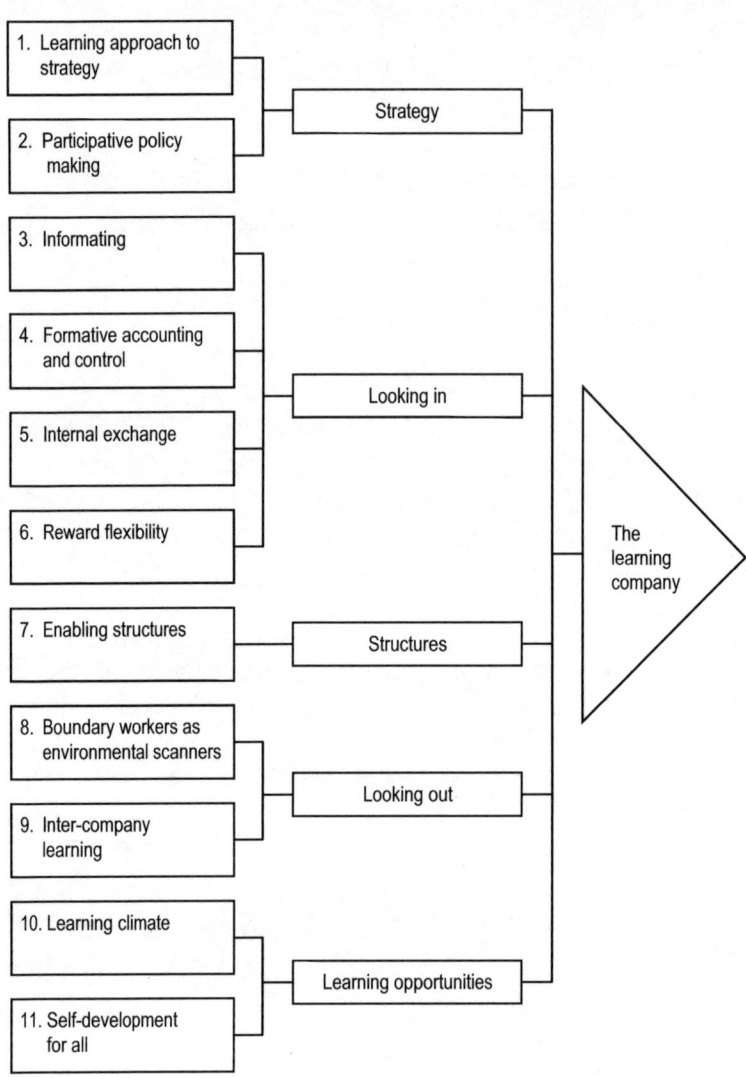

Source: Pedler, Burgoyne & Boydell 1991:25

In the book, Pedler, Burgoyne and Boydell are not accounting clearly for the interrelationship of various elements of the models – nor for the one termed *Blueprint*. Several of the sections in the book describe these relations randomly. Only the section "Glimpses of the Learning Company" suggests possible interrelationships among elements of the model. If you are looking for a starting and closing point in the model you are left to incorporate it yourself. If you want to determine the dynamic relations of the model more explicitly you have to import them from the so-called glimpses or introduce them yourself. This is both the strength and the weakness of the model.

There is no doubt that the elements included in the model are relevant, but nevertheless the model is difficult to work theoretically. Precisely because the contents of the individual elements and their interrelationships are left to the reader or the user to determine, the reader may easily shape the model to fit the most serious problems of the organisation.

It appears from the so-called *Blueprint* that structure is not given much attention. When structure is mentioned it is as enabling structure. Implicitly structures must enable the very diverse processes that individually and combined can contribute to the development toward the vision of the learning organisation. Thus the juxtaposition of concepts emphasises the importance of organisational processes.

Structure is about norms, rules, routines, relationships between superiors/subordinates, and information and communication channels whereas processes concern various types of behaviour that employees demonstrate in their targeted performance. Structure entails control and management while processes concern actual behaviour. With a view to processes, Pedler, Burgoyne and Boydell (1991) have advanced a model of energy flows in the organisation. The ideal process in the learning organisation is one that integrates that individual and the collective levels.

Figure 1.4: The energy flow model of the learning organisation

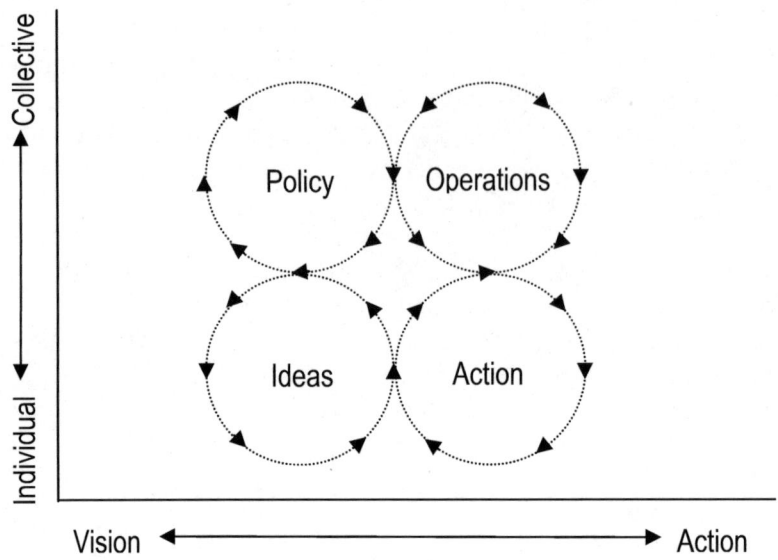

Source: Pedler, Burgoyne & Boydell 1991:32

B. The learning organisation and the five disciplines of learning

In "The Fifth Discipline" Peter Senge (1990: 3) defines the learning organisation as:

> "Organisations where people continually expand their capacity to create the results they truly desire, where new and expansive patterns of thinking are nurtured, where collective aspiration is set free, and where people are continually learning how to learn together."

The definition immediately lacks clarity and precision which is a good reason for including Senge's model in assessing the appropriateness of the definition.

The model comprises five elements or disciplines. Systems learning, personal mastery, mental models, shared vision, and team learning. Among these elements or disciplines systems thinking is assigned significant importance. This element is important because it forms the basis for the function and interaction of the remaining elements. According to Senge, systems thinking constitutes the template for the interrelationship of structure and process. Senge (1990: 69) describes systems thinking as:

> "I call *systems thinking* the fifth discipline because it is the conceptual cornerstone that underlies all of the five learning disciplines of this book. All are concerned with a shift of mind from seeing parts to seeing wholes, from seeing people as helpless reactors to seeing them as active participants in shaping their reality, from reacting to present to creating the future. Without *systems thinking*, there is neither the incentive nor the means to integrate the learning disciplines once they have come into practice. As the fifth discipline, *systems thinking* is the cornerstone of how learning organisations think about their world."

In several chapters Senge discusses the most important elements of systems thinking, such as in his account of the law of the fifth discipline that appears as series of proverb-like statements of the type today's problems derive from yesterday's "solutions" and "the cure may be worse than the disease". The statements are, however, not very different from those advocated by systems theorists many years ago. Here, we shall confine ourselves to a brief summary of the contents of systems thinking:

> "*Systems thinking* is a discipline for seeing wholes. It is a framework for seeing interrelationship rather than things, seeing pattern of change rather than static *snapshots*." (Senge, 1990: 68)

Strategic plans and analyses typically do not have the desired effects. Strategic planning is often conventional coupling potential future situations to certain sets of solutions. Senge refers to the complexity that conventional planners attempt as *dynamic complexity*. While *detail complexity* concerns uncovering potential individual situations and possible solutions, strategic planning as *dynamic complexity* also includes the interaction of situations over time. This approach increases the possibilities of seeking out likely target areas and the lever effect of planned changes.

Senge states the essence of systems thinking to be that one:

- focuses on interrelationships rather than on linear chains of cause-effect, and
- focuses on change processes rather than snapshots of change.

At least two things are important in connection with systems thinking, feedback and systems patterns. Within systems thinking, the content of feedback differs from that of linear thinking:

> "It means any reciprocal flow of influence. In systems thinking it is an axiom that every influence is both cause and effect. Nothing is ever influenced in just one direction." (Senge, 1990: 75)

Two types of feedback stand out in Senge's book: reinforcing feedback and stabilising feedback. Reinforcing feedback is when several processes integrate and collaborate toward the same goal. Reinforcing feedback can be both positive and negative.

Stabilising feedback implies that processes working in one direction become influenced by other processes, and in effect the former are modified or stabilised. Such processes may be implemented deliberately or be non-recognised and opposing processes.

Feedback is thus fundamental to systems thinking. The precondition for managers and employees being able to understand the dynamics of the organisation is that feedback processes, their way of functioning, context and effect are transparent.

Systems thinking also enables exposure of recurring patterns, i.e., interrelationship of systems elements that occur repeatedly. Senge labels these patterns "systems archetypes". Recognising systems patterns makes it possible to identify places in the system where the lever principle will yield the greatest effect. And exposing systems patterns makes it possible to get an overview of wholes and parts simultaneously. Consequently employees and managers are better able to react fast and appropriately to external and internal changes.

We have seen that Senge perceives systems thinking as fundamental to how organisations function. But Senge also points out that mastering systems thinking requires mastering the other four disciplines. Therefore, we shall summarise these disciplines and their interplay.

According to Senge, "personal mastery" is the term that my colleagues and I use for the discipline that concerns personal development and learning. Individual learning is the very prerequisite for organisational learning. That individual learning occurs does not, however, guarantee organisational learning.

Personal mastery entails more than competence and skills though the discipline is also based on competence and skills. But according to Senge, it entails more than mental openness, though this is a basic requirement. Senge (1990: 141) defines personal mastery as:

> "It means approaching one's life as a creative work, living life from a creative as opposed to a reactive viewpoint."

When personal mastery becomes a discipline, i.e., when it becomes an activity that we integrate in our lives, it implies two underlying movements. The first concerns the continuous realisation of what is important for us. This means that reflection on direction and circumstances are often much more important that the details. The second movement concerns the continuous learning of how to interpret the given situation. This implies strengthening one's interpretive capabilities continuously, i.e., getting better in difficult situation at distinguishing between important and less important issues and at seeing things as wholes rather than losing oneself in details.

The background for developing personal mastery into a discipline is the personal vision. A personal vision is an inner desire typically tied to objectives, which implies tensions between the concrete vision and the more abstract objectives. In connection with behaviour that aims to transform the vision into reality *creative tension* occurs (Senge, 1990). It is a positive force that facilitates the transformation. Another force occurring is *emotional tension*, which is a negative force that come into effect when the transformation is unsuccessful, when the conditions are not present, and when existing patterns in the organisation function as barriers to transformation. The discipline personal mastery involves overcoming the conflict between one's self-perception and capabilities and the contents of one's vision. Thus, personal mastery also concerns personal development and the adaptation of visions.

Mental models must be perceived as an important discipline in that they are the templates for human and organisational actions. Mental models are significant for interpreting existing situations and for behaving according to this interpretation. Senge (1990: 8) understands mental models as:

> "Mental models are deeply ingrained assumptions, generalisations, or even pictures or images that influence how we understand the world and how we take action."

Mental models are not static in that the assumptions, generalisations, and images underlying the models are continuously challenged by reality and personal or group reflections. Interpersonal communication is one of the most important preconditions for criticism and reflection, and is thus the basis for reinterpretations that might in turn cause criticism and reflection.

Shared visions are another of Senge's disciplines, which he defines as:

> "A vision is truly shared when you and I have a similar picture and are committed to one another having it, not just to each of us, individually, having it. When people truly share a vision they are connected, bound together by a common aspiration (...) Shared vision is vital for the learning organisation because it provides the focus and energy for learning (...). A shared vision is a vision that many people are truly committed to, because it reflects their own personal vision." (Senge, 1990: 206)

A shared vision is fundamental for moving from *them-interpretation* to *we-interpretations* in relation to organisational issues. It is also vital for what learning is to comprise, what should be changed and how. One of the most important objectives in the context of developing a shared vision is the creation of compliance among employees, middle managers, and mangers.

Shared visions are often rooted in individual visions. Individual visions concern beliefs and attitudes toward people, groups, the organisation, society, the environment, etc. Open and supportive environments facilitate mediation and discussion of personal visions and, in particular, integrate personal visions into a shared vision. A shared vision implies higher tolerance of new procedures, of experiments, and of committing errors under new and complex conditions.

The last of Senge's disciplines is team learning. Team learning starts from the personal visions and a shared vision. In this context 'alignment' is important. Alignment facilitates a shared understanding and purpose. Alignment in team learning is what actually links people's independent behaviour to collective behaviour toward the purpose of the group or the organisation. Both elements are necessary for achieving the desired development.

Dialogue and discussion are prerequisites for team learning. In these forms of interaction the existing situation and defensive routines are clarified. One's own beliefs and those of others are communicated and debated. In general this involves moving from original mental maps to other mental maps or elements of these.

C.   The learning organisation and the interaction of aspects of learning

In the following we shall discuss a model for developing the learning organisation focusing on organisational management processes and issues of import for the production company. The model is described in Neergaard (1994) and is related to the following expositions: Riis & Fick (1991); Riis & Neergaard (1994a) and Riis & Neergaard (1994b).

Theoretically Neergaard's (1994) model rests on assumptions about the mutual interaction of four aspects of learning, and a framework for four development stages in learning. Neergaard (1994:
78-91) discusses the preconditions and contents of the model of assumptions concerning the mutual interaction of: (1) individual behaviour; (2) management systems and organisational structure; (3) corporate culture; and (4) decision support.

Neergaard (1994: 137-141) modifies the model defining the above mentioned aspects as being part of the internal environment and by adding a series of components that constitute the external environment. The latter are components such as customers, competitors, suppliers, technology and socio-political conditions. The modification concerns the external environment of a production company. If applied to a public organisation, the components would be different. Here interaction among the four aspects of learning and the external environment is implicit.

Figure 1.5: Model of assumptions about mutual interaction among the four aspects of learning

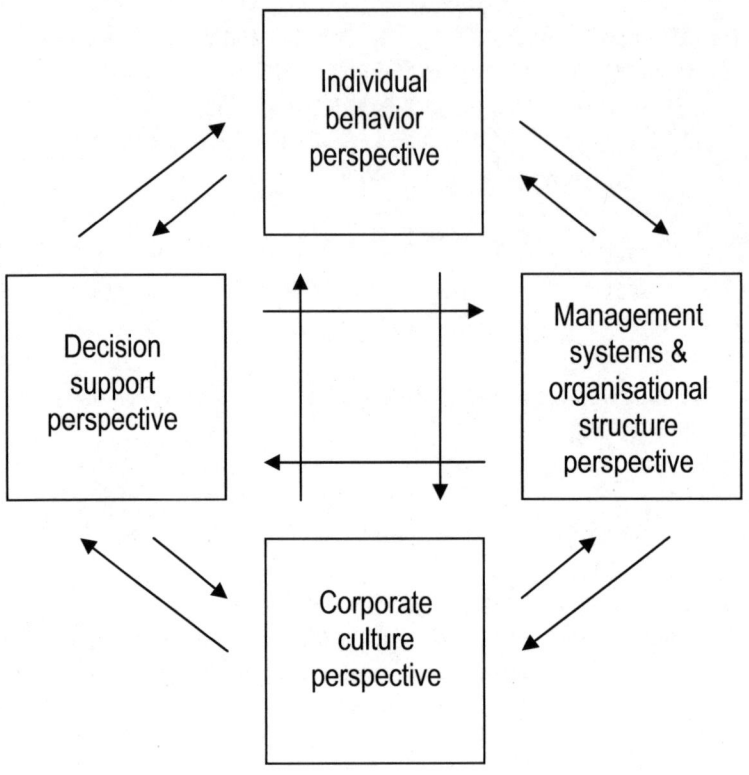

Source: Neergaard 1994: 86.

The framework includes four phases of learning (Neergaard 1994):

Phase 1:   The need for learning: Identification of core competencies.
Phase 2:   Analysis and diagnosis: The current situation.
Phase 3:   Towards the learning organisation: Solution elements.
Phase 4:   Implementation: Incremental and innovative changes.

Figure 1.6: The framework of the four phases of learning

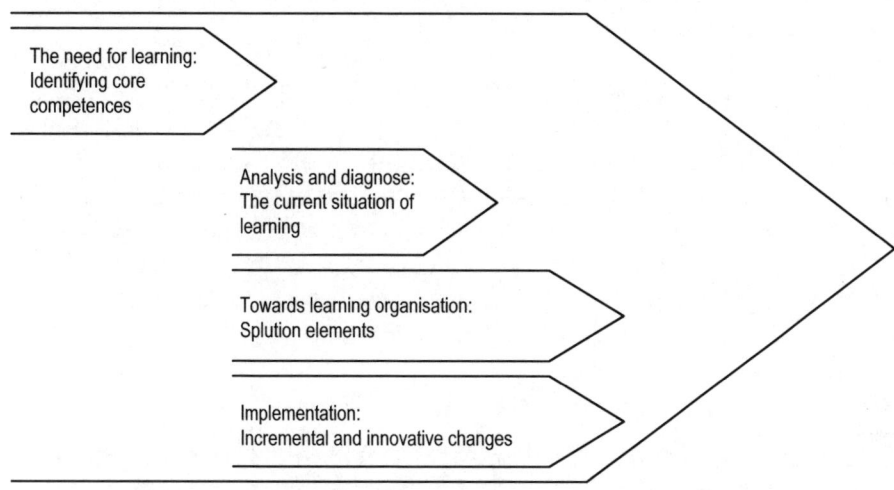

Source: Neergaard 1994: 100.

Individual behaviour is expressed through organisational processes. Combined and individually personal behaviour, decision support, and corporate culture constitute fundamental parts of organisational processes. The management systems and the organisational structure govern the processes.

The purpose of the model is to identify the individual behaviour that can be labelled individual learning (and the collective behaviour as organisational learning), innovation, change preparedness, etc. The relations of the elements and their interaction make it possible to examine individual behaviour. What are the demands of individual and organisational learning to the other aspects of learning? What should decision support include in order to support the individual behaviour that takes the shape of individual (and organisational) learning? What are interesting in this context are the available information technology and its institutionalised knowledge. It is thus the formal aspects of decision support that should be given weight in relation to learning, innovation, and change preparedness. Management systems and organisational structure are important for the organisation's formal processes. How planning and control conducted and what are the contents? How are policies and strategies designed and what are the contents? How are procedures and routines established and for what? How are information structure and incentive structure designed? These questions can be summarised to questions about to what degree the managerial system and the organisational structure push or pull individual (and organisational) learning, innovation, and orientation toward change.

Corporate culture constitutes the collective framework of values for managers and employees in an organisation. It includes general ideas, norms, and rules. Furthermore, it includes ideas, norms, and rules upheld by smaller units and which might be challenging the general and dominant ideas, norms, and rules. Corporate culture includes formal and informal communication and interaction. The collective framework of values that the corporate culture stipulates strongly affects individual behaviour and consequently also individual and organisational learning.

How Does the Organisation Become Learning?

As the previous sections reflect, organisations that have the vision of becoming a learning organisation should not expect to be able to fully realise the vision. The society, the organisation and the individual are far too complex. The same applies to the previously mentioned concepts of the learning organisation. The organisation will always be in the processes of becoming a learning organisation but never reach the goal. Nothing in reality corresponds to a vision or an ideal. Pedler, Burgoyne and Boydell (1991) demonstrate this fact in their account of problems and solutions as continuously alternating. When one problem has found its solution, one or more new problems emerge either from the original problem or for other reasons. Therefore orientation toward change and continuous learning are vital for organisational development. What distinguishes the traditional organisation's way of functioning from the organisation that strives to become a learning organisation is that in the latter change and learning have been integrated into the life of the organisation.

In the previous sections we have focused on various models of development under the concept of the learning organisation. We have accounted for the authors' perception of the concept or vision of the learning organisation and the most important factors and relations among these in connection with development processes. In the following we shall discuss the same authors' perceptions of what approaches might strengthen the development under the concept of the learning organisation.

Pedler, Burgoyne and Boydell (1991:66-67)) refer to their practical approaches as "starting points" for companies that wish to pursue a "Learning Company" strategy. They suggest the development process to include:

- Work with the board of directors.
- Begin with diagnosis
- Start with a 'Big Event'
- Run a development program to raise consciousness
- Work out from the human resources department
- A joint union and management initiative.
- Set up a series of task forces.
- Work with the strategic planning cycle.
- Major on a priority Characteristic.
- Start with one department

The elements are the vein of what is recommended in books and articles on general organisational changes. See for instance Harvey and Brown (1996) and Borum (1995).

Senge's (1990) recommended approaches to implementing development under the concept of the learning organisations are scattered all over the book. However in the chapter on the disciplines of learning (pp. 373-377) Senge systematises his recommendations and states that the five disciplines of learning are conceivable as consisting of three separate levels:

- Practices: what do you do
- Principles: guiding ideas and insights
- Essence: the state of being of those with high levels of mastery in discipline

By applying the three levels to the disciplines (systems thinking, personal mastery, mental models, shared vision, and team learning) Senge gives the reader an idea of the complexity involved in developing toward the learning organisation. Here we shall focus on the level of practices - that is the concrete approaches related to each of the disciplines in the development.

Systems Thinking: - system archetypes are coupled to considerations on effect of change
 - simulation

Personal Mastery:	- clarifying personal vision - holding creative tension by - focusing on the result - seeing current reality - making choices
Mental Models:	- distinguishing "data" from abstractions based on data - testing assumptions - say what one usually does not say
Shared Vision:	- support the visioning process - sharing personal visions - listening to others - allowing freedom of choice - acknowledging current reality
Team Learning:	- suspending assumptions - acting as colleagues - practicing ideas and visions

The practical approaches are thus characterises by, on the one hand, a coupling of new ideas, visions, and conditions and, on the other hand, the conditions for translating these into action. Senge's practical approaches reflect Pedler, Burgoyne and Boydell's relations individual-collective and vision-action.

In Neergaard (1994) the four phases of the framework for developing learning constitute the point of departure for recommendations and practical approaches:

Phase 1: The need for learning: Identification of core competencies
Phase 2: Analysis and diagnosis: The current situation
Phase 3: Towards the learning organisation: Solution elements
Phase 4: Implementation: Incremental and innovative changes.

Phase 1, identification of core competencies, includes the following questions:

1) What tasks should the organisation be able to manage in the future?
2) What areas of competence will be important?
3) How can we assist managers in being attentive to these areas?
4) Are existing models in the literature applicable for identifying and discussing within which areas it is important to build competencies?

It appears that the content of phase 1 concerns establishing coherence between objective/tasks and resources/competencies. This implies learning in connection with the organisational change resulting from new objectives/tasks and the organisational change brought about by general competencies and new key competencies.

The analysis and diagnosis in Phase 2 is an in-depth exploration of the nature of current learning, applying the model of mutual interaction among the four learning aspects: individual behaviour, decision support, corporate culture, management system, and organisational structure. In analysing the individual aspects, problems related to these or their interaction is identified. By changing problematic elements of these aspects it becomes possible to establish consistency among aspects and hence effective learning in the organisation.

In relation to the mentioned analysis and diagnosis one could focus on current and desirable conditions for learning. This might lead to the following questions:

1) What is the contents and direction of current learning in the organisation, etc.?
2) What learning processes are taking place? What are their forms? And what are the results?
3) Which persons in the organisation are learning something, and which are not?
4) What are the conditions and potential for individual and collective learning?
5) In which areas should the organisation improve its learning capacity?

In Phase 3 we have reached recommendations and solution proposals that must take the organisation through the change process. And in this phase, the authors define the concept of the learning organisation as:

> "An organisation having an appropriate combination of the four types of learning capable of mutually supporting one another enabling the organisation to continuously develop its preparedness for external and internal changes." (Riis & Neergaard, 1994 b)

Here, the question of the four learning aspects of the general model and their interaction must be in place. Contents of and interaction among the learning aspects must be supportive of a development that concerns the following elements:

1) Choice of development tasks
2) Choice of learning level in connection with the chosen tasks
3) Selection of methods or approaches to implementation.

Phase 4 concerns implementation of innovative changes in the organisation. The author continues the contents of the previous phases in this phase and asks the following question concerning implementation:

1) How should the implementation process take place and who are involved, when we are focusing on the continuous change?
2) How can we stimulate and establish learning mechanisms and which methods are applicable when focusing on continuous development changes?
3) What conditions should be taken into consideration in a development project focusing on innovative changes?
4) What procedural approaches will be appropriate when focusing on innovative changes?

The practical approaches suggested by Neergaard (1994) have much in common with those suggested by Kanter (1983) and Pedler, Burgoyne and Boydell (1991). The significant difference consists in the author's systematic coupling of approaches to the general model applied.

The previous sections have demonstrated that the learning organisation is a vision or conceptual framework difficult to manage. Translating visions or conceptual frameworks into practice is also difficult. Solutions to these difficulties are suggested in Nielsen and Ariensen (1996) and in Madsen and Vikøren (1996). These works are proviso, and comments are thus confined to a general level.

Nielsen and Ariesen (1996) discuss how knowledge is exchanged in a certain part of a company. It appears that knowledge is primarily exchanged within areas where results are visible and measurable. Formalisation and traditional attitudes will impede the exchange of knowledge while positive experiences from previous knowledge exchange and the managers' positive perception of employees and positive attitudes toward learning are supportive of knowledge exchange. Madsen and Vikøren (1996) discuss the operationalisation and development of tools for identifying the degree of consistency between the actual development of the company and the contents of the concept of the learning organisation.

New literature, neglected literature and new problems.

The first new problems to be mentioned relate to the content, usefulness and transferability of the concept *the learning organisation.*
Hildebrandt (1997) and Brandi & Hildebrandt (1997) were the first Danish authors to raise some important questions on the concept of the learning organisation. In this chapter, the author offers his modest attempts at explaining what practice means in Kanter (1984), Pedler, Bourgoyne & Boydell (1991), Senge (1990) and Neergaard (1994). This question was and still is, very important.
In Etienne Wenger: "Communities of practice. Learning, Meaning and Identity". The Cambridge University Press 1998 this question is related to our daily work and our learning situations.

> "People that work, organise their lives together with the nearest colleagues and customers to get the work done. They develop or preserve a sense of them self that they can live with, they have fun and fulfil the demands made by their employer and customers. No matter where their job description is leading them, they create a practice that consists of what there has to be done."
> (Wenger, 1998, p.16)

> "Communities of practice are an integrated part of our daily life. They are so informal and so ordinary that they seldom will come in direct focus. Just for this reason they are quite well known. The word is maybe new, but the experiences are not."
> (Wenger, 1998, p.17)

Lave & Wenger: "Situated Learning. Legitimate. Peripheral. Participation". Cambridge University Press, 1991. In this book, the authors examine the social frame of learning and theory of learning.

And now back to Hildebrandt (1997) and Brandi & Hildebrandt (1997), who not only raise the question on practice, but also a number of fundamental aspects of the concept the learning organisation:

1) What is a learning organisation?
   We need a more plausible and empirical well-founded definition of what characterises the learning organisation including more precise formulation of how one in practice with the implementation of the learning organisation

2) What is management in a learning organisation?
   We need a more practical instruction on what management is and how management is put into practice in the learning organisation.

3) To what extent is the organisation learning?
   The important question is about measuring: There is a need of ascertain to what extent an organisation has developed over a certain period of time and what rate of learning an organisation possess at a certain point in time.

Until now, these questions have not been answered, but several authors have presented good contributions in relation to providing some useful answers.

Pernille Bottrup: "Læringsrum I arbejdslivet – et kritisk blik på Den Lærende Organisation" ("Room of learning in work life – a critical look on the learning organisation"), Forlaget Sociologi, 2001. A very good and critical book on the concept *the learning organisation.*
After a long passage presenting several empirical cases, the discussion shifts its focus and its course on the subject. The author questions the concept of the learning organisation and concludes that the concept in future should be excluded from use.
It is easy to agree in most of the critical remarks in Bottrup, but that does not mean rejecting the entire concept. Bottrup suggests using *room for learning* instead of *the learning organisation*. However, in my opinion, the concept *room of learning* does not itself possess the clarity asserted to be missing in *learning organisation.*
About the same time as our two Danish books were published, a number of foreign books trying to shed light on the content of the concept *the learning organisation* were published as well.
Janice A. Cook, Derek Staniforth & Jack Stewart (ed.): "The Learning Organisation in the public services", Glower 1997. The authors discuss the concept generally and in relation to the special conditions present in different part of the public services in UK.

A very interesting book, which really managed to put *the learning organisation* on the agenda. The postscript of the book shows that putting the learning organisation into practice is far from easy, and that working under this concept does not automatically lead to profit and happiness.

Michael D. Cohen & Lee S. Sproull (ed.): "Organisational Learning", 1996. This book is based on papers from an earlier conference, where the participating authors came from universities all over the USA. In the book, many theoretical aspects of organisational learning are treated and at the same time the concept seen in relation to different forms of practice. The interesting thing about the book is that well-known as well as almost unknown authors has participated writing this book.

Einar Marnburg: "Den selvutviklende virksomhet. Idepilarer i lærende organisasjoner". Gyldendal akademisk, 2000 ("The self developing company. Conceptual basis for organisational learning").
Marnburg is a Norwegian author. He is included here, because his book is interesting and because he is an example of the many Scandinavians interested in the concept of the learning organisation or organisational learning. In Marnburg's book, the problems in relation to the learning organisation are treated as a desirable situation, where necessary change and necessary organisational learning in its sustained form is mentioned as the self developing company.

The authors mentioned so far are critical in a very constructive way. Now we move to authors dealing with bitter experiences on the learning organisation. Bente Elkjær: "Det er længe siden at nogen har talt om den lærende organisation." ("It is long time since anyone talked about the learning organisation"), Periodical for working life, no.4, 1999. In this article Elkjær examines how contrasting assumptions can constitute a barrier to work under the concept of the learning organisation. The article, which is a theoretical statement, related to the relevant parts of a change project, tells a sad story about a public-service institution within social sector that wished to introduce the learning organisation. The introduction of and work in relation to the concept of the learning organisation in this institution was marked by several conflicts of interest. The fatal thing was that the management failed to understand that such extreme points of conflict of interests are incompatible. The extreme points were rationalisation through TQM and developing the employees through the learning organisation; focusing on quantitative conditions as well as focusing on qualitative conditions; control in contrast to degrees of freedom and

individualising in contrast to collectivisation. Such sets of extreme points can not appear at the same time as preconditions for introduction of and work under the concept of the learning organisation. An organisation can contain the extreme points of conflicting interests, but not untreated and not as
Simultaneous preconditions for introducing and working under the concept of the learning organisation. In her article Elkjær concludes that this institution no longer works under the concept.

For some authors the experiences with the concept of the learning organisation has moved their focus to other organisational areas: Knowledge, knowledge creation, knowledge management etc
E.g. to Nonaka & Takeuchi: "The Knowledge creating company". New York 1995 or to Davenport & Prusak: "Working Knowledge. How Organisations Manage What the Know", Harvard Business School Press. Boston 1998.

Conclusion

As a result of the growing complexity characterising society and organisations the life of the individual is also becoming increasingly unpredictable. In our attempts to systematise and form a general view of life, we try to construct templates and simple frameworks.

The concepts and juxtaposition of concepts of the learning organisation proposed by the various authors discussed can be understood as templates or frameworks. The problem is, however, that their concepts are not simple and clear. Though they are sufficiently spacious to take into consideration bottom-up innovation, organisations may not exploit this possibility. Respect and reciprocity constitute the prerequisite for initiating and profiting from learning and change through the concepts of the learning organisation. However, the discussed concepts are so complex that organisations will be inclined to prioritise certain "starting points" and then perhaps supplement with a few more. The immediate risk is that the desire for learning, participation, and change will be translated into a series of segmented courses and seldom into a whole of temporally fixed and coherent changes. The risk is also that management will identify the areas of priority, which at best will lead to fixed and limited employee participation, and at worst to actions fairly similar to the current.

Importunate internal entrepreneurs and other employees capable of managing "wild" problems will not necessary obtain support if the organisation attempts to translate the concept of the learning organisation into narrow frameworks and rules.

The concept of the learning organisation necessitates resources if it is to function reasonably well in practice. A large share of small and medium sized companies characterising the Danish industrial structure has probably modest resources and will thus be prone to apply the concept somewhat more rigorously. In recent years, public institutions have spent vast resources on rationalisations and reorganisations. Therefore, the problem of resources might prove decisive. What can be done about this? Organisations and institutions could attempt to attract attention and support from interest organisations. They could also combine forces or establish networks in order to procure the necessary minimum resources. Collaborating or forming networks will not effect competitive conditions or the desire of independence, but will solely be directed toward gathering information, developing knowledge, documentation, and exchange of experiences. Thorny issues can be negotiated in advance or left out. And it is left to the individual organisation to gather information, knowledge, and documentation specific to the organisation.

There is no doubt that learning, renewal, and change is essential for most organisations and institutions regardless of size and sector. In the daily life of organisations and institutions this is reflected in the considerable scope of training offered and demanded. It is also reflected in changes related to production and information technology. Finally, both public and private organisations experience reorganisations, renewals, and organisational changes.

What can the concept of the learning organisation contribute with in this context? The concept can contribute to establish a direct link between the objectives and learning needs of the organisation and factual learning and training. The concept can also contribute to broaden the forms and possibilities of learning. Learning can take place in relation to most of the organisation's activities and in ways different from traditional courses. It could be team learning, user-teaches-user, etc., and the occasion could be professional activities or participation in strategic or policy development. Within this area the significant strength of the concept is that learning becomes oriented toward problematic and often alien areas.

The relationship between individual and organisation is part of the concept in several ways. The five disciplines in Senge's (1990) concept operate with this relationship, and it is part of the organisational energy flow in Pedler et al.

(1991). Finally Neergaard (1994) discusses the relationship in his account of the elements of the model.

The relationship between individual and organisation is important because it constitutes a significant coupling in translation and integration. Here is the interaction between individual and common visions, between control and self-management, between individual and shared translations, between individual and organisational learning, and between differentiation and integration. Against this relationship the strength of the organisation for learning, change and renewal can be measured.

Seeing wholes and human resources as the foundation for the future development of the organisation is both sympathetic and necessary. But by including limits of traditional design in the actual change projects that can be designed on the basis of the concept of the learning organisation, the intentions of integrative thinking as wholes, of change orientation and ability for change, and of utilization of undiscovered human resources may result in yet another managerial tool.

References

Argyris, C. & D. A.Schön (1996): *Organisational Learning II. Theory, Method, and Practice.* Addison-Wesley, Reading, Massachusetts, 1996.

Argyris, C. & D. A.Schön (1978): *Organisational Learning: A Theory of Action Perspective.* Addison-Wesley, Reading, Massachusetts, 1978.

Borum, F. (1995): *Strategier for organisationændring.* Handelshøjskolens Forlag, København, 1995.

Burns, T. & G.M.Stalker (1961): *The Management of Innovation.* London: Tavistock, 1961 (2. udgave 1966).

Harvey, D. F. & D. R. Brown (1996): *An Experiential Approach to Organisation Development.* Prentice-Hall Int. Upper Saddle River, New Jersey, 1996.

Kanter, R. M. (1983): *The Change Masters. Corporate Entrepreneurs at Work.* Routledge, London & New York, 1983.

Kofoed, L. B. (1994): *Uddannelsesmodel for integreret anvendelse af Informationsteknologi: Tværfaglig kompetence og organisatorisk læring - nye muligheder for et godt arbejdsmiljø.* Aalborg, 1994.

Lindholm, M. R. (1995): *Det skal Danmark leve af. En nyvurdering af Danmarks udviklingsevne.* Mandag Morgen, København, 1995.

Madsen, C. Ø. & C. B. Vikøren (1996): *Novi - en lærende organisation?* Specialeafhandling (Klausuleret) Aalborg Universitet, 1996.

Nielsen, L. S. & W. Ariesen (1996): *Udveksling af viden i Danisco.* Specialeafhandling (Klausuleret) Aalborg Universitet, 1996.

Morgan, G. (1986): *Images of Organisation.* Sage Publications, London, 1986.

Neergaard, C. (1994): *Creating a Learning Organisation. A Comprehensive Framework.* Department of Production, Aalborg University, Denmark. October, 1994.

Pedler, M., J. Brugoyne & T. Boydell (1991): *The Learning Company. A Strategy for Sustainable Development.* McGraw-Hill, Maidenhead, UK, 1991.

Riis, J. O. og J. Frick (1991): *Organisational Learning: A Neglected Dimension of Production.* Management Systems Design Proceedings og the APMS 90 conference in Finland, Edited by Eero Elorante, North Holland, 1991.

Riis, J. O. og C. Neergaard (1995): *Managing Technology Projects: An Organisational Learning Approach.* Paper presented at the HIESS conference in Hawaii, jan.1995.

Riis, J. O. og C. Neergaard (1994a): *Project as Means for Developing the Learning Organisation.* Proceedings of INTERNET 94, 12th World Congress on Project Management, Oslo, Norway, june, 1994 (a).

Riis, J. O. og C. Neergaard (1994b): *The Learning Company: A New Manufacturing digm.* A Paper Presented at The Annual CIM Europe Conference In Copenhagen, oct., 1994 (b).

Senge, Peter (1990): *The Fifth Discipline. The Art and Practice of the Learning Organisation.* Century Business, London, 1990.

Taylor, F. W. (1911): *The Principles of Scientific Management.* Harper, New York, 1911.

van Hauen, F., V. Strandgaard og B. Kastberg (1995): *Den lærende organisation, - om evnen til at skabe kollektiv forandring.* Industriens Forlag, København, 1995.

Chapter 2

Images of Learning and the Development of Learning Behaviour in Organisations

By Erik Laursen

Introduction: A Few Popular Concepts

During the 1990s the concepts of learning and organisational learning became popular also in Denmark. They became widely used in everyday language and within a series of more specialised fields. During the last decade of the nineties the two concepts soon became catchwords.

Learning implies both a very old and a quite new concept. Traditionally, the Danish language you are expected to "learn something" ("lære") in school or from working as an apprentice. One learned from experience and from life in general. In relation to events from which one perhaps did not benefit much – materially – the saying has for years been 'well, what did we learn from that?' "To learn" ("at lære") is a broad concept in Danish, covering both processes of learning and teaching. Compared to the Danish usage of "learn", the British usage of "learning" is confined to the acquiring of knowledge or skills. Imitating this concept the modern concept of "læring" has emerged in the Danish language. Politiken's Dictionary of Modern Danish defines "læring'" as: "to acquire the knowledge and skills that one needs by taking actively part in the process." (1987: 677)

But not only does the scope of "lære" and "læring" differ in Danish. To learn is a verb that must link up with a subject implying that if we talk about "at lære"(to learn) we must also deal with, who learns.

"Læring" (Learning), on the other hand, is a noun that refers to a process. Learning can be complex, independent, or organisational, but does not require a subject. This is actually paradoxical: The modern concept of "learning", which strongly emphasises the role of the subject, refers to a process without an accompanying subject as opposed to the traditional concept that also embraces passive learning processes in that its word class emphasises the subject. The concept of "learning" immediately makes us talk about processes void of subjects – processes the outcome of which is increased human wisdom.

The outcome of the process may very well benefit the individual, but the process, learning, remains surprisingly anonymous or collective. If we attempt to make the process personal, the language becomes ponderous, clumsy, and strange as when we are talking about "Peter's learning" as if it were a sandwich box or a scarf that he brought along.

The concept of "learning" thus tends to cut off the individual from his or her actions. This is inappropriate unless the goal is to emphasise the relational or procedural aspects of processes. In other words the point is that learning may result from the active actions of the individual – but by nature the process is collective, systemic, and relational.

"Lifelong learning" – to take another one of the contemporary catchwords – demonstrates the impersonal nature of the concept. I can formulate it as my personal life project "to learn all my life", or I can optimistically say that "in all my life I have learned a lot of things and I wish to continue doing so". This is then my project and my life, whereas "lifelong learning" is a social demand or a social option targeted toward a larger or smaller group of people in society.

Organisational learning is an even more pronounced catchword than *learning*. If lifelong learning is a moral demand today, directed toward the entire normal population in western societies, organisational learning is even more pronounced in organisations – public or private. One of the most significant mantra since the 1990s has been "learn or leave" – especially in business life.

The popularity of the concept does not refer to its descriptive qualities. All human learning by and large takes place within social frameworks that make the learning processes meaningful, necessary and possible. *Organisational learning* is therefore almost synonymous with "learning". But the concept has gained ground as a managerial and organisational concept.

In recent years scholars have increasingly been distinguishing systematically between organisational learning, i.e., the organisation as the room for or framework of the employees' learning, and the learning organisation, which in part refers to an organisation that learns, and in part to the concept of dynamic management and organisational development. The latter has two aims. First, it is a way of considering all work processes and work relations as actual or potential learning processes. Second the staging of targeted and systematic learning efforts includes all members of the organisation. This distinction between the two senses of the concept of 'the learning organisation' may immediately seem to be a distinction between means and ends. Can an organisation wanting to learn and become wiser realise this goal in other ways than by optimising employee learning? This viewpoint is both right and wrong. An organisation can "become wiser" in two senses. An organisation has become wiser when its total scope of knowledge or competence increases. This is only possible through employee learning. But an organisation can also be said to have become wiser if it demonstrates wiser actions – when it learns from experience. This might be the effect of the individual employee improving his or her performance, but it could also result from management decisions of a higher quality. However, there is no necessary correlation between employee learning, competence scope, and the quality of management decisions. If we briefly look at some of the possible success criteria for the growing 'wisdom' of an organisation, such as that it yields higher profit, higher growth, and productivity, we seriously begin to have our doubts. Does this always and necessarily involve "learning" and growing competencies? Hardly. On the other hand, there is currently a close relationship between realising most of the success criteria of the organisation and its ability and readiness to change.

We have now reached the third and broadest translation of the concept of organisational learning according to which the learning organisation simply is the organisation capable of changing. If we view organisational learning as a concept of management and organisational development, it is evident that it concerns the development of both the employees' ability and readiness to change and their professional competencies (van Hauen, 1995; Senge, 1999).

The Fragile Point of Convergence

Why have learning and organisational learning become such popular concepts? First, a large share of contemporary organisations in the western world lives from supplying or selling information and knowledge. Second, the services and products supplied by modern organisations have high contents of information and competence. This has made it clear to organisations that employee competencies are key resources. Third, knowledge production in the western world is growing rapidly. Fourth, the speed of change in society is high, and the pressure on organisations to change becomes correspondingly high.

To these conditions – those are both very general and have consequences for both public and private organisations, the individual citizen, and the individual employee – other factors can be added that have consequences for the individual in particular.

First, the assumption underlying the concept of learning: that we learn from our actions and that we, in keeping with the spirit of time, must be active in order to become wiser and more competent. As a consequence human development is perceived as produced by the social actors and as something for which they should assume responsibility.

Second, embedded in the concept are four elements of positive connotation: personal development, growth, competence, and career.

Looking at contemporary society one can easily get the impression that, learning is the prevailing and most acceptable way of describing positive personal changes. Thus we use the concept to understand change and to describe the processes, actions, interactions, and situations that we find to have changed us.

In order to be able to describe personal change as "learning" and "development", the change must include an element of progression and/or growth. The growth element is prevailing in the way the concept of learning refers to personal development. The general concept seems to be that learning is a process comparable to saving money and depositing it in the bank: the more and the longer you learn, the more competence and knowledge will you accumulate, and the more competent you become as a person, employee and human being. Thus the relationship between personal change and growth is evident.

This savings bank concept of human learning is, however, only accurate if we consider learning within a very narrow perspective. If I, for instance, as an experienced driver take a couple of lessons in driving on greasy roads my driving competence will be greater after the lessons. If, on the other hand, I am a forty-five year old checkout assistant in the supermarket who decides to study for the Higher Preparatory Examination, the situation is much more complex. I will become wiser and more competent in certain areas, but I will also lose knowledge and competence. Much of what I know and am skilled in, is no longer relevant, it is no longer used. I will forget or de-learn it sooner or later, and my way of organising my total knowledge and capability will change. The ways in which what I know and what I master affect my total personality and my identity changes. I change. Not only do I become richer in knowledge and capability, but I also lose something.

These reflections are immediately transferable to organisations. The total capability and knowledge of organisations that learn to the extent that they undergo transformations does not grow unequivocally. They also lose capability and knowledge, and large parts of their total competence will be organised in new ways and be ascribed different meanings.

Why does modern man hold such positive attitudes toward personal change in the sense development and growth?

There are several explanations of which the most important ones are based on how modern man experiences society and the life course of human beings, that is, as the framework for a series of unique self-identity projects (Giddens 1991; Beck 1992). In this context I shall not discuss the ways in which the post-modern ideology affects how people get involved and motivated in private and working life. I shall only briefly comment on one, though important, aspect: the relationship between career and lifelong education.

A growing share of the population is currently experiencing their life as a *career*. One reason is that since the 1960s the so-called "new middle class" has constituted an increasingly larger share of the population. Another reason is that in the same period the coupling between people's life and the social background of their parents has been strongly weakened. The individual has gained a larger social space for making decisions relevant for his or her life. Simultaneously, education and the acquiring of qualifications have come to play a much more important role in modern careers than earlier. It is thus no exaggeration to claim that in our society any career requires lifelong education. However, we could also rephrase this simple fact and claim that most of the lives that today are experienced and lived as careers are, in reality, lifelong re-education (Sennett, 1999).

The classic career was not merely a version of the pilgrimage of the Catholic Church (Bauman, 1997). It was also a journey in three dimensions. First of all in time, second in status and position, from low to high status, and third in a clearly defined hierarchy of qualifications from novice to virtuous master (Dreyfus & Dreyfus, 1986; Benner, 1984). The modern career is, on the other hand, increasingly characterises by the terminal point being unknown. The process itself is fragmented and unpredictable. Rather than moving towards a known and well-defined "virtuosity" one learns something quite new continuously throughout life, albeit the process is more based on education than was previously the case. For instance some one with twenty-thirty years of professional experience may have to "go back to school" time and again in order to learn something quite new and only be able to draw on existing knowledge and capability to a limited extent. In the modern career we are not only novices when we start our career, but several times during our life.

It is in relation to modern careers that personal growth has become a motivational parameter on a par with status and salary.

In my opinion, the popularity and force that the learning organisation has enjoyed as a management and development concept is rooted in the fact it has formulated a point of interest convergence. Convergence between management desires for optimising the change and adaptive capabilities of the organisation, e.g. through employee flexibility – and the employees' interest in making career, becoming the manager of one's own life and staging one's personal growth. Through continuous learning and training, reflexive interdisciplinary teams of highly competent professionals and dedicated participation in challenging and developing work processes.

The learning organisation is also a concept of motivation and like any other concept of motivation it must, apart from rhetoric and ideology, have real, effective substance in order to have any affect. In other words, if learning and personal growth can be reduced to pure demands for flexibility, and if all talk about career paths are reducible to a predictable route through organisational positions that neither goes uphill nor downhill, but are rich in ruptures, changes in functions, and new beginnings, then the concept does not hold much motivation, and the fragile convergence of interests, which is the real foundation and true raison d'être of the learning organisation is gone.

Where Does the Organisation Learn?

In an excellent summary of the various ways in which organisations learn, Andersen and Hansen (1999) distinguish between four arenas for learning: (1) *Institutionalised education*, such as adult education or training supplied by public or private institutions. (2) *Institutionalised workplace based learning.* Short and most often tailor made courses in the organisation that are designed and offered by external suppliers, such as AMU (public institution that offers labour market courses). (3) *Structured and planned "on-the-job" learning*, such as colleagues teaching each other, development projects, discussion groups, autonomous learning processes under supervision. (4) *Informal and internal learning through work*, i.e., learning is a natural and integrated part of the job. The nature of this learning is often intuitive because learning emerges spontaneously in connection with the various types of problem solutions applied in the work process.

It immediately appears that the learning processes within the four arenas can be distributed on a scale the extreme values of which are: internal-external (in relation to the organisation); formal-informal; integrated-separated (from the work process); planned-spontaneous; controlled by others (external people or management) – autonomous, based on outside assistance – self-based (on external or own competencies).

The diversities seem to contain two major dimensions. First a difference between learning processes referring to competencies already possessed by some of the organisational members and processes refer to "external". Second a difference between learning processes that are closely integrated knowledge to be "imported" by the organisation into the work processes in the organisation and processes separated from and generalised in relation to the work processes.

Two efficient theses about the learning organisation's way of functioning could be:

Thesis 1: The quality and dynamics of organisational learning processes depend on the interplay between the opponent dimensions of the two concepts.

The important question to ask being: Is the balance and interplay between internal and external learning processes appropriate and between learning processes integrated into and separated from the actual work processes? And how efficient is the coordination of the totality of learning processes taking place in the organisation?

Thesis 2: The dynamics of organisational learning processes depend on the 'strength' of the learning processes embedded in the work processes, and on how much space, time, and status they are allocated.

One extreme could be a group of doctors, engineers or economist working on solving a mutual theoretical or practical problem. It is evident to all involved professionals and to the surroundings that the knowledge and information available, be it technical books, articles in journals, and "experts" is the most important basis for working with the problem in a qualified way, but in itself this cannot provide solutions. Solutions in this context will probably emerge from collective reflection on the concrete problem based on two things: (1) *A varied, detailed account of the nature of the problem.* (2) *Putting the problem into a broad perspective based on the accumulated experience of comparable cases.*

Another extreme could the long standing discussion of the duration of coffee breaks within the public health sector. I am not concerned with the discussions, whether the staff is spending an unreasonable amount of time drinking coffee together, rather than spending time with the people, they are supposed to nurse. I am much more concerned with the premise for the discussion: colleagues spending time together during working hours are almost by definition wasting time compared to what they should be spending their time on: working in the front line. In my opinion there is a strong connection between, on the one hand, the possibility to qualify the social learning and reflection processes emerging immediately from problem solving related to the work processes and, on the other hand, the possibility of giving these processes sufficient status and space in the organisation.

In an earlier study I have tried to describe the conflict that may emerge in organisations between the high status external management courses and the low status work based learning activities, such as reflecting teams and collegial supervision (see Laursen 1996 and 1997); in other words, the relationship between the external and the internal element of structured and planned learning on the job. The problem often seems to be one of lacking time for internal learning activities, but it is just as much about the status of these activities and of qualifying them, which in the end is a question of professional self-confidence and professional qualification in a broad sense (see Senge op.cit.).

Donald Schön (1983; 1987) uses the concepts of *competence-in-action* and *reflection-in-action* to characterise learning from the very work process. He uses competence-in-action about routinised, tacit competence. What we do without thinking about it and do not know how we learned it. We just do it. Therefore, we often find it difficult to verbalise, what we are doing and why. Such competencies and actions function well in unproblematic situations – because they develop normally compared to our experiences and expectations – and they are competencies and forms of actions, which are extremely appropriate in situations of heavy time pressure.

On the other hand, Schön uses reflection-in-action to describe situations in which we for one reason or another think about, what we are doing. Situations, in which we note, if the given situation differs from similar situations – something that we might have overlooked earlier. It could also be reflections on whether we have made errors, or whether we have misinterpreted the entire situation and hence the problems implied. Perhaps the situation should be interpreted completely differently.

These are reflection that we typically make in situations that develop counter to our intentions and actions. In the first place they are reflections 'on the spot' while we are in the situations. These are often fast and more or less systematic – from the professional systematic and cool "it did not work, what can be wrong…" – and to the first cold sweat of panic "something is totally wrong – nothing is as it should be".

Against these situational forms of reflection and action Schön now introduces a third form of reflection, *reflection-outside-action*, which in many ways resembles *reflection-in-action* but with certain significant differences. This reflection often takes place outside the action in terms of time, function and space. Therefore the problems are at a distance and can be placed in a different perspective. There is more time to reflect upon which perspective to choose. There is time to search for supplemental information, such as literature, databases, and collegial advice. But first and foremost there is time to discuss the problems with colleagues and other people of insight.

If we are to relate Schön's three forms of reflection to Andersen and Hansen's three internal arenas for learning in an organisation, then competence-in-action and reflection-in-action refer to learning through work, whereas reflection-outside-action primarily refers to structured and planned learning on the job. This is also, where the organisation has the best possibilities for increasing the quality and scope of internal learning processes.

With the purpose of identifying a possible field of potential learning I will include another set of concepts to describe the fundamental learning processes – Kolb's learning circle (Kolb, 1984).

Kolb's model is primarily based on the ideas of John Dewey and Jean Piaget that human learning emerges from reflection upon problem solving and experimental actions (Piaget, 1971; Dewey, 1974). For Kolb human learning and cognition is a circular process that begins and ends with goal-directed actions.

According to Kolb the reflection process has three moments: (1) The actual experience (immediate experience) in which the individual registers the action and its consequences through the sensory-motor apparatus. (2) The reflecting observation (reflected experience) where the individual either alone or with others reflects upon the image of the action and its consequences registered in the previous phase. (3) Abstract conceptualisation (conceptualisation through understanding that is drawing on concepts, models and theories of abstract or general nature) where the individual brings the reflected experience into general models of broad application. Then the learning process returns to its last (and first) moment: Active experimentation (action).

Figure 2.1. Kolb's Learning circle

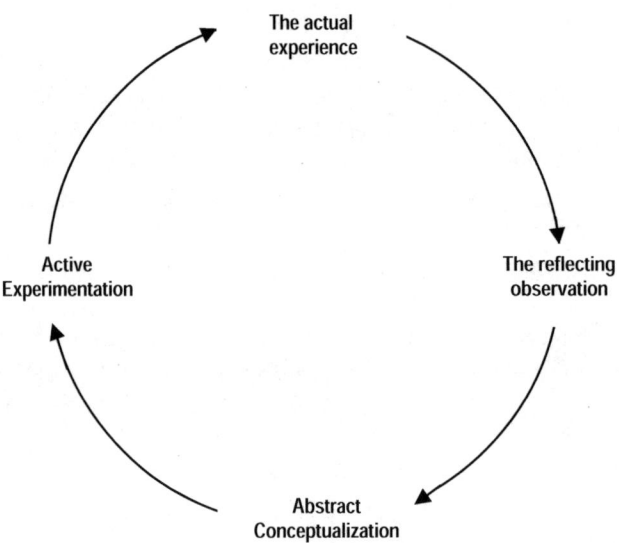

Kolb's learning circle is an ideal model in the sense that it holds all four possible phases in the process. In real life the learning and cognition processes are often cut short.

Two well-known shortenings are the never ending practician and the chronic theorist. In both cases the learning cycle is broken, is reduced to a closed cycle between two moments. The never ending practitioner cycles between practical action and immediate experience from action. He or she acts intentionally and registers subsequently whether the consequences were as expected. If so he or she will repeat the actions by and large unchanged, and if not he or she will change the action. This type of thermostat-learning or "success-failure-learning" is what Argyris and Schön (1977) describe as single-loop learning. This is learning-by-doing in a very narrow sense. What has been learned is what is relevant for the given action. What the experience revealed by the action tells us about other aspects of reality is not turned into a theme for reflection.

The chronic theorist cycles between reflected observation and abstract conceptualisation or from data to theory and back. In this context data is always processed experiences that have been filtered and transformed through several intermediate phases. It is probably not the theorist's own experiences, and if it was, they would have changed radically from how they were sensed originally. Here sensing is subsumed form and the concrete is subsumed the general. Conception is deduced from the abstract concepts and not from the actual sensing of success or failure, pleasure or pain, profit or loss.

Argyris and Schön's basic view on optimising learning within organisations can be summarised as *the closed cycle of the the never ending practitioner must be broken* – primarily by virtue of collective reflection processes. Or as they themselves formulate it: the preoccupation of single-loop learning with the consequences of actions in a narrow sense must be expanded with the reflections of double-loop learning on the frames of reference that we draw on to realise and explain the consequences of the action.

Returning to Andersen and Hansen's four arenas for learning, this can happen by establishing appropriate coordination between the structured and planned learning-on-the-job and the informal internal learning through work.

The key to developing dynamic organisational learning processes is to establish appropriate coordination of experimental actions, immediate experiences and reflecting observations closely tied to the work processes – reflecting observations and abstract conceptualisations that can be established among colleagues on the job and in everyday life. This primarily involves making learning teams function in relation to organisational work processes, as described by e.g. Peter M. Senge (see Senge, 1999; Schön, 1987; Strandgaard et al. 1996; Bohm, 1996).

Some Reasons for Organisations having Difficulties in Learning

What are the typical obstacles to develop learning processes in organisations? In an attempt to answer this question, I shall start by categorising a number of highly diverse problems that may characterise organisations of highly different nature into general types of impediments to learning and subsequently focus on one single factor that I shall discuss in the remainder of this chapter. This factor is the images of learning that we apply when trying to learn, or understand situations and events from which we expect or want to "learn".

I shall point out six significant reasons for organisations facing difficulties in learning:

1. *Experience possibilities are too weak.* The dynamic key element in the organisation is on-the-job learning. That is, it is a necessary (but not sufficient) condition for developing useful learning processes in the organisation that work processes can yield learning. The work processes must contain an element of problem solving, of demands to the performers for developing their qualifications, fantasy, and innovativeness. This is clearly a variable that includes a very broad spectrum of different work situations. Nevertheless, one very simple, trivial but at the same time fatal reason for non-learning in organisations is that there is nothing to learn. Developing learning processes necessarily require interesting and demanding work processes.
2. *Supply of information and knowledge is too weak.* This concerns the institutionalised education that organisational members have received either as basic education or as further training while working in the organisation, including institutionalised, workplace based learning. In other words the recruitment and training policy of the organisation.

The last four factors concern various problems related to making the structured and planned learning-on-the-job function. As mentioned earlier this involves team-learning and collegial reflection processes.

3. *Reflection possibilities are too poor.* These are the most obvious, trivial reasons why team-learning is not practiced (enough). There is too little

time and too few tools and competencies to do it – or the attitude towards team-learning is one of resent.
4. *Inappropriate understandings of learning.* The employees' understandings, models, and images of learning processes are either inappropriate for effectively acquiring knowledge and capabilities or obstructing the learning processes, which the organisation wish to stage within a collegiate framework.
5. *Little motivation for learning, innovation and risk taking.* In general this entails two issues: What are the actual contents of the organisation's learning processes and demands for learning? Are the demands merely for flexibility or for genuine qualifications? And how are the employees experiencing the demands? I have earlier stated there is always the reverse of profound and broad learning processes. They always involve both gains and losses, which is why rejecting learning is rational in many cases (but also has its price). Other aspects of significant effect may be deficient remuneration of innovativeness and risk taking, hierarchical structures, and resentment in the workplace towards competition.
6. *Inappropriate informal organisational patterns*, implying especially three dimensions:
   a. Qualification hierarchies in a flat organisational structure
   b. Hierarchies based on criteria other than qualifications
   c. Collective, professional inferiority.

In general, structured and planned learning on-the-job rests on a flat non-hierarchical organisational structure. The central idea is that the involved parties learn from each other through sharing experiences and interpretations of experiences. Nothing prevents incorporating differences among participants in insight, experience, knowledge, and capability into the organising of such learning processes. But it implies that differences are explicit and recognised and not reflecting a workplace culture holding that "in this department we are all equally good" (i.e., "equally wise"). It may prove difficult for establishing effective learning teams and the like, if the team consists of employees being part of a status-hierarchy based on criteria other than competence, such as seniority, gender, age, and ethnicity. Another significant problem is that if the team is characterised by collective professional inferiority making it difficult for both the team itself and the environment to seriously accept spending time on things like that.

Example:

Attempts to improve the quality of care and reduce work related psychological strains.

I have earlier described this example (Laursen 1996 & 1997) of organised and planned learning processes in three hospital wards aiming at:

1. Strengthening the quality of care toward patients and their families.
2. Develop capabilities for processing and reducing the psychological strains related to this type of work.
3. Develop competencies in undertaking collegial supervision.

The planned and implemented process ran over nine months with a combination of external courses, workshops, internal supervisions assisted by external professionals, and internal collegial supervision assisted by external professionals.

Compared to Andersen and Hansen's categories, this process takes place within two arenas: the *institutionalised workplace based learning* (course, workshop and series of supervision assisted by professionals), and *the structured and planned learning on-the-job* (supervision assisted by external consultants).

As described elsewhere, this learning process only proved partly successful. There were several reasons for this outcome, which I shall not discuss in this context, but rather focus on a series of factors that, in my opinion, are telling of the (difficult) conditions for learning within the two arenas:

1. *We have a "problem"* (**a.** the psychological strain related to "normal" work is too high, or **b.** we wish to improve the quality of care).

    - But who is experiencing the problem?
    - How different are their perceptions of the problem?
    - And is it a problem at all?

    Learning processes of this nature imply that the employees involved clarify and define the problem. When the problem is "psychological strain" and "care" the task may prove complex. For instance, certain of the doctors working in the ward had refused to having experienced psychological strain. In our context psychological strain is defined as the emotional strain caused by, for example, having to tell people that they

are suffering from terminal cancer. Therefore, it is suggestive if the staff is experiencing great difference in psychological strain. In this context "experienced strain" will often be translated as an expression of whether or not one is committed to the work.
Nor is "quality of care" unambiguous and clearly defined.
Therefore, prior to initiating the learning process, the involved parties must attempt to determine norms, standards and objectives.

2. *Who must (can) participate in the learning process?*

In this case the process involved the nurses, but not the auxiliary nurses and the doctors. This delimitation was only in part justified by the differences in individual experience of strain. The most important reasons were probably the status and power relations among the professional groups.

3. *How is the interaction of learning processes integrated into and separated from the concrete work processes?*

In this case the external teaching was both of high quality and strongly relevant. The problem was that the autonomous collegial supervisions claimed over time to be lacking input. In other words, the link to concrete work processes was not sufficiently strong. However, the problem was rather that the outcome of collegial reflection was assessed to be too modest.

4. *How was the internal distribution of qualifications among the participants in the learning group?*

Among the nurses there was no formal hierarchy. There were differences in seniority and thus in experience and competence, but not in professional competencies. This apparent ignoring of significant differences in competencies was even more pronounced for differences in attitudes toward commitment and work. Furthermore in effect of high personnel turnover in the three wards experienced employees were scarce commodities. Combined these aspects made, e.g. learning from 'symmetrical' collegial supervision difficult. At the same time the fact that the workplace culture did not explicitly recognise experienced or proficient employees as "experts". Furthermore there were in fact only a few experienced employees available, which naturally impeded the learning processes based on the relationship between novice-expert.

Structured and Planned Learning "On-the-Job"

In the following we will take a closer look at organisational structured and planned learning on-the-job. This is, as indicated earlier, a somewhat motley affair. It covers diverse activities, such as learning from the neighbour, development projects, discussion groups, collegial supervision, and team learning. On the one hand, the field is delimited in relation to institutionalised workplace based learning in that activities are not based on external competencies and teaching. On the other hand the field is delimited in relation to informal, internal learning at work, i.e., learning processes that are not immediately integrated parts of the work processes but are separated from these in time and space. However, though the latter arena of learning processes is internal, informal, and separated from the work process in time and space, its contents is strongly related to employee experiences and problems encountered in the actual work process which is self-governed.

In continuation of the two major theses formulated earlier, this arena for learning raises the following key questions:

- Does it sufficiently and adequately incorporate experiences and problems from the organisational work processes?
- Is it sufficiently supported by external teaching, information, and supervision?
- Does the organisation – including the employees – allocate sufficient time, space and status to the learning processes to make them sufficiently "powerful" in their way of functioning and their consequences?

The latter question is rather complex in that it involves factors, such as management relations, organisational culture, the relationship between various professional groups in the organisation, the self-identity of the individual professional groups, culture and tradition within the given area, and, finally, the professional identity of the individual employee and perception of learning and qualification.

In the last part of this chapter I shall focus on one factor related to the employee's subjective perception of learning. Why is the factor relevant in relation to structured and planned learning on-the-job? In my view the participants' subjective perceptions of learning and learning models are central to any learning process. However, they are particularly important in relation to this specific learning arena (i.e., the structured and planned learning zone), because of the relatively open character of the learning activities.

In general, learning activities within this arena primarily concern presentation of experiences, collective reflections, problem solving and developing ideas, and they must be fitted into the existing organisational structure temporally and physically. They are activities that take place "when time allows" and wherever there might be "vacant rooms". They are activities almost exclusively based on dialogue – the spoken word and typically across the table. If passions run high, participants might even use the whiteboard to illustrate their arguments. In other words they are activities of relatively weak *context cursors*. The framework is not signalling "learning" unambiguously and conspicuously in the way that a classroom or a lecture room does. Furthermore, the organising of the learning process will often differ from the learning models of the participants. In addition these learning processes in general lack technologies (see Senge, 1999) and consequently must be supported by an explicit learning model.

Meta-Cognition and Learning Processes

Meta-cognition can be defined as conscious "awareness of one's own cognitive processing" (Mayer 1992:256) or, somewhat more detailed – as our "knowledge and control of the cognitive domain" within our own behaviour repertoire (Breuer 1998:685).

One example of attention could be the control of understanding that in the experienced reader is an integrated aspect of the reading process making him or her ask himself or herself more or less implicitly: "Do I understand what I am reading?" and "does this make sense?"

From the two above definitions it appears that the concept of meta-cognition covers two things:

First, the concept refers to our knowledge about personal cognitive processes. This knowledge is, on the one hand, available to us explicitly and, on the other hand, it is generated at a relative late stage in our development. It might be our knowledge about the limits of our memory ("I have a poor memory of names"), about what certain types of problems require, or about the most adequate solution strategy to a given type of problems.

Second, the concept refers to our ability to control cognitive processes such as control of understanding, when reading texts. This ability is in general relatively specific to the problem, task and situation, and is not transferable in the same way as our knowledge about cognitive processes.

Meta-cognition can take as its object any cognitive field, including learning. Within this field too meta-cognitive activities have two aspects: (1) our knowledge about and image of the learning processes; (2) our ability to control and regulate learning processes.

Bearing in mind Kolb's learning circle, learning processes contain four elements: (1) targeted actions (active experimentation); (2) immediate experience from action and its consequences (concrete experience); (3) reflected and communicated experience (reflective observation), and (4) understanding through abstract conceptualisation. Of the four elements, the first refers to the learning subject's relationship to the world, while the remaining three elements in principle refer to the subject's mental processing of experiences with the world, but the latter need not only refer to mental (internal) processes. For instance, reflected experience may be a dialogue between two people. In consequence, most definitions of the learning process embrace both external relations to the world and (internal) mental processing.

> "Here learning refers to relatively common changes in individual competence resulting from interaction with the world" (Ellström 1996:147).

Or more detailed:

> "(...) learning is perceived as an integrated process comprising two interrelated and interacting sub-processes. First, the interaction process between the individual and the world (...) Second, the internal psychological learning from and processing of this experience leading to the outcome of learning." (Illeris 1999:16)

Likewise the images of and knowledge about learning processes, which individuals generate, embrace two elements: the external relation or the interaction process and the internal processing.

From a general point of view these images contain certain significant considerations of classification and strength, questions such as: What are the internal and the external elements of the process? And what is the relative strength of the efforts of individual and of the environment? And of the internal and external aspects of individual efforts? Is learning perceived as a process that predominantly is facilitated by powerful persons that possess resources and authority (or vice versa as "blocked" by incompetent or malignant persons), or is learning perceived as a process the outcome of which depends on the individual's own actions? Is learning perceived as a process the outcome of which primarily depends on one's internal, mental space such as *intelligence*, *memory*, and *number sense*? Or does the process depend on the qualities of the external social space, such as good environment, "clever, but not devastatingly clever colleagues", and interesting tasks?

The relationship between cognitive processes, including learning, and meta-cognitive images and reflections on these contain several complex aspects that still needs elucidation. For example, to what extent and in which ways is it possible to optimise cognitive processes through the images that we generate from them? And what are the limits of this learning strategy?

Models of Social Learning

We will now proceed to a special case of metacognition, i.e. the relationship between meta-cognitive images of social learning contexts and the social staging of similar processes.

In the following we will focus on, how employee images of, or knowledge about, learning may facilitate or block the diverse ways of staging learning processes within the framework of an organisation.

We are primarily interested in learning processes that are organised as structured and planned learning on-the-job. The models of learning processes that employees in an organisation apply in part result from life experiences and life-long learning processes, and in part from the organisational culture characterising the given workplace with its specific combination of individuals, professional groups, and organisational history.

However, even though any organisation in many ways represents a unique space for learning with its own learning culture, the organisation shares its images of learning with the society and historical context in which it is embedded. Images of learning are rooted in the North European culture and its values, norms, and worldviews (King 1983; Watt 1970; Nellemann 1966).

Images of learning are "cognitive schemata" (see Mayer 1992) that organise our experiences and direct our behaviour. They are the frameworks or perspectives by which we make sense of the meaningless (Goffman 1986). They help us identify social situations as places where we can expect 'learning to take place' and direct our behaviour in these situations. Below six of the cognitive schemata related to learning are summarised based on the factors participants, space, knowledge, and process.

A. Models "with a teacher"

The core of this cultural tradition is three classical models of learning that I have chosen to label "filling station", "apprenticeship", and "greenhouse". These images are not only deeply rooted in history and tradition, but also in our consciousness and they strongly affect, how we, as individuals think and act, in relation to learning processes and education.[1]

A.1. The filling station

Student: The empty, open container. Knows nothing.
Teacher: The full container. Filling station attendant, the versed in the Scriptures. Knows everything.
Room: Classroom. Lecture room (back of the shop = the study).
Knowledge: Based on books. To knowing- that. Declarative knowledge.
Process: Sermon on a text. Examination = evaluating the reproduction of text and sermon.

A.2. The apprenticeship

Student: Apprentice, novice. Knows nothing.
Teacher: Journeyman, the expert. Knows everything.
Room: The workshop.

---

[1] The six learning models are generated from two different sources: an open-ended questionnaire about learning and learning locations that we used in connection with a larger study of youth educations. Findings from the study are reported in the book "Unge i Uddannelse" (L.B. Andersen et al., 1997) and my notes from an exercise ("when and under which circumstances did you learn something important?") that I for a number of years have used when teaching adults. In consequence, the typology is a hypothesis rather than based on empirical data.

Knowledge: Practical knowledge. Knowing-how. Procedural knowledge. The use of well-known methods to accomplish well-defined objectives.
Process: Imitation. Demonstration, instruction, monitoring, and "commenting".

A.3 The greenhouse

Student: A seed. An acorn. A sum of potentials. Carrier of the "good". In the beginning almost ignorant.
Teacher: The old gardener, guru, therapist. Knows a lot. About students. About the "path" and about the field of knowledge and especially concerning, which route to travel in order to acquire it.
Room: A workshop-like structure with a broad or narrow spectre of open facilities and tools (extremes: an artist's room or meditation room).
Knowledge: Actualising potentials. Both knowledge and capability.
Process: self-creation through externalisation. Development through creative and self-actualising process. Using a broad variety of methods to reach an often ill-defined objective.

The first image, the filling station could have been labelled the old grammar school. It is firmly rooted in the way that teaching has been organised in the western world since the Middle Ages (Eisenstein 1970; Bourdieu 1970). The model is embedded in the organising of public school systems emerging in the nineteen century and materialised in the thousands of school all over Europe. In the early twenty-first century, the inner classroom is still embedded in the consciousness of the majority of the Western population. Unless we consciously begin to scrutinise this idea, we will for the rest of our lives spontaneously contribute to stage the social arrangements characterising the filling station, even though we may rarely find ourselves in situation, where its premises are met.

The main principles of filling station teaching should be well known, and I will only emphasise a few of the most important characteristics:

- The classroom is organised physically in a way that the majority of the individuals (the students) face one person (the teacher) and the majority of activities only require activity from one or at the most two persons while the rest are passive observers or taking notes.
- The teacher is the decisive element in learning processes or, in other words, apparently main responsible for learning.

- Teaching and learning is continuously referring to the universe of texts and written materials which become the contents of and key to learning.
- Activities are based on two dimensions: (a) The teacher's professional competence (omniscience) that as a rule is considered as indisputable and self-evident. If questioned seriously teaching risks collapsing; (b) Students preparing themselves in their studies and focusing attention on class teaching.

In consequence of this image of learning the process of learning becomes strongly focused on the teacher while the students learn to occupy a relatively passive role.

As an image of learning, apprenticeship is as old as the filling station, and it is socially rooted in vocational training related to crafts, professions and communities of practice, the competencies of which must be handed over from one generation to the next (Nielsen & Kvale 1999). Its two most important elements are that it is based on practical, rational and goal-oriented actions, and on an unequivocal distribution of competence between teacher (master) and student (apprentice). The point of departure is that the teacher masters everything and knows the right way of doing things, while the student either does not know how to do it or is doing it the wrong way. The student starts as a novice (Benner 1984; Dreyfus & Dreyfus 1986) in the periphery of the community of practice (Lave & Wenger 1991).

The greenhouse is the last of the classical images of learning in our culture, though it is not as widespread as the two others are. Compared to the "filling station" the relationship between teacher and student is one of dialogue. Fundamental to this image of learning is the development of the student's potentials (Grue-Sørensen 1966). Naturally the unfolding of the potentials requires professional space, a pre-existing socially constructed field of organised knowledge that the teacher must master competently. But just as important in facilitating this unfolding is the teacher's knowledge about the potentials of the student, and the teacher's ability to create situations for and insights with the student. An illustrative example of this relationship is the Socratic dialogue.

B. Models "without a Teacher"

But there are other learning models that play an important role in our culture. In the following we shall discuss three important forms of learning established within structured and planned learning on-the-job in work organisations. They are: "the asphalt gang", "the chat group", and "the exploratorium".

B.1 The asphalt gang

Participants: Competent practitioners, dabblers.
Room: The workshop
Knowledge: Bits and pieces usable for the present purpose. Mostly procedural knowledge. Knowing-how.
Process: Neighbour teaching. Exchange of tips and "tricks". Well-defined objectives and well-known, though fragmented knowledge.

B.2 Chat group

(including: Study group/reflecting team/supervision group)

Participants: Competent practitioners, interested novices. Students.
Room: Can take place everywhere. Typically chairs placed around a table, in a circle or horseshoe.
Knowledge: Knowledge, experience, How to do things. Concepts. Evaluating used methods in relation to accomplish certain objectives. Ontological premises or values.
Process: Learning through dialogue.

B.3 Exploratorium

(including: Project group/workshop/kindergarten)

Participants: Innovative practitioners, curious actors. Students.
Room: Workshop.
Knowledge: Both procedural – and declarative knowledge.
Process: Emphasis on two phases: Innovative development of new methods and even objectives. And on the other hand the analytical oriented discussion of process and outcome.

Contrary to the first three models of learning, the latter three are based on *symmetric role relations*.
The situations are characterised by an equal exchange of knowledge and information.

The *asphalt gang* ("workroom") in most cases represents the situation of "learning through the job". Jointly the gang or the team attempts to solve different problems that occur in the work process. No expert or manger is immediately present, and usually problems are solved on the spot when occurring. The point of departure of collective problem solving is always concrete, but participants will be drawing on common knowledge and experience, that is primarily on similar situations solutions to which are transferable.

The *chat group* represents situations in which points of view are discussed and exchanged. The primary purpose is not to solve actual problems, but rather to create a more broad and general understanding or insight. The point of departure for the study group is typically the interpretation and understanding of a given text. The study group could be described as a filling station without teacher. Discussions refer to the text, but the processing and understanding of the text is based on common experience and understanding that play a much more vital role than in the filling station. The reflecting team, however, refers to experiences from identical or parallel practice situations and types of problems.

The *Exploratorium* basically resembles the *asphalt gang*. Dialogues, reflections, and learning refer to a mutual here-and-now practice situation and related problems. The asphalt gang in turn much resembles the apprenticeship, because practice concerns goal-oriented, sensible (wage) work the purpose or result of which is well defined. The kindergarten and the workshop are, on the other hand, relatively open and free structures consisting in tools and facilities that offer the learners fairly great freedom of action and hence of learning. It is a context constructed with the primary purpose of learning and to produce goods of utility and exchange value.

The project group is both a way of organising work processes and a teaching tool the primary purpose of which is to create learning through designing a project.

Especially the latter two images of learning are interesting in this context, because it is primarily variations of these that are brought into play in structured and planned learning in work organisations.

Conclusion:
The Weak Frameworks, the Absent Teacher, and the Well-Established Rights

Concluding we will look at two factors that make these learning processes difficult: The weak frameworks for learning processes and the assumption of symmetrical role relations. In this context we shall be drawing on the previously mentioned case from the hospital field.

The weak frameworks

Successful learning within a weak framework requires strongly committed participants. This can, for example, imply a strong identity as learner – a strong individual or collective vision of change and development through acquiring new competencies, and strong symbol indicators and rituals signalling that now we are in a learning situation.

Collegial supervision, for example, will typically take place in a meeting room with a table and chairs and sometimes a whiteboard. In other words, in a room that in many ways is suited for the purpose, but which is also used for various other meeting activities. It requires strong context switchers to mark that something quite different is going on. A strong context switcher might also be able to change other meetings, such as group conferences in the wards, and make the participants discuss the type of problems (emotional strain) that supervision is meant to alleviate.

Groups function compared to the three learning models Collegial reflection and learning processes require, as among others Senge points out, capability, enthusiasm, and "props" (op. cit.: 225cont.; Schön 1983:157 cont.).To this we could add individual and collective self-discipline and the desire to learn from each other and use each other in a way different from the usual work routines.

Symmetrical role relations are, in general, a precondition for the three latter learning models though not unconditionally. Differences in competence, not to mention competence hierarchies, are manageable provided that the learning group openly recognise and accept such differences. On the other hand, pronounced differences in commitment, attitudes, and values may constitute serious obstacles to making learning without teacher.

In my view the greatest problem in this context is that people often find it difficult to commit themselves whole-heartedly to learning processes in which they have to learn from colleagues at their own competence levels. The most serious obstacle is not the relationship to the colleagues, but that they experience the situation through an inappropriate learning model. Within the model of the "filling station" individuals may find it more motivating to participate in supervisions conducted by an external competent psychologist than being in the situation of sharing a room with a number of well known faces. Something similar could be said about other types of learning that fall within the three latter images of learning. But what can we do about this type of problems?

First, it is important to get accustomed to thinking learning and learning processes - not only in relation to the three former traditional models, but also to the latter three: the asphalt gang, the chat group, and the exploratorium. And in continuation to develop the learning competencies required for these methods of work.

Second, the (too rapid) decline in participant spirit and commitment toward collegial team learning is often caused by the fact that the coupling is too poor between these types of learning and learning through work processes and external learning, respectively.

It could be that employees have too few or too irrelevant possibilities for external training. Or maybe the organisation has not developed routines for incorporating into the collegial learning processes on-the-job the knowledge and capabilities that certain employees gain from external courses. Or important aspects of the organisational work processes are not discussed for some reasons and consequently not incorporated into the collegial learning processes. The informal (and perhaps tacit) norms governing from which frame of reference or perspective work related problems are discussed could be too traditional or too narrow-minded to yield much learning from the collegial dialogue.

One could claim that important aspects of these problems not necessarily have much in common with learning. I fully agree with this viewpoint. From the general point of view, I think that the reasons why an organisation does not learn sufficiently (whatever this might be), are not related to the learning processes. They stem from the deeper layers of norms and values characterising the organisational culture and to the well-established rights of employees and management.

References

Andersen, Karsten Bøjesen & Claus Agø Hansen (1999): *Intern læring - tayloristisk praksis eller helhedsorienteret udvikling?* I: Tidsskriftet for Arbejdsliv nr 4. 1999. Odense.

Andreasen, Lars Birch (1997): *Unge i uddannelse. Valg og vurderinger af ungdomsuddannelserne.* Udviklingscentret for folkeoplysning og voksenundervisning. København.

Argyris, Chris & Schön, Donald A. (1977): *Organisational Learning: a theory of action perspective.* Addison-Wesley. Reading, Massachusetts.

Bateson, Gregory (1973): *Steps to an ecology of mind.* Paladin.London

Bauman, Zygmunt (1997): *Postmodernity and its discontents.* Polity Press.Cambridge

Beck, Ulrich (1992): *Risk Society.* Sage. London.

Benner, Patricia (1984): *From Novice to Expert.* Addison Wesley. San Francisco.

Bohm, David (1996): *On Dialogue.* Routledge. London

Bourdieu, Pierre (1971): *Systems of Education and Systems of Thought* i: Young, Michael F.D. (red): Knowledge and control. New directions for the sociology of education. Collier-Macmillan.London.

Bruer, John T. (1998): *Education.* I: William Bechtel & George Graham (red): A companion to cognitive science. Blackwell. Oxford

Bruner, Jerome (1998): *Uddannelseskulturen.* Munksgaard. København

Dewey, John (1974): *Erfaring og opdragelse.* Christian Ejlers. København.

Doise, Willem (1991): *System and metasystem in cognitive operations.* I: Carretero, Mario m.fl.(red): Learning and Instruction. Vol 3. Persamont Press.Oxford.

Dreyfus, Hubert & S.Dreyfus (1986): *Mind over Machine.* The Free Press. New York

Eisenstein, E.L. (1970): *The Impact of Printing on European Education.* I: Musgrave, P.W.(red): Sociology, History and Education. Methuen & Co Ltd.London.

Ellström, Per-Erik (1996): *Rutin och reflektion.* I: Ellström, Per-Erik m.fl (red) (1996): Livslångt lärande. Studentlitteratur. Lund.

Giddens, Anthony (1991): *Modernity and Self-Identity.* Polity Press; Cambridge.

Goffman, Erving (1986): *Frame Analysis: an essay on the organisation of experience.* Harper & Row. New York.

Grue-Sørensen, K. (1966): *Opdragelsens historie 3.* Gyldendal. København.

Hauen, Finn van, Vagn Strandgaard, Bjarne Kastberg (1995): *Den lærende organisation.* Industriens Forlag. København.

Illeris, Knud (1999): *Læring.* - Aktuel læringsteori i spændingsfeltet mellem Piaget, Freud og Marx. Roskilde Universitetsforlag. København

Nielsen, Klaus & Steinar Kvale (1999): *Mesterlæren som aktuel læringsform.* I: Nielsen, Klaus & Steinar Kvale (red): Mesterlære. Læring som social praksis. Reitzel. København.

Kolb, D.A. (1984): *Experiental learning. Experience as source of learning and development.* Prentice-Hall.New Jersey.

Laursen, Erik (1997): *Glemsel, leg og hierarkisering. Nye muligheder og gamle barrierer for organisatorisk læring.* I: Christensen, Allan (red): Den lærende organisations begreber og praksis. Aalborg Universitetsforlag. Aalborg.

Laursen, Erik (1996): *Fra den "todelte hjælper" mod "reflekterende teams".* LEO-serien nr 13. Aalborg Universitet.

Laursen, Erik (1994): *Problembaseret projektarbejde.* Evaluering af den samfundsvidenskabelige basisuddannelse. Aalborg Universitet. Aalborg.

Lave, Jean & Etienne Wenger (1991): *Situated learning.* Legitimate peripheral participation.
Cambridge Uni. Press. Cambridge.

Mayer, Richard E. (1992): *Thinking, problem solving, cognition.* W.H. Freeman and Company. New York.

Nellemann, Aksel H. (1966): *Den danske skoles historie.* Gjellerup. København

Piaget, Jean (1969): *Barnets psykiske udvikling.* Reitzel. København.

Politiken (1987): Nudansk Ordborg. Politikens Forlag. København.

Schön, Donald A. (1983): *The Reflective Practioner.* - How Professionals think in action.
Harper Collins Publ. New York

Schön, Donald A. (1987): *Educating the Reflective Practioner.* Jossey-Bass Publ. San Francisco.

Senge, Peter M (1999): *Den femte disciplin.* Klim. Århus

Sennett, Richard (1999): *Det fleksible menneske.* Hovedlandet. Højbjerg.

Strandgaard, Vagn, Finn van Hauen & Bjarne Kastberg (1996): *Det samarbejdende menneske.* Industriens forlag. København.

Chapter 3

Personal development - for whose sake?[2]

By Jan Brødslev Olsen

Organisational learning involves not only learning in a narrow sense but personal development in a broader sense. But what does the concept "personal development"' really cover? The concept is used in many different areas from the basic training in social work and health care, from business courses and evening classes in psychology and communication, to job training for social security clients.

Two main approaches to personal development immediately stand out.

The first approach is *problem oriented*, dealing with the reparation functions and is typical for the public, social sector. Its purpose is to repair the social and mental damage, which a part of the population has incurred in life through different forms of collisions with modern society. From this perspective, personal development seeks to free the individual from various destructive patterns (work-shyness, addictions, lack of social skills etc.), which restrain the individual from taking actively part in productive society.

The other main approach is *growth oriented*, dealing with development functions, and this approach is typical for the public sector of education, basic education as well as supplementary education, and in the private sector's multifarious businesses of education and consulting services. Its purpose is typically to make effective persons even more effective, because the goal is to adjust people's values and attitudes to their jobs. For instance by making them more flexible, co-operative, responsible etc.

---

[2] The article is a translation of Brødslev Olsen (2000): Personlig forandring – for hvis skyld? In: Kognition & Pædagogik, nr. 38, december 2000, Dansk Psykologisk Forlag, with a minor supplement from Brødslev Olsen 2006a & 2006b, Brødslev Olsen 2007 and Keldorff & Brødslev Olsen 2007.

Personal development in the context of organisational learning will mainly focus on the growth-oriented approach but might also involve problem-oriented elements.

The individual as a means

The two approaches to personal development above might look very different and are probably also seen that way by the individuals involved. Despite of that, I will claim that what they have in common is that they have the individual as a means and not an end. Whether we are talking about the young claimant, who has to develop his ego structure to learn to go to work, or we are talking about the successful managing director, who is on a management course to learn stress reduction, both are subjects to an adjustment of personality with a special object in view. The manager will probably have a better chance of maintaining the illusion of him "doing it for his own sake" than the claimant, who has been sent on the course with the threat of losing his benefits if he does not turn up. But the fundamental end is the same: to develop the individual with a view to an end outside the individual. The individual has become a means. This is the source of the alienation which latently or manifestly threatens the sense of identity, and which I will return to.

The individual as an end

On the other hand, another approach to personal development exists: this approach involves efforts directed towards the individual as an end, typically various forms of courses and master/student relationships, where the only target is to cultivate human nature. The cultivation may be to develop cognitive as well as emotional and active aspects of the individual. Taken as a whole, you can say that the purpose of these endeavours is that the individual can become himself, and that is the sole purpose. Personal development in that sense often involves precisely the opposite of personal development with the individual as a means: that the individual moves away from the social performance. This type of personal development - to become your self - is metaphorically described by the Danish engineer and philosopher Ludvig Feilberg. He writes (Feilberg 1918, p. 7):

> "On a dark winter's day, a man walks down the street of Gothersgade and reaches the square of Kongens Nytorv. If a person is mindful of his own inner state, he will often observe how seemingly minor changes in the surroundings may cause major changes in mood, as for instance here the shift from the dirty street

with its annoying traffic, slush, shouting and rumble of wheels to the large quiet square where the noise is heard at a distance, where houses and lampposts seem to recede. It is as if you have peace to expand and collect yourself, to look at the weather and the sky. Our man felt freer at heart; instinctively he was walking more slowly."

Most people know the two mental states, which Feilberg describes. One is marked by noise, hectic activity, lack of presence and attentiveness. The other is marked by silence, the opportunity to collect oneself and to be present. It is this difference that interests Feilberg in his works. According to Feilberg, the point is that we as humans have living space to do, what comes natural in relation to our abilities and personality, and that we can be present in relation to what the situation offers. In Feilberg's example above it is evident that Feilberg connects civilisation to one type of existence, the hurried, stressed life, while he connects the possibility of withdrawing from the pressures of civilisation on human nature with the other type of existence. In brief Feilberg wanted "(...) simply to find out what it is that at times makes us feel that we really live, and what it is that other times makes us feel that everything is dead, empty, trivial, unimportant, cold, dark, low, sad." (Pahuus 1986, p. 14). Feilberg's answer certainly does not turn out to the advantage of civilisation. That also goes for a corresponding endeavour to describe man's possibility of happiness, which is a quarter of a century later than Feilberg's. In 1926 a young English psychologist Marion Milner began with unusual systematic endeavour to study what made her happy. An endeavour, that lasted all her life with systematic records of her life. The starting point for this endeavour was Milner's own sudden realisation of her emotional despondency. One of Milner's central findings relating to the reasons for her lack of happiness and joy was a painful realisation of her deep dependency on her surrounding's opinion of her and her fear of offending them or not doing the right thing (Donaldson 1992, p. 262ff.). A reflection, many people probably recognise.

End or means?

We thus have two types of self-development: processes, which have an end *outside* the individual, and processes, which have an end *inside* the individual. There are developmental processes, which have higher productivity, better service, higher quality etc. as their end, and development processes, which only have the individual as the end. The question is, whether these two types of processes can be merged and perhaps enrich each other, or whether they are by nature incompatible. I will pinpoint this problem through three examples.

Supervision and personal development

The first example is of a forty something woman. She experiences increased fatigue and lack of vivacity in almost all her spheres of life. Tests have disclaimed the suspicion of somatic illness or disease. Only with a violent effort of will can she do her daily chores at work, at home and in her family. Particularly her job is influenced by her condition, where work is piling up, and the woman finds herself in a state of increased chronic stress. The situation draws to a dramatic high point. At her manager's suggestion, the woman now begins an individual supervision course paid by her employer. Here the woman learns some mastering strategies, which reduce her stress and give her a bust of energy. After six months the woman is almost up to her usual form. She has learned to say "yes" and "no" at the right times and places, she has reduced a number of unhealthy job habits, and she has conquered self-destructive automatic thoughts and feelings. The woman finds herself more sparkling and with strength to cope with life at home as well as at work. The concrete, operational yield from this process is that the woman can once again work effectively.

Is there a clash of interests between the individual as a means and the individual as an end? No. But you only have to alter the story slightly to reveal that the clash is latent. We may imagine the following quite realistic possibilities:

- The mastering strategies, which the woman has learned in order to handle her thoughts, feelings and actions, gradually turn out to be in conflict with both the manager's management style and demands and the culture of the firm. To sum up, you may describe the job's norms as markedly we-oriented without personal space to any large extent. As the woman begins to deviate from this prevailing norm through her now distinct character, the manager and some of her colleagues begin to doubt the value of her supervision course. They had not expected her development to take that direction. They only want her "back in the pen".

- During the supervision course, it becomes still more evident for both the supervisor and the supervised that the problems they are working with are only symptoms of her being in a more extensive mid-life crisis. The woman now begins to see a totally different working life with a different content and form. In other words, she is about to change her path in life.

- To the supervised, the supervision course reveals that the manifest problems in question mirror a more extensive life long problem: that the woman at an earlier point of her life took an educational and job path for which she had basically neither talent nor interest. As in the previous development version, the woman now begins to see a different kind of working life.

The three possibilities above illustrate how the process, "the individual as a means", can easily be corrected by the other process, "the individual as an end". Harmony between the two types of processes *is* possible, but things will not always turn out that way.

Supplementary education and self-development

Another example is of a group of health care workers who participate in supplementary education. Here they learn a number of philosophical and psychological theories. Some of these theories point to human needs and forms of interaction which - if they are taken seriously - also point to some destructive or at best very limiting factors in the health care sector. All the participants agree that the theories contain some good ideals for the health care sector, but here the group is divided into four:

- *The pragmatists* who go home to their jobs and try "to make the best of" the reality they are part of.

- *The disillusioned* ones who at home have to forget or repress the knowledge they have gained, but who partly or wholly still experience the pain and suffering of not being true to what they now know to be the truth.

- *The revolutionaries* who attempt to change the structures and work habits that oppose their newly found ideals.

- *The immigrants* who have to acknowledge that they cannot realise their newly found ideals under the existing conditions, and that they cannot make or do not believe in the possibility of basic changes.

The four strategies are all attempts to master the conflict between "the individual as an end" and "the individual as a means". In real life it is quite possible to shift between these positions. Thus a usual path is that you begin as a revolutionary, then you become disillusioned and in the end you become a pragmatic or an immigrant.

Therapy and personal development

A man who works within a highly specialised technical area goes through two years of cognitive therapy because of some phobic conditions he experiences in certain job situations. At the end of the therapy his phobia is practically gone, but in the last sessions of therapy he has begun to see that to a large extend he has reduced a great deal of his human capacity to obtain the success he enjoys. However, he also has to acknowledge that the realisation of a wider section of his personality will cause a lowering of the high and ambitious activity level he has within his field. An existential dilemma thus exists.

An inner or an outer conflict?

The two first examples illustrate the conflict between the individual as a means and the individual as an end as a conflict, which takes place between the individual person on the one hand, and the social surroundings on the other. It is thus the classic conflict between the individual and society, the inner and the outer world, the life world and the systems world. The two worlds are easily identifiable. Nevertheless, the third example above shows that the conflict could just as easily have been an inner existential drama where the individual is in a real inner dilemma. In some instances the dilemma can be solved with the aid of various kinds of life adjustments where the individual to a certain extent opens up to the aspects, which demand attention. In other instances the dilemma will be an inner psychological tension through perhaps many years. It is probable that in the majority of cases the conflict between the individual as an end and the individual as a means will result in an outer as well as an inner dilemma.

The individual and the community

So far I have assumed and tried to illustrate that an individual can develop with the sole intention of inner growth or with the intention of a goal that lies outside of the individual. The examples above show that in every personal development process there is a latent or manifest conflict between these two goals. Nonetheless, it is relevant at this point to question this assumption. To realise the individual as an end I have so far uncritically connected to the realisation of *the individual*. But could we not just as easily imagine that the realisation of the individual as an end takes the community into consideration? That is, "the individual as an end" is connected to the community with regard to universally humane values. Yes, indeed we can, because "the individual as an end" is not attached to the individual as such but to the qualities connected to being human and living in a human community. Two problems can clarify this point: the instances where it is the individual who uses the outside world and the community as the means to his own end, meaning the instances where the individual's end is selfish, and the instances where the end is universally altruistic.

The selfish goal

It is well-known that the individual can use the outside world, the others, to realise his own selfish goals and nothing else. In that case the individual does not perceive the outside world to any other extent than that of fulfilling his own needs. The outside world is perceived and evaluated from a utilitarian perspective. The others are perceived and evaluated not as the persons they are but as (potential) objects for satisfying the individual's own needs. Philosophically this line of thought can be traced back to Jeremy Bentham (1748-1832). To Bentham any talk of especially noble and eternal rules was "nonsense on stilts". Everything, an individual does is (Fink 1995, p. 91):

> "(...) an attempt at attaining happiness and avoiding unhappiness and pain. Things, which bring happiness, man calls good and useful and things, which bring unhappiness is called evil and wrong. Each time an individual acts, he will choose and should choose the act, which, all things considered, looks as if it will lead to greater happiness than any other act possible in the given situation. How great the happiness is depends on how intense and durable it is."

According to this idea, in a narrow sense man is nothing but a self-centred needs oriented being, and it is certainly possible to live that way.

The altruistic goal

Opposite the selfish goal is the universally altruistic goal. That the goal is universally altruistic means that it realises the values which bind us together as humans, i.e. core-values such as trust, honesty, kindness and caring. A core-value is a quality that – if it was not in your life – your existence together with other people would seem shallow, grey, conflict-ridden or even without hope. To develop your self with that end can hardly be said to have the individual as a means because the end is beyond the individual. Especially people working in leadership, counselling, teaching, etc., must emphasise the maintenance and development of core values in support of themselves as well as their staff, clients, pupils, students or patients. Maintenance of core-values is just as important as the maintenance of professional knowledge (Brødslev Olsen 2006a, 2006b, 2007 and Keldorff & Brødslev Olsen 2007). That a health care worker participates in supplementary education to improve his patient care has exactly the individual as an end. Here it is about learning something for the common good. But still the question is not that simple. Because what if the person in question against his will has been sent on this course by his departmental manager because the manager believes that the employee lacks competence and a sense of responsibility? The employee is thus the means of his own manager's ideal of the individual, i.e. the patient, as an end.

Self-realisation through universal altruism

The considerations above lead to the conclusion that the individual as an end can only be realised to the extent that the individual person as well as universal altruism is realised. The perspective can be an inner or an outer perspective, i.e. that of the individual or the social surroundings. From *the inner perspective*, self-realisation has to go beyond what is purely selfish to the social surrounding through the realisation of the universal values. From *the outer perspective*, self-realisation of the individual has to be made possible by the social context having the universal values as its end.

"The golden rule"

The golden rule is an attempt at a brief guide as to what the individual can do to do good for him self as well as for others. We find the golden rule in a negative and in a positive wording. As the classic Chinese philosopher Confucius (551-479 BC.) puts it in a negative wording:

"Never do unto others as you would not have them do unto you."

In his guide on how to follow the golden rule, Confucius refers to five cardinal virtues: compassion, generosity, sincerity, honesty and kindness.

About 500 years later Jesus phased the same principle this way (Matthew 7:12):

"Do unto others as you would have them do unto you."

We find the golden rule and the individual cardinal virtues with the Danish philosopher K E Løgstrup (1956, 1968, and 1972). As humans we have to realise ourselves - or perhaps rather the human aspect - in the meeting with others as we then realise what Løgstrup calls a spontaneous and sovereign manifestation of life such as trust, mercy, love, frankness and kindness. It is only through the meeting of humans where I open up to others and their situation that I can realise what is essential as a human. I can only realise myself by being obliging and open to what other humans need. To Løgstrup, self-realisation is thus all but a selfish goal. It is the opposite. I can only do well to myself by doing well unto others. There is no clash between the individual and the community; on the contrary, the community is the condition for the individual. But is not any kind of community. To Løgstrup it is only through the community, which realises the spontaneous and sovereign manifestations of life, such as trust, honesty and kindness that the individual can realise himself as a human. We cannot become humans in just any community. In communities where there are revolving thoughts and feelings such as distrust, bitterness, hatred, resentment, envy and jealousy, we cannot realise ourselves because we cannot realise ourselves as humans.

Personal development with the individual and the community as an end

The conclusion to this multitude of considerations points to only certain types of personal development and only certain social conditions being able to handle the double movement of realising the individual for his own sake and realising the universal values at the same time. It is my belief that there is much work to be done in order to reach a greater precision within this field than the case is today[3]. As the individual is becoming an ever greater part of job qualifications and education, it is necessary to know for whose sake you attempt to develop what qualities. Only then it is possible to clarify the end of the endeavours of developing your personality, and only then might you avoid some of the mistakes which often occur within this field, such as private or public companies setting personal development processes in motion on behalf of their employees - processes which the managers in reality have neither the intention nor the resources to accomplish. Or it might be educational institutions that leave

---

[3] In the book "The world of the self" I have extensively defined and discussed the relationship between the individual and the social surroundings from the perspective of developmental psychology and life history.

students with unrealised developmental needs or overstep their personal boundaries. You can also say that there appears to be a lack of professional dialogue as well as ethics in this field (Keldorff og Brødslev Olsen 2007). Personal development in the context of organisational learning will meet the same challenge to develop such a dialogue and ethics.

References

Brødslev Olsen, Jan (2000): *Selvets verden* (The world of the self). Systime Academic 2004.

Brødslev Olsen (2000): *Personlig forandring – for hvis skyld?* In: Kognition & Pædagogik, nr. 38, December 2000, Dansk Psykologisk Forlag

Brødslev Olsen, Jan (2001): *Personlig forandring – for hvis skyld?* In: Frederiksen, Klee & Nefer (ed.): Individualitet, værdier og fællesskab. Dafolo Forlag 2001

Brødslev Olsen, Jan (2006a): *Core Learning* ICEL 2006. (International Consortium for Experiental Learning), Lancaster University, UK. Conference presentation.

Brødslev Olsen, Jan (2006b): *Essensvejledning.* In: Andreasen & Giehm-Reese (2006): *Perspektiver på vejledning.* Udviklings- og Videnscenter for Vejledning.

Brødslev Olsen, Jan (2007): *Genopdagelse af det menneskelige.* In: *Voksenpædagogisk tidsskrift* 1/2007.

Donaldson, Margaret (1992): *Menneskets psyke.* Hans Reitzels Forlag 1998, translated from: *Human minds,* Penguin Books, London 1992.

Feilberg, Ludvig (1918): *Samlede skrifter.* Gyldendalske Boghandel - Nordisk Forlag.

Fink (1995): *Samfundsfilosofi.* Aarhus Universitetsforlag.

Keldorff, Søren & Brødslev, Jan (2007): *Hvad er meningen – Og er der en åndelig?* In: Joel Haviv (2007): *Medarbejder eller modarbejder – religion i det moderne arbejdsliv.* Klim.

Løgstrup, K E (1956): *Den etiske fordring.* Gyldendal 1991.

Løgstrup, K E (1968): *Opgør med Kierkegaard.* Gyldendal 1994.

Løgstrup, K E (1972): *Norm og spontanitet.* Gyldendal 1993.

Pahuus, Mogens (1986): *Livsfilosofi: Lykke og lidelse i eksistens og litteratur.* Forlaget Philosophia.

Chapter 4

The "Must" of Sensibility in the Knowledge Society. On the Psychological Roots of the Developing Work and the Learning Organisation

By Søren Keldorff

Revisiting the Accumulation of Work Needs

After having been away from the field for some years, I returned to the conceptual universe of contemporary industrial psychology[4] some years ago and got the feeling of a déjà vue. The very same concepts that I had left in the 1970s seemed to be having a renaissance in the 1990s. The 1970s were the palmy days of sensitivity training and group dynamics. At the courses where I worked as assistant coach, we got our material from American social psychology research in the 1950s. Scholars such as Kurt Lewin, Solomon Asch, Friedrick Herzberg, John McClelland, Sherif & Sherif, and Robert Bales were translated into popular Danish texts and practical exercises. The Dane Arne Sjølund published his book "Gruppepsykologi" (Group Psychology) in the 1960s summarising American research results. Those of us that were "ordained" to the fairly profitable clergy got access to Sjølund's exercise book, and after having communicated its message virtually any educational institution in Denmark had been subjected to training in group dynamics. Those were the years of "democratising" medium and long-term educations and of bringing to light the so-called reserve of talents from village ponds, cottages, and worker ghettoes in order to use this powerful mass to "smoke" the last professors out of the ivory towers. A few years later we would occupy the Danish educational society that had been liberated by the student revolt and the OECD education economists. Bear in mind that the concepts were "reserve of talent" and "human capital". At that time any idea of applying the same group dynamic exercises to common industrial workers would not only have been reprehensible, but would have been

---

[4] Being a psychologist I deliberately choose to call much of what others refer to as "organisation psychology" for "industrial psychology" as that is what I have learned: "applied social psychology" is equivalent to "industrial psychology" Hosking and Morley (1991) says it like this "Organisation people get a distant look in their face when psychologists talk – and vice versa".

the worst kind of class betrayal and social partner ideology. The workers had to be understood as alienated[5] and exploited, even though it was not until later in the 1970s that the theoretical fundamentalism of university Marxism made it totally impossible to undertake any practical work related to the workers. Nevertheless I did succeed in producing a number of critical student reports in my capacity as external expert on the collaboration between "workers-academics", an organisation that then published a series of much discussed critical reports on working environment.

Against this background it is perhaps not strange that I was surprised to find that the positive message about development in work, performance requirements, self-realisation, etc., had re-entered the scene in the early 1990s. On the other hand, I soon realised that the truth of the 1990s differed from that of the 1970s – but perhaps it has meanwhile become possible to communicate the good message from that time to the industrial wage earners. Could it really be true that politicians, unions and managers had resumed their talk about "reserve of talent" and "human capital" – now just using different labels (the learning organisation and the developing work) and targeted at common industrial workers? Were they advocating changing the organising of work towards allowing employees greater responsibility, personal development, and furthering training? And was this attitude no longer solely based on considerations of productivity?

Marx and Industrial Psychology

When we, in the early 1970s, attended optional afternoon lectures on Capital Logic at the Student House in Aarhus, one of the key messages was the development of forms of co-operation. This was the lesson on how the artisans during the first tentative years of capitalism were collected under one roof to stand side by side performing their work. It was called "simple co-operation" – they could and did whatever they had done before, but now there were many of them doing the same at the same time. But having had to surrender their large toolboxes in return for being entitled to use a tool at the assembly line for repeating the same function changed the nature of work qualitatively. In addition the command of work had moved to the cage of the foreman. Gone was not only the diversity of artisan capabilities and ingenuity, but the workers were also

---

[5] Joachim Israel's book on "Alienation" (Copenhagen 1970) among other things presented Blauner's industrial studies which at that time was a must – just as the critical Swedish book "Konsten att dressera Människor" ["The Art of Training Human Beings"] (Stockholm 1971).

expected to leave their brains outside the factory gate – they were no longer required to think, but only to perform according to the orders of the foreman. Within industrial or organisation psychology this development is referred to as Taylorism or Fordism and it was by and large identical with any pre-psychological thinking about the organising of work: assembly lines that lead to alienation and reduce man to the state of stupidity. The perception of man underlying "the economic man" – the calculating worker who only works out of pure necessity for earning money to survive/consume during leisure time. This is, among other, Mc Gregor's theory X. The management's perception of the ideal worker was "the tireless ox" that could work infinitely without thinking:

> "Now one of the very first requirements for a man who is fit to handle pig irons as a regular occupation is that he shall be so stupid and so phlegmatic that he more nearly resembles in his mental make-up the ox than any other type. The man who is mentally alert and intelligent is for this very reason entirely unsuited to what would, for him, be the grinding monotony of work of this character." (Taylor 1967:59)

Frederic Winston Taylor, who wrote this in 1911, was himself promoted from machine worker to foreman. No matter how scientific his management theory attempted to appear, his main "plot" was that from his time as common worker he knew the types of resistance to exploitation. The Norwegian Sverry Lysgård has later on described this brilliantly in his book "Arbeiderkollektivet" (the Workers Collective) However, Lysgård's theory was never adopted by the great American industrialists. During these years the American unions doubled their membership. The workers reacted by resorting to strikes, slow-down actions, and low performance. Henry Ford was shrewder than the small manufacturer's "pet", Taylor. Ford made the products of his assembly lines – cars – attainable for his own workers, and was a kind of precursor of what we have later come to understand as "Japanese management style"[6]. However, the industry could not continue to manage without a more positive psychological theory of the working human being.

---

[6] Among other things Ford built houses in ghettos for his workers and installed a kind of "a corps of snoopers" to stop the workers from spending their weekly wages in the pubs.

The Great Revolution: Discovering Needs

The great revolution in industrial psychology was the discovery of social needs in the 1930s and 1940s in the U.S.A. So far the increased efficiency of assembly work had rested on intensive time studies of the monotonous work. Taylor's methods for rationalising the movements of the workers represented the precursor of later piece-rate systems based on time studies, but the so-called scientific management already began cracking in the years prior to World War II. The majority of line workers proved not to be the tireless oxen that Taylor's ideal prescribed. Hundreds of rationalisation experts visited factories in attempts to solve the line workers' problems of boredom and loss of meaning. Especially the Hawthorne experiments focused on the workers as social beings, which led to a new epoch in industrial psychology. The catchword of the new managerial form, "human relations", was established in a series of books, such as Mason Haire's Psychology in Management (1955).

In his book Haire refers to Walker and Guest's comprehensive study of assembly line workers.[7] Typically workers would say that they would prefer not working at the assembly line if they could obtain the same wage. Haire finds that such responses reflect that people have learned to accept more money to compensate for less of something else, such as less time to talk and joke with fellow workers – one of the reasons why they did not like their work. Their complaints concerned all aspects of the work organisation, which made work impersonal and resulted in reduced requirements for proficiency. This situation was clearly brought about by the mechanisation, which had turned work into routine functions and thus increased the efficiency in all technical and mechanical parts of the factory. But what about the human efficiency?

The evident answer was the lacking attention in production to human needs thus introducing the focus of the new industrial psychology on the necessity of paying attention to and invest managerial efforts in human needs as production factors.

According to Hair, the moment that we become aware of all the possibilities for meeting the social and selfish needs prevailing in the workplace they seem to exist everywhere. Creating good social relations among workers need not clash with the interests of production. In many cases it suffices to satisfy the workers' feelings of belong the group they are part of, and hence satisfy their social needs.

---

[7] Walker & Guest (1952) The Man on the Assembly Line.

Sociality as Compensatory Necessity

The very choice of words in the 1950s seems to imply compensatory measures rather than a genuine interest in employees as human beings. The idea seems to be that since studies have demonstrated that workers have social needs, it must be possible to exploit these needs by coupling workers in groups. However, Haire is fully aware of the fact that he is advocating changes which the post-war American managers profoundly oppose as they are still strongly influenced by McGregor's theory X which presents workers as lazy free-riders. So it will take both pep talk and success stories to make managers consider his ideas. He compares his good message with the popular idea that for medicine to work it must taste nasty. This is not necessarily the case of human relations, he says. The message may be true even though it is positive.

But preferably the companies should gain something from changing the organising of work, e.g. cost reductions. Haire tells a tale from a public office where one hundred women work in a large room sorting exhibits. They make numerous errors, have a high rate of absence due to illness, and the personnel turnover is also high. In order to change the situation, the room was been divided into smaller sections holding groups of maximum ten women – and look what happened. Fewer errors, less absence due to illness and lower personnel turnover! Haire personifies the story by quoting one of the women who wakes up in the morning with a cold thinking: "I have better go to work, because if I don't Else, Karen and Gerda will have to make up for me".

Haire's Model of Needs

It is typical of these early theories of industrial psychology that they approach the theory of needs from the behaviourist perspective. Admittedly we are introduced to a kind of Y-theory about humans/workers as susceptible creatures, but often in the shape of Hull's theory of remuneration of appropriate and punishment of inappropriate behaviour which is, to a large extent, based on experiments with rats and other creatures searching labyrinths for food.

Nevertheless at the bottom of his model is a kind of need hierarchy consisting of three layers: 1) physical or organic needs (food, oxygen, sleep, etc.); 2) social needs consisting in establishing relationships with and among human beings, that is the need for being with others, for being tied to others (the previous "herd instinct")[8] and finally 3) the selfish needs such as the need for domineering others, hold one's ground or be recognised for one's efforts, etc.[9]

Haire's need model resembles hundreds of other models, but it is important to add that it is somewhat limited compared to the later humanistic models. It does not, for instance, operate with independent "inner" motives for acting as a human being. This is in part due to the underlying theory of science. Behaviourism has never recognised inner experiences as evidence of anything. In principle, it views human emotions as a "black box" – psychological statements can only be based on observable behaviour.[10]

Abraham Maslow and Frederick Herzberg

The model was, however, soon updated with the motivation theories of humanistic psychology and in particular by the psychologists Henry Murray and Abraham Maslow. The later one well known tentative hierarchy of needs was introduced and later on rendered probable with Herzberg studies of what motivates man to work. In the preface to the Danish translation of Herzberg et al.'s *Motivation to Work*, Finn Junge-Jensen writes that the book breaks with both the theory of scientific management about wage and with the theory of human relations about social aspects as being decisive. Higher wages, friendly superiors, longer vacations or the like is not decisive. "To motivate people requires attaching great importance to issues that can meet the needs for self-

---

[8] In all fairness it should be mentioned that Haire elaborates on the social needs with reference to the work place. He thus mentions the need for feeling accepted as a member of a group, the importance to getting into a "good gang" – and even the de-selection of a better job to stay with colleagues /friends – and the effect of group pressure on dissidents, e.g. those breaking the price rates.

[9] Haire mentions an illustrative example from the hotel industry with a women in charge of the seafood buffet but who would not tolerate being referred to as the " fishwife" by the management and colleagues. Only through diplomatic intervention did the management succeed in persuading her to stay in her otherwise satisfactory job. Who we are and how we think that others perceive us may fill us with both pleasure and deep disappointment.

[10] Emotional life remained scientific taboo after the so-called "cognitive revolution" within psychology in the late 1960s. According to Goleman (1997:67), cognitive psychologists continued to view intelligence as hyper-rational, dry information bytes unsoiled by emotions, the incarnation of the idea that emotions are incompatible with intelligence and only confuse our image of conscious mental life. It was, amongst others, cognitive psychologists (Bruner, Berlyne and others) who provided the ammunition for introducing "the scientific curriculum" in order to bring out "the hidden intelligence reserve" in the early 1970s.

realisation, which are, among others, recognition, performance and responsibility (ibid:7).

The studies by Herzberg and others in the 1960s provided the justification for distinguishing between so-called maintenance factors and genuine motivation factors – that is the difference between basic factors that must satisfied and in order and satisfactions that really count in terms of motivation.

Figure 4.1 Maslow's & Herzberg's models

MASLOW	HERZBERG
SELF-REALISATION Having the opportunity for unfolding one's capabilities CREATIVITY	CHALLENGES AND PERSONAL RESPONSIBILITY IN THE JOB
RESPECT ONESELF AND BE RESPECTED BY OTHERS Being accepted for what you are SELF-ESTEEM	RECOGNITION OF ONES EFFORTS AND BEGINNING ALLOCATION OF RESPONSIBILITY
SOCIAL ATTACHMENT Belonging to and feeling that some people care about you SOCIAL NEEDS	BEING SURROUNDED BY LOYAL WORKERS AND COLLEAGUES
MATERIAL AND PERSONAL SAFETY	SAFETY, WAGE, ENVIROMENT AND GOODS
HAVING ONES PHYSIOLOGICAL NEEDS SATISFIED	HAVING A JOB

Figure 4.1: Comparison of Maslow's and Hertberg's models for the hierarchy of needs from satisfaction of basic physiological needs/having a job to the most important needs: self-realisation/challenges in the job (modified after Schein 1990:93).

The two top sections concern growth or actual motivation factors. The remaining three sections concern so-called deficiency or maintenance factors. The most important difference is – apart from Herzberg's model solely concerns work – that in Herzberg's model satisfaction of maintenance factors at the most evoke a neutral feeling and not outright dissatisfaction. Satisfaction of the three needs lowest in the hierarchy will not result in direct motivation, but "must be satisfied" in order to evoke actual motivation (the two top sections).

Hunt and Hill[11] have juxtaposed Maslow's hierarchy of needs with Herzberg's two-factor theory and it appears from Figure 4.1 that Maslow's two top levels correspond to Herzberg's actual motivation factors. These are factors are "directly related to the job and the individual' ability to manage his job satisfactorily... the very experience of success (goal fulfilment), being recognised for having done a good job, the nature of tasks and the opportunity for stimulation and personal development – apart from the responsibility for the tasks."[12]

Proposal for the Design of Jobs: Make Work Richer and Freer!

Herzberg's focus on the individual's need for self-realisation in the job via assuming greater responsibility and being free to set his own performance goals broke decisively with the tendencies at that time to make jobs as specialised as possible. Therefore he was in a position to list quite precise proposals for the design of jobs:
1) Removal of control functions, but keeping responsibility; 2) increasing the responsibility of the individual within his own domains; 3) freedom in the job; 4) communicating directly with the individual worker rather than through his foreman; 5) introduction of new and more demanding tasks; 6) allocation of specialist tasks to the individual workers making it possible for them to become experts within certain areas (Junge-Jensen ibid.:17).

Industrial Psychology as Trouble-shooter

After having discussed the transition from meaningless work at the assembly line and the two schools solutions to the problems of motivating people to wok, it might be a good idea to summarise schematically the different approaches (see figure 4.2) before turning to the learning organisation.

---

[11] According to Junge-Jensen ibid:9.
[12] Henning Wilhelm-Hansen *Arbejdspsykologi* 1992:36.

If we decode from the history of industrial psychology the problems that it has had to resolve to make people work/give them a feeling of meaningfulness and coherence in work, we can list three ideal-typical major problems of psychological nature corresponding to the three phases of organisational composition of work. During the stage of assembly line work, the problems were "fatigue/boredom" the solution to which was piece-work based on time studies (worker ideal = the tireless ox preferably without mental alertness and intelligence), and overview and control were literally placed above the worker in the foreman cage. In the subsequent stage, the problem was lack of (social) meaning in the work. The solution was the formation of groups that were allocated partial or total autonomy. In this process, sociality and, to a certain extent, do-how competence were restored among the workers. The basis for this solution was, among others, Maoy's Hawthorne experiments.

With the third stage we have approached the current problem. This can perhaps most concisely be described as dissatisfaction with/insufficient use of knowledge and capabilities among the individual workers. Setting free as production factors, the creativity and the desire for acting and mastering among workers would, viewed in their perspective, be experienced as self-realisation and mastering one's own life and thus constitute a more genuine restoration of the know- and do-how qualities.

Changing factors within the schools of industrial psychology

SCHOOLS	PROBLEM	WORKER IDEAL	SOLUTION	MOTIVATION FACTOR
Approx. 1920-1950 **SCIENTIFIC MANAGEMENT** (W.F. Taylor) (Henry Ford)	Tiredness, boredom, low quality/performance, personnel flow, absence due to illness	The brainless ox that works itself to the bone, holding its tongue and consenting, leaving its brain outside the factory gate	Time studies of motion patterns, placing the "brain" and the command in a foreman cage	"homo economicus": obtain the highest possible wage for the least efforts (McGregor's X-theory)
Approx. 1940-1970 **HUMAN RELATIONS** (Elton Mayo, Roethlisberger & Dickson)	Lack of meaning and sociality in the work	"homo sociologicus" the social man who trusts and respects others	Autonomous groups and in part restoration of do-how among the workers	A sense of community and growing independence in work + groups pressure
Approx. 1960-1980 **HUMAN RESOURCES**	Lack of flexibility and mobility in job functions and lack of opportunities for stimulating the individual to better performance/development	The growth oriented performance man/the struggler or "entrepreneur" who prioritise own development over solidarity with others	Job enrichment/job change – increased allocation of responsibility and competence to the individual who wants and masters it	Challenges in terms of growing responsibility and demands on the capabilities of the individual. Competence and status are motivation factors – wages and environment in themselves are not stimulating (McGregor's Y-theory)
The 1990s **New HRM (Human Resource Management)** Hybrids: LO/DW et al. (Peter Senge) (John Storey)	The nature of work changes toward the service- and information society: Growing competition creates needs for continuous innovation, creativity, quality and customer friendliness	"Man in a constant state of learning and reflecting". Development of workers professionally and personally. Both the right and the left side of the brain must be mobilised.	Internal and external training activities, equalisation of the organisation into flatter structures. Staking on "soft" qualifications – "Japanisation" of company culture	Development of the whole self – make the aspects of life – work, leisure time and social life – coherent to the individual worker. It must be "fun" to be used fully.

Figure 4.2: Overview of the schools within industrial psychology related to the problems they have had to resolve – the prevailing worker ideals, the solutions suggested and the corresponding competencies and motivation factors.

The Development of Needs is Cumulative

In consequence of the above it is my assertion that the development of industrial psychological needs is cumulative viewed from the perspective of employees. In other words, it is not contingent that we are now confronted with the need for refining the Human Resource School. But it is oversimplified to claim that we with the synonyms for modern work, such as "the developing work" and "human resource management" are abandoned to the individual, self-determined universe and its psychology. The emerging needs for learning among employees, caused by changes in the nature of work, are cumulative. What is on today's agenda is a combination of the requirements and capabilities necessary for being able to work in or cope with committed teams, including changed demands on the individual to demonstrate "sensibility toward using herself or himself fully". Self-development and learning in the organisation must be viewed in part as a need for productive results through allocating responsibility to the modern well educated manpower, and in part as a need for fulfilling employees' possibilities for development, thus enabling them to stay employable. In addition the employees themselves are increasingly demanding life to be holistic, coherent, and developing, which is naturally related to the growing pressure from "the impact of modernity on consciousness". Here the "great narratives" and cultural traditions, habits and lifestyles are subject to intense challenges.

Light year from the alienating work in the 1970s (though it still exists) there are today – within advanced industries – explicit needs for being successful and develop one's personality in and with the changing work. Naturally one can, taught by history, sense that all the new and fancy ideas and innovations will be yet another exploitation factor. In a sense this is true, but it becomes increasingly difficult to stick to this rigid attitude the more modern man explicates the need for learning and development. Moreover, it is only relatively recently that common wage earners have been given the chance of viewing themselves as individuals of change.

The Worker Assumes Character as a Masterful and Free Human Being

When we view personal development in an historical perspective it is identical with talking about the "profanation" or dissemination of subjectivity to comprise common workers - like what the history of childhood devotes to the right of being a child. In the pre-modern society, "childhood" as a separate phase in life characterised by play and gradual socialisation to adult life did not exist.

Children did not exist or they were non-adults expected to assume, as soon as possible, the adult obligation to work. Nobody cared about what characterised the personality of children. The interest in child development first arose among the aristocracy and in Court circles and along with the societal development among the common citizens. In the eighteenth century, the philosophers of the Enlightenment (Rousseau and Kant) advocated the idea of childhood as a separate phase in life. In parallel the humanistic oriented industrial psychology can be view as a modern variety of Enlightenment philosophy when it propagates the right of workers to subjectivity and individuality. First with the Human Relation School in the 1950s and later on with the Human Resource School in the 1960s.[13] Having initiated this process the full set of particulars characterising the western perception of subjectivity and individuality applies:

> "Subjectivity is the freedom for which man, striving to attain authority is responsible. It is the self-consciousness deriving from reflection on one self and thinking about thinking.
> Subjectivity is furthermore setting free individual powers for the purpose of self-realisation… ..[…] In relating to himself critically and keeping a certain distance to others, the free human being must attempt to create a productive live and fill his own life with sustainable contents. Ideally, modern man combines reflexively his self-perception with meaningful activities while simultaneously recognising the relativity of his own interpretation as a condition for tolerance toward those of others." (Martin Doehlemann (1991) *Langeweile? Deutung eines verbreitendes Phänomens.* Suhrkamp Verlag).

It is exactly this civilisation movement or transformation that the quotation states to constitute the continuous historical subjectivisation – first encompassing only

---

[13] Johano Strasser (1993:89 cont.) notices that that the fight for individual freedom has been going on ever since the French Revolution: "Die Freiheit des männlichen Besitzbürgers wird under dem Druck des universellen Freiheitsversprechens zur *Freiheit auch der Arbeiter*, der Frauen, der Kinder und schliesslich auch der unterdrückten und kolonialisierten nichteuropäischen Rassen" – and he maintains that the tendency of radical modern individualisation itself is a product of the modern industrial society with the inherent "cultural contrasts of capitalism", such as the strongly increased pressure for mobility and consumption. The paradoxical result is that the very same process that subjectively is describable as radical individualism viewed from the outside is a process of uniforming the masses through consumption. (From the book "Individualisierung und Solidarität – über die gegärdung eines Grundwertes. Bonn 1993).

the social classes of wealth and education, and later on common people. Today it is conceived as a right applying to all people, including the semi-skilled industrial worker. Doehlemann specifically stresses that the process runs along diverse paths, but it is fundamentally linked to the capitalist industrialisation that in consideration of the employer's freedom needed and still needs the free individual who is willing to work, and the (politically conscious) consumer "seeking meaning". When both employers' associations and unions are currently talking about the necessity of staking on the "soft qualifications" or manpower connoted with concepts such as "personal development" "managing one's own life and qualifications", then "sensibilisation" becomes a necessary qualification to which I shall later return. "Sensibilisation" implies involving oneself in the work as an awakened, emotional, and thinking individual, who actively seeks new challenges, solves problems, and employs intuition and creativity. These are the properties of sensitisation. However, this post-modern orientation toward the individual also implies potential isolation of the single individual. The individual may be referred to him- or herself and possibly isolated. Against these new features of the social cosmos of interaction the individual must interact and develop. Ultimately the individual is referred to himself or herself, a situation that is becoming increasingly difficult with the post-modern collapse of values and the rate of change in society and in work especially.[14]

In exchange for evoking individuals at the marketplace of subjectivity and the related increasing demand for personal loyalty in work toward the company, the

---

[14] Here it is important to keep a clear head in the new individualistic age. The old distinction between consensus oriented North American and conflict oriented critical European sociology repeat itself like the ghost of the headless women in black in the castle. Naisbitt and Aburdene (1990) describe the 1990s as the "victory of the individual". The individual changes before beginning to change society and realise the new golden age in which man earns his living by virtue of his personal creativity and not as wage slave. The worker is remunerated for his unique capabilities, intelligence and creativity and not for his stamina as part of a collective labor force. Thus the authors view it as possible to construct a community of human beings that voluntarily unite.

Opposite the German sociologist Ulrik Bech's description of the same phenomenon: "Today setting free is not similar to setting free from the feudal and religious society of pre-modernity, but setting free from the paradigm of rationality governing the industrial society to engage in the reflexivity of the risk society. Individualisation is not the end of every form of community nor is it a comeback of bourgeois individualism. It is the product of safety disintegrating in the industrial society which forces the individual to find new forms... in this sense individualisation and interdependency become two sides of the same coin as reflexivity... only is possible through communicative interaction with others" (Beck according to Jens Rasmussen 1996:28 cont.).

freedom of the wage earner has been limited, freedom in the sense of being part of or belonging to a non-subjective mass or class of informal collective powers to safeguard the conditions for sale of labour. This is what the industrial sociologist Karen Legge (1992:19 cont.) warns against in her Hyman inspired criticism of Human Resource strategies: if the worker in exchange for sweet words and commitment to job and company abandons his free right to sell his labour – inflexibility and conservatism may emerge among workers.

Action Once More becomes at more Important than Needs: The Concept of Competence in the 1990s

Why is the interest now shifting from needs to action? Within psychology this issue has continuously been discussed – both as a question of whether mental issues can and must be justified by applying the methodology of natural sciences or that of the humanities. It is a question of social and personality psychology versus cognitive psychology. In other words, the question of what is most interesting: the cause of/background for versus the meaning of a given human action? It is difficult to say what has caused the shift in focus toward the action aspect at the expense of needs and causal relations, but it is probably rooted in the current focus on the competencies/qualifications required for holding against the international competition.[15]

Right from the Beginning HR Involved "the Meaning of" or the "Meaningless" work

But right from the beginning there was "meaning" in the madness. Schein (1996) mentions that it has always been possible to interpret advances in industrial psychology from the perspectives of both social psychology and cognitive psychology. Research on human relations in the 1950s applied the perspective of social psychology in analysing data, but it might as well have been analysed from the perspective of cognitive psychology. The alienating and demoralising effects of the assembly line on the labour were primarily caused by the social isolation of the workers though the work team to some extent compensated for this isolation. But the studies strongly evidenced that alienation of the workers – or loss or meaning and overview of the entire production process – was caused by boring, repetitious piecework.

---

[15] Hans Siggård's review of "De Menneskelige Ressourcer" in Dansk Pædagogisk Tidsskrift 5/95:282-86.

This epistemological advance is important. The moment we introduce "meaning" or "overview" the interest shifts from outer to the inner motivation/incentive/ action factor. What the HR school had done was to evoke interest in positive, inner motivation factors. It changed radically the previous perception that only external force/control would make people work. The discovery of the social factor furnished the workers with the freedom to let their needs for informal collegial interrelationships unfold, at least to the extent allowed by changed HR inspired management styles. In other words, for better or for worse the work team became the new external regulator of work in that pressure from the group functioned to set the norms that regulated work, such as breaking the piece rate contract or being disloyal to the group.[16]

The Theory of Self-Realisation Gains Ground

We are now approaching the personal level or the assumptions that man has an inherent tendency to seek wholeness and meaning in work if possible. This is the foundation of McGregor's theory Y or in the words of Schein:

> "The issue is not whether the employee can fulfil social needs; this issue is whether the employee can find meaning in work, which gives him or her a sense of pride and self-esteem." (Schein 1980:69) – and "The original interviews which employees at the Hawthone plant and of other companies studied in the 1920s and 1930s were actually as much evidence for employees' needs to find challenge and meaning in their work as they were evidence for social needs." (ibid:70).

What is unique about this theory about the individual's striving toward self-realisation is that the incentive is embedded in the task itself. It is the challenge of the problem/task that motivates the individual to do his or her utmost that is

---

[16] The Swedish labor market researcher Paavo Bergman (1997) draws attention to the fact that the idyllic myths about the Hawthorne study has suppressed the important information that next to the ideal unit performing tiger leaps in production at each change in their external working conditions was an "impossible" unit that stubbornly resisted any changes the researchers might introduce and constantly produced below standard fearing that they might run out of work (ibid.:49). Bergman also mar the myth about the good unit by citing M. Rose for saying that in the beginning of the experiment the informal leader of the girls, an assiduous Italian immigrant, drove them to increasing productivity continuously. In other words "the real Hawthorne effect" might as well consist in "driving leadership" as in a combination of benevolent supervision and "participation" (Rose according to Bergman 1997:51).

employ his or her capabilities and creativity in resolving the task and hence develop or realise him- or herself.

Already in its earliest version Maslow's theory of self-realisation or self-actualisation comprised the aspects of emotion and rationality. He did not distinguish between cognitive dimension the nature of which was aspiration, and the conative (desire and will). Man's perpetual search for understanding and meaning was an incentive inherent in the highest levels of the hierarchy of needs. The inner incentive for self-realisation was so strong that Maslow compared it with the musician that cannot help playing, the painter that cannot help painting, and the poet that must write poems. Maslow introduced one important exception to his hypothesis of hierarchical needs – needs at the lower levels must be satisfied before the higher needs can ascend into the sphere of satisfaction. The fact that artists or researchers can become totally carried away with the creation process demonstrates that something can be so important for man that he – at least temporarily – brackets all other needs at the lower levels. Introducing this hypothesis about "functional autonomy" made room for the numerous myths about truly great art being created by starving artists.

Sensibilisation as Qualification – Sensibility as Competence
The Learning Organisation (LO) and the Developing Work (DW) as concepts void of the subject

In much of the literature on LO and DW these concepts appear as independently acting subjects – inspired by a specific strength to initiate various processes. This may derive from the so-called "organismic" thinking in older sociology, or from previous tendencies within management thinking to skate over the fact that in most case it is the management that thinks and implements changes. However, I agree with Nonaka and Takeuchi (1995) that blurring the nature of the actual agents or actors is especially misplaced in relation to the learning organisation or the developing work, which they prefer to call "the Knowledge-Creating Company":

> "Although we use the term "organisational" knowledge-creation, the organisation cannot create knowledge on its own without the initiative of the individual and the interaction that takes place within the group." (Ibid:13)

Thus, in relation to learning or knowledge-creating organisations, the stage is populated with individuals who want change and learning.[17] And the organisations carrying or transforming this learning are primarily "groups" or teams characterised by the abilities for turning the novel into shared knowledge and subsequent useful action through dialogue, discussion, experience sharing, and observation:

> "Knowledge can be amplified or crystallised at the group level through dialogue,
> discussion, experience sharing and observation." (ibid:13)

It follows from this that the learning and knowledge-creation in question are outcomes of the efforts of specific people and must be considered as "democratising development for all categories of employees – or DW (the Developing Work) to use another subjectless abbreviation.[18]

What I hope to have said in the first section on the history of needs is that

1. individuals as agents are behind any effort of organisational change – including the learning organisation
2. the individual must be understood as a whole comprising sense and sensibility and – creative thinking "plays on" both body and soul
3. individual ideas are transformed into the organisation through man's social communicative abilities – that is, through the team's ability to transform and share experiences
4. learning requires that the individual wants change.

The most natural place to begin for a psychologist is with the subject or the individual. Then the learning organisation must be viewed in the perspective of whether it actually comprises people who actively attempt to make sense of or give meaning to change, especially when it, as in this case, involves their daily working conditions. What is it that makes people intentionally throw themselves into the troubles of changing from the known to the unknown?

---

[17] Peter Senge (1990) touches upon the recondition for the learning organisation: "Organisation can not learn until their members begin to learn".
[18] Henrik Holt Larsen. Det udviklende arbejde – et debatoplæg. In Det udviklende arbejde. Centralrådet for for Statens Samarbejdsudvalg, 1996. Larsen's discussion paper, however, yields to the same tendency: "… a learning organisation is curious, diagnoses its situation, open up for experiments and evaluates efforts of development." (Ibid:13).

Sensibilisation – in two equally important senses of the word

The word sensibilisation, to increase sensibility, might denote what is brewing in relation to the demands for personal change in the learning organisation. I am using this meaning of the word to emphasise the necessity of both mangers and employees during modern organisational changes (HRM, LO, DW) are emotionally awakened and demonstrate a positive attitude toward change minded and using their emotional intelligence.[19] These are important premises for learning and knowledge-creations, but it not the only ones.

But I also wish to use the word in the sense where "sensible" is synonymous with reasonable or making sense. In using sensibilisation and sensible I wish signal that if we are to understand the conditions for LO and DW, we must include both sensibility and sense.[20] In the Learning Organisation and in the Developing Work "They learn to use both reason and intuition to create" (Senge 1990). Emotions must be awakened in order to activate so far unheeded abilities of the right cerebral hemisphere, such as intuition, holistic thinking, and creativity in order for these to merge with the analytic, rational, problem solving abilities of the left cerebral hemisphere (see Figure 4.3).[21]

---

[19] Several authors emphasise the importance of being "awakened" – among others Senge (1990): "in a way those who work in a learning organisation are "fully awakened" people… engaged in their work, striving to reach their potential by sharing the vision of a worthy goal with team colleagues." (LO Homepage 1997). In regard to "emotional, intelligence" see Daniel Goleman. Emotional Intelligence.

[20] Sensible = sensitive/acting with good judgement (Cassells Concise English Dictionary, 1994). That acting on the basis of good judgement is not only a linguistic subtlety appears from Senge's description of creative tension, i.e. the difference between actual and attainable future function level. Personal Mastery (dimension 1 of Senge's five dimensions) presumes a clear concept about the actual reality: "One must be able to see reality as it truly is – without biases or misconceptions" (LO Homepage, 1997:3/21).

[21] Patrick Magee (1997) writes in his self-instructive book "Brain Dancing" that the concept emerged as a symbol for making the two hemispheres interact better in terms of "mental synergy": "Right-brain creativity" gives the left side more and better ideas to analyse… the result is a dynamic loop between the two hemispheres – a "brain dance".

Figure 4.3

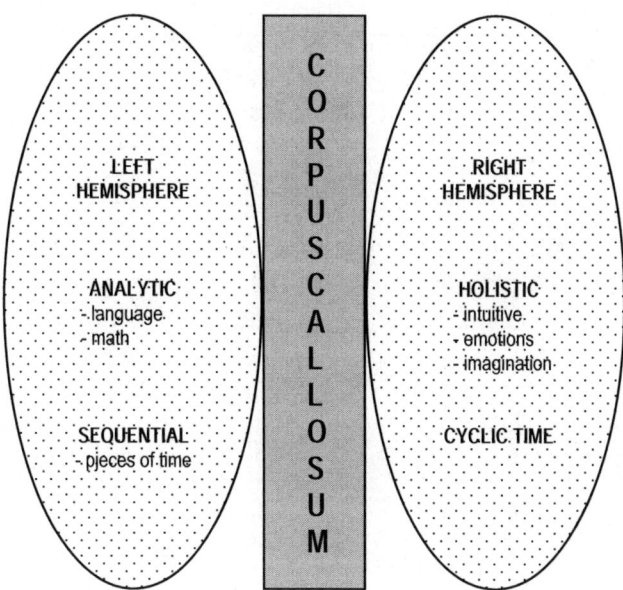

Figure 4.3: Stylised illustration of the functionally divided cerebral hemispheres, the left one is in particular analytical and sequential and the right one is the seat of perception and emotions. The secret of human intelligence is of course that the two parts interacts across the corpus callosum. Therefore, the purpose of emphasising the functional division of the brain is primarily to demonstrate the widespread "cultural confusion" in the western world giving one-sidedly preference to the left side.

It is this the "double" meaning of sense that Mr. Learning Organisation himself, Peter Senge, attempts to capture with his systemic thinking which was launched to introduce a holistic perspective. But, as Nonaka and Takeouchi point out, Senge's system is not sufficiently precise about the difference between body and mind, that is the difference between bodily acquired human knowledge (tacit and most often not immediately accessible for cognition) and the more normal (left cerebral hemisphere) analytical way of conscious knowledge creation. There are several explanations of why it is becoming increasingly important to relate to this coupling under the conditions of the new working conditions at both the individual and the global level.

INDIVIDUALLY – **cognitively**: Western man is said to use only ten percent of his brain capacity due to, in particular, the cultural "lateralisation" which implies overtraining and dominance of the linquistic-mathematical-analytical abilities of the left cerebral hemisphere and under stimulation of the abilities of the right cerebral hemisphere for empathy, fantasy, thinking in wholes and perceiving time and space cyclically. If this is true there are significant dormant potentials to actualise by increasing the synergy between the left and the right cerebral hemispheres (cf. e.g. Howard Garnener's studies of the brain).[22]

INDIVIDUALLY – **attitudes**: With the dissolution of well-established societal ritual and values in the post-modern era, it is becoming increasingly difficult for the individual to orient himself or herself. In trying to succeed as an adult with a fixed identity, a permanent job, and a permanent family, the individual is continuously subject to "fast-food", "fast" in the sense often changing family and individual constellation demand continuous thoughtfulness and attempts to "stop the carousel" in order merely to survive as an individual with a relatively fixed identity.

NATIONALLY – Competition among organisations increases and the demands for quality, change, and customer service are becoming increasingly important parameters for survivability. Attempt to increase productivity through controlling/exploiting old-fashioned process dependent worker skills seem to be exhausted. Management is now directing focus toward process independent qualifications, that is, moral and personal qualifications. The Developing Work and the Learning Organisation can be seen as attempts of the two sides of industry to cope with this development.

GLOBALLY/INTERNATIONALLY – The rate of technological development and the steadily growing dependence on the global market provoke changes – not only in terms of managing day-to-day affairs nationally, but particularly in terms of ensuring that one is just inches ahead of the competitors and still better than the "yellow danger" in the price and cost low East Asia. Today 20-30% of the labour in the West is "knowledge and symbol workers" and the rate of turnover is steadily increasing with the information and knowledge society.

---

[22] The Japanese take their criticism of, among others, Senge so far that they claim Western thinkers never to have transgressed the Cartesian Split – that is never have been able to merge body and mind or sense and sensibility. They claim Japanese organisational theory not to be characterised by this problem as the underlying Zen-Buddhism does not distinguish between body and mind (Nonaka & Takeuchi 1995:29).

Personal Mastery – the Master Violin or the Diamond as the Ideal

Some find the change of language from "teaching" to "learning" somewhat popish. Nevertheless the change reflects a highly important difference. In this context learning must be understood an active, self-imposed process. This leads to a different understand of the process of developing or improving one's skills. Earlier such processes were typically associated with "being taught" – that is, the individual was perceived as an object contrary to as a subject in a change process. This is what Peter Senge (1990) calls "Personal Mastery", the fist of his five dimensions of the Learning Organisation.[23]

Organisations do not become learning unless the organisational members change perspective and develop their abilities to think critically and creatively. Personal Mastery has two components: 1) trying to generate a result and 2) having a true picture how close one is to achieve this goal. Senge talks about "vision" which is perhaps a better term than result and goal, because reaching the goal is a lifelong endeavour. Antonius Stradivarius spent his entire life on perfecting the sound of the violin, but we do not know, according to Senge (1995) whether he actually reached his goal. We only know that throughout his entire life he pursued this goal. The alternative management education in Aarhus – Kaospiloterne – must have listened to these high aspirations for personal development or mastering. Their leitmotif for the mandatory participant project is the "coal-and-diamond strategy" – "that it is more important to have too high ambitions than too low ones... and to create situations in which the participants are subject to pressure, perhaps caused by too high ambitions, and which symbolically are comparable to pressuring coal into diamonds – at the risk of destroying the coal by a erroneous pressure" (Langager 1994:124).

"Peak experiences", "the marshmallow test" and "self-efficiency"

In his hierarchical ordering of human needs, Maslow exemplied needs in the top of the hierarchy by referring to qualitative interviews with, in particular, his prominent contemporaries (Mahatma Ghandi, Einstein, Mrs. Roosevelt, Albert

---

[23] Peter Senge's five dimensions of the learning organisation are: 1) Personal Mastery; 2) Mental Models; 3) Team-Learning; 4) Shared Visions; and 5) Systemic Thinking.

Sweitzer, Aldous Huxley, Danilo Dolci[24] etc.) and biographies of unique historical personalities (Spinoza, Goethe, Haydn, Renoir, Thomas Morre, Benjamin Franklin, etc.) In summary he describes these people in relation to other less self-actualised persons as possessing:

1. more well-balanced/having a better understanding of reality
2. greater self-respect and respect of others
3. greater spontaneity and naturalness
4. better focus on problems
5. greater self-dependence and independence of surrounding culture and norms
6. greater ability to assess recurring experiences in life in a positive perspective
7. greater unselfishness, democratic attitude, and solidarity
8. greater non-aggressive sense of humour
9. greater creativity/ability to adopt a new perspective on issues
10. more peak experiences

Maslow was, however, rather self-critical of the methodology underlying the composition of these idols/ideals, and referred to his effort as "a poor or insufficient experiment" (Madsen 1986:105).

McClellan took a much more empirical approach in demonstrating what distinguished the "performers" or the "ambitious" from other people. Performers driven by a high "success motive" in general managed better than others even if their basic conditions were identical, e.g. IQ. Furthermore, performers were more prone to accept pre-calculated risks[25], meaning that they were not "gamblers",

---

[24] I have met the Sicilian Danilo Dolci who impressed me. Throughout his entire life he has combated the Sicilian Mafia using non-violent methods. See my description of him and Mahatma Ghandi in: Keldorf. Hvorfor krig? (Why War?) Aalborg University Press, 1984:79-124.

[25] The ambitious ones are, according to McClelland, characterised by: 1) preferring to work independently; 2) be less affected by remuneration in terms of money; 3) inclined to accept moderate risks; 4) inclinked to apply for managerial positions within industry, trade, and the financial sector. The less ambitious ones prefer working within science, education or art – he actually says so!

"but primarily sought out situations and tasks through which they could demonstrate their unique abilities, and they often had a realistic perception of their own abilities... in pure gambling their proficiencies would not have been put to a test." (Madsen 1968:59)

It is beyond doubt that Maslow's and McClelland's interests in the exorbitant unique or geniuses recur in the current interest in what distinguishes the problem solutions of geniuses or experts from that of pure competence or routine (Schön, Dreyfuss, Polanyi, Csikszentmihalyi and others)[26]. Goleman (1995:82 cont.) describes in the chapter on "The Master Aptitude" how well known cultural values, such as being able to sublimate needs in order to achieve higher goals, are still valid. In a mean experiment a group of four-year old American children, we subject to the so-called "marshmallow test". Placed on the table in the room with the children was a bowl of marshmallows. The experimenter told the children that if they could wait until he had run an errand they could have two marshmallows for at treat. But if they could not wait, they could have one and only one now. Some of the children could wait until he returned, but the majority grabbed one immediately. A subsequent experiment comprising the same children at the age of 12-14 demonstrated that those able to sublimate their temptations for at higher goal at the age of four were later on in life also more inclined to resist immediate satisfaction of needs in pursuit of higher goals. The children that immediately succumbed to their needs proved later on in life to be more inclined to be paralysed in stressed situations, to be mistrustful, to be prone to jealousy and envy, and to be offensive and aggressive if they did not find that they "got enough". Goleman (1995:82) writes: "some chilldren, even at four, had mastered the basics: they were able to read the social situation as one where delay was beneficial, to pry their attention from focusing on the temptation at hand, and to distract themselves while maintaining the necessary perseverance toward the goal – the two marshmallows."

Tested again when the children were leaving high school, those demonstrating patience at the age of four were more academically competent that those in the group who had acted on whim. The former was better able to formulate their ideas, to reason, make plans for the future, and more eager to learn. The psychologist Walter Mischel, who did the study, concludes that combined

---

[26] For a short introduction to these, see among others Laursen, E. "Den geniale fusker" (The Brilliant Bungler), in Dansk Pædagogisk Tidsskrift 2/1993. The other articles in this volume are also relevant in this context.

emotional intelligence and cognition function as a "meta-ability" which determines how good or bad people are at utilizing their various mental capacities and that both impulse control and exact reading of the social situation can be learned (ibid: 83). This demonstrates that Maslow's intuitive method for tracing features of self-actualisation was not half bad. The difference between Maslow's study and the above study rather seems to be that a considerable larger number of "common" people are able to learn self-realisation by becoming conscious of the right conditions for performing better. According to recent research, optimism, hope, and good moods seem to be rather the conditions for than the outcome of good performances:

> "Good moods, while they last, enhance the ability to think flexibly and with more complexity, thus making it easier to find solutions to problems, whether intellectual or interpersonal... Laughing, like elation, seems to help people think more broadly and associate more freely, noticing relationships that might have eluded them otherwise – a mental skill important not just in creativity, but in recognising complex relationships and foreseeing the consequences of a given decision." (ibid:85)

The psychologist Albert Bandura, Stanford, claims that optimism and hope as well as the opposite helplessness and despair are learned. These attitudes relate to degrees of "self-efficiency", that is, to what extent one believes to be in control of one's own life. Becoming competent in doing something strengthens one's feelings of self-efficiency, making one prone to dare more, to undertake difficult tasks and be better at not abandoning projects from the start. Abilities are not static and determined once and for all. Growing self-efficiency will lead to growing self-realisation.[27]

---

[27] Naisbitt & Aburdene (1990:353) have a suggestive interpretation in "Megatrends". In Chapter 10 talking about the victory of the individual they say that this involves a new respect of the individual in the 1990s. It is misleading to talk about mass as a prefix: The environmental movements, the women's movement, and the anti nuclear power movement has emerged from one mind at a time, from one individual who believed in the possibility of creating a new reality. In my book on the worries about nuclear war and the peace activism in the mid-1980s, I actually use a theory parallel to "self-efficiency", the so-called "locus-of-control" theory the meaning of which is the same. The most persistent peace activists were exactly those who believed their resistance to have an impact (Keldorf: Bekymring for atomkrig (Worries about Nuclear War). Edupax 1989:49).

Gardener's Seven Intelligences

The core of the recent attention in psychology toward performance, knowledge, and competence is that the scope of these are not fixed once and for all either as inheritance or predetermined. We must expand the concept of intelligence beyond the torso on which we have been used to base our understanding of intelligence since Binet and Simon invented their intelligence test in the early twentieth century. The Harvard psychologist Howard Gardner departed decisively from this determinism in his book "Frames of Mind" (1983). Having studied, among other things, "wonder children" and children with brain injuries for ten years, he documents that IQ tests only measure traditional cultural skills, such as linguistic and logical-mathematical abilities. Such tests by no means reflect man's multiple and complex mental equipment and potentials. Gardner identified seven independent intelligence modules:

1. linguistic (understands and uses verbal language)
2. musical
3. logical-mathematical
4. spatial (ability to work with spatial relations)
5. body-kinetic (ability to use and control body)
6. personal (ability to understand and use own mind)
7. interpersonal (ability to understand other minds)

According to Gardner, everybody can reach a certain competence level within the seven modules – and certainly learn much more than we have been used to think based on the idea of inherited talents. Like Maslow Gardner had studied unique peak-performing historical personalities (Einstein, Ghandi and Picasso) and he makes it clear that none of these people have contributed creatively without having spent at least ten years full time on learning to master the tradition of their professional field. There are not smart shortcuts to competence and creativity (Fibæk Laursen 1996). Gardner does not neglect that certain people are born with special talents. But decisive for the unfolding of such talents seems to be how they themselves and their surroundings administer the talents – which such people, have been given the opportunities to actualise their potentials. Furthermore, the majority of peak-performing people always seem to have been reflecting systematically on their experiences and development over time – reflected in e.g. diaries.

Gardner is actually approaching a structural theory of intelligence and knowledge comparable to Senge's systemic theory. Gardner breaks with the conventional idea that intelligence is traceable to the nob. According to Gardner, intelligence is distributed, meaning that the culturally accumulated knowledge auxiliaries must be included in our concept of intelligence. Our intelligence is also reflected in books, computers, tools, etc. – and intelligence is also to be able to incorporate auxiliary tools and symbolic systems. In this context it is tempting to twist C.G. Jung's concept and talk about "the collectively conscious" – cf. my earlier claim that labour needs are cumulative. Prior to the acquiring of knowledge being organised socially, knowledge consisted in being apt at doing the right things jointly with others in certain situations using tools and other means. Gardner speaks in favour of reviving craft apprenticeship, because formal education has eliminated the context in which knowledge is best acquired, that is, the practical context. In other words, knowledge within a profession is use rather than something in textbooks.

Social and Emotional Intelligence

Even though Gardner's theories are subject to criticism today, much attention has been given to his personal and interpersonal forms of intelligence. This is perhaps not very surprising. A growing number of jobs require people to work in teams in which mutual understanding and sociability are key values. Simultaneously, the management form is moving from the aggressive, manipulating leader to the sensitive and intuitive leader. Possessing personal and social intelligence is practical and appropriate for both manager and employee. The psychologist Salovey has elaborated on Gardner's forms six and seven and listed five areas of emotional intelligence (see figure 4.4)

Figure 4.4: Salovey's translation of Howard Gardner's personal and interpersonal intelligence within five areas: Self-awareness, self-control, self-motivation, empathy, and sociability and the corresponding competencies in social and emotional intelligence (adapted from Goleman 1995:43 cont.)

1. Self-awareness: Knowing one's emotions	2. Self-control: Managing emotions	3. Self-motivation: Motivating oneself	4. Empathy: Recognising emotions in others	5. Sociability: Handling relationships
The ability to recognise feelings from moment to moment – if unable to do so one becomes the victim of one's feelings. Certainty about feelings makes one a better pilot of one's life and better able to make decisions	Is closely related to and rooted in 1. Important is the capacity of soothe oneself and to shake off anxiety and the feeling of failure, gloom or irritability. People mastering self-control bounce back more quickly from life's setbacks and upsets.	Builds on being able to sublimate – to delaying gratification of needs until better times in order to achieve a goal. Being able to do so, one will find it easier to get into the "flow" states that enable outstanding performance. This ability is self-fuelling.	Rests primarily on 1. the self-awareness that fertilises the ability to listen with the heart because success is dependent upon being able to put oneself in others place. Being tone-deaf creates distance to others – as opposed to closeness and hearing "the social grass growing": sense what others need	Related to skills in managing emotions in others. Popularity, leadership, and interpersonal effectiveness. People who excel in these skills do well at anything that relies on interacting smoothly with others.

In many cases psychologists are most funny when they move into fields about which they only have little understanding, such as the social field. McClelland has actually risked his neck by attempting to do cross-cultural comparative studies of the performance motive. In a study comparing American Jews and Protestants with Irish and Italian Catholics he found that the Jews scored highest and the Italian Catholics lowest on identical performance tests. His explanation is interesting. The Jews have always been an outsider group forced to fight for any position (independence as survival condition). The Italian Catholics, on the other hand, have had to cross two barriers: the authoritarian religion and the mom-culture populated with buxom mothers to whose apron strings they could tie themselves (dependency creating barriers to independence).

More up-to-date motivation researchers have recently supplemented motivation theory with concepts such as goal-setting and personal values – the idea being that it is decisive to look at what people want with their actions and what their underlying attitudes are. A Greenpeace activist and a "Pretty Women" will take a very different stand on the choice of winter coats. The mere idea of "Venus in a sealskin coat" will make the former cross herself whereas the latter will enjoy it.

Team Building and Team Learning

With concepts such as empowerment, coaching, synergistic dialogue teams have once again become hot stuff as parameters for organisational change. And teambuilding is one of Senge's five dimensions. Like in the case of the individual, there is a long tradition within social psychology for studying groups and the impact of factors such as roles, size, composition, management and stress in determining success. World War II supplied an abundance of data. For the first time officers and sergeant were leading combat groups in open fields so it was vital to know how the individual member of the team would react. And ever since the question of what make teams "peak-performers" and more successful than others has been the subject of numerous studies.

Morgan (1957) discusses a team performance task within the British Secret Service during the war with the purpose of finding the persons most suitable for functioning as spies and saboteurs behind enemy lines. The most well functioning groups were characterised by enthusiasm for the task, high spirit, loyalty, and friendly interrelationships. Fights among themselves, on the other hand, characterised the poorest functioning groups and lacking belief in being able to do the job - and even outright cheating. Morgan (1957 in Harrison 1972:462) summarises the factors that seem to distinguish the groups and to being important for a group's problem solution:

1. degree of intercommunication
2. degree of conformity or creativity
3. group moral
4. type of leadership

In a more recent study of as different teams as world cup football teams and teams of cardiac transplant surgeons Larsen and LaFasto (1996) have identified eight features that seem to characterise "peak-performing" teams:

1. a clear goal/a clear task
2. goal-oriented group structure
3. individual competent members
4. coordinated engagement
5. good collaboration climate
6. fixed proficiency standards
7. external support and admiration
8. firm management

Lippitt views teamwork as the way in which a group resolves its problems or as its ability to investigate how it continuously improves as a team. This involves, among other things, how it nourishes its ballast of mutual trust and openness ensuring free communication and tolerance of diverse opinions and personalities.

Within small group research Robert Bale et al.'s studies in the 1960s of problem solving in groups are classical. These studies point to social support in the intellectual process as being important for the quality of the solutions. I recently did a case study myself drawing on Bales. The study involved a selected group of first year students over a semester, and the social mediator role(s) was decisive of the group's success.[28]

Belbin's Types

One of the central questions in recent years has been how different types or roles in a group are supplemental or opposing. The Belbin test, names after Dr. Robert Meredith Belbin, characterises the ideal role structure of teams as:

> "The useful people to have in teams are those who possess strengths or characteristics which serve a need without duplicating those already there. Teams are a question of balance. What is needed it not well-balanced individuals but individuals who balance well with one another. In that way human frailties can be underpinned and strengths used to full advantage." (Belbin according to Hoskin & Morley 1991)

Belbin and his team approached systematically the task of determining what roles are required for a group to succeed. During seven years they studied hundreds of middle managers attending a ten-week course at the Administrative Staff College of Henley. In a simulated management game they studied what characterised the personal pattern of the winning groups. Several findings were surprising, such as that groups composed solely of people with high IQs lost compared to groups composed of people with more average IQs. This confirms the hypothesis that too many of the same kind in a group are counterproductive to achieving the goal. If a team is composed of nothing but ambitious, analytically intelligent, and performance oriented individuals, they will only

---

[28] See Søren Keldorf: Tæt på en gruppe (Close to a Group). Edupax 1996.

produce mediocre results.[29] Additional tests led to the identification of eight types of roles required for the team to be successful (see Figure 4.5).

Belbin et al.'s studies thus seems to corroborate the thesis that winning groups must not include too many of the same types/resources, but must hold complementary roles. On the other hand, there are certain roles that must be represented in the group. Winning groups are characterised by:

- being organised differently from losing groups – and in particular nobody works alone and everybody possess identical information about what has happened and why
- all members are willing to and capable of performing the eight roles – if the group comprised less than eight people some of them would perform more than one of the roles
- had leaders who would combine features of the roles of chairman and shaper and were capable of sustaining leadership without domineering the others or forcing certain functions or ways of making decisions on the group
- harbouring at least one innovator, one contact creator, one analyst, and one social mediator

In contrast the loser groups were characterised by:

- too many members did not assume responsibility for any particular role
- the members worked "solo" and made few efforts of coordinating activities
- none of the members were clearly creative or analytical
- the social mediator was absent

---

[29] Contrary to the known formula for group synergy: 2 + 2 = 5, Belbin's formula for the co-called Apollo teams is: 1 + 1 + 1 + 1 = 2 (Belbin's The Apollo Syndrome, cf. http://www.teamtechnology.co.uk/tt/t-articl/apollo.htm).

Figure 4.5: Belbin's Roles within groups (Hosking & Morley 1991:198)

1.A: Company worker Personality: disciplined, conscientious, tough-minded, practical, trusting, tolerant, and conservative. Role: turns concepts and plans into practical working procedures. Varries out agreed plans systematically and effectively.	5.E: Resource investigator Personality: enthusiastic, extroverted, and open. Develops ideas or fragments of ideas originated by other people. Role: liaison. Looks for help inside and outside the group.
2.B: Chairman Personality: realistic, calm, disciplined. Strong commitment to basic goals and objectives. Extrovert capacity of enthusiasm, but otherwise prone to detachment in social relations. Role: presides, coordinates, facilitates. Willing to listen to others but quite capable of rejecting their advice. Knows how to use and organise resources within the team, and brings the best out in other people. Imparts a sense of direction and purpose.	6.F: Monitor Evaluator Personality: strives to follow paradigm of rational actor and makes deliberate, considered, calculated choices. Critical analytical thinker. Role: specialises in analysing and evaluating ideas. Will raise critical issues, however uncomfortable. May help to deal with lack of consensus when crucial decisions are to be made.
3.C: Shaper Personality: tough, anxious, extrovert, impatient for achievement. May overreact to disappointments. Prone to challenge, to argue, and to disagree. Role: classic dominant task leader. Motivates slow moving systems. Negotiator who is a major force for change.	7.G: Team worker Personality: trusting, sensitive. Sociable without being dominant. Wants to meet people and talk to them. Role: social specialist who smoothies potentially disruptive conflicts. Skills in listening and managing awkward people.
4.D: Plant Personality: introvert but nevertheless forthright. Role: originator of ideas on strategy and other major issues. Expected to be the most creative members of the group	8.H: Completer-finisher Personality: introverted perfectionist who pays great attention to detail. Role: shows how ideas work out in detail and ensures that nothing is overlooked. Worries about schedules and specialises in administrative staff work.

It may sound rather trivial when Senge (1990:236) says that "talented teams are made up of talented individuals", but Belbin's role perspective shows that there is more to it than meets the eye. In connection with my case study of a group, I stumble on a neglected group theorist, W.F. Bion. Having spent most of his professional life on studying groups and working with group therapy, Bion demonstrates that the good team is characterised by the individual member never merges into the wallpaper. It is characteristic of the problem solving group that the members are qualified to do something alone and together with the group. The most important component in teamwork and team learning is the dialogue. The members must suspend their biases against and assumptions about one another and view each other as equal colleagues. Furthermore, the group must include at least one leader who maintains the substance and context of the dialogue.

Golemann (1995:225 cont.) claims that a group or team composed to solve a problem is characterised by a "group IQ" – the aggregate sum of the involved talents and competencies. The key to a high group IQ is not the group's academic-analytical skills, but its emotional intelligence, its ability to create "social harmony" and to adapt to each other. This is what makes certain groups particularly talented, productive and successful.

Work Ethics –From External Coercion to Internal Will and Self-control

In effect of the introduction of the concepts of the Developing Work and the Learning Organisation, the quality and nature of the concepts of work and work ethics have also changed (Inglehart 1970; Villemoes 1991). The old-fashioned industrial worker is a dinosaur – counting scarcely 200,000 workers in Denmark left in the "lower end". A growing number of companies are doing business with each other in new ways. Immaterial "goods" such as service, knowledge, consultancy, and know-how amount to approximately half of the GNP. This in itself changes the picture of qualifications and competencies. The ethics of duty and authoritarian management are fading parallel with the growing demand for meaningful work and satisfied individual desires and needs.

Responsibility and Mental Health

According to the industrial psychologist Eggert Petersen (1996:38 cont.) it was necessary to introduce a new psychological variable in the empirical universe in the 1990s: responsibility. He has identified an increasing tendency among the population to assume responsibility[30] – not only related to age and political attitude (from left to right), but also independent of gender and income: most pronounced among women, young people below thirty years, students, low-income groups, left-wing constituents, and public/private servants. On the other hand, among skilled and unskilled workers the tendency to assume responsibility has been steady. In general this seems to indicate that significant groups of labour, of people who will soon be entering the labour market, and of the traditionally welfare oriented groups of the population are becoming increasingly inclined to assume responsibility. This might help lift a corner of an empirical redemption of the ideal of a healthy lifestyle described by the WHO as health to everybody in year 2000 as the capabilities that enable people to control and manage their lives and thus live in a healthy way. These capabilities include formulation of problems, finding solutions, making decisions and acting in

---

[30] Eggert Petersen et al. Danskernes trivsel, holdninger og selvansvarlighed under "opsvinget" (Job satisfaction, attitudes and self-responsibility during the "boom"). Publication 14, Department of Psychology, Aalborg University 1996.

accordance with these, solve conflicts, communicate effectively, take a critical stand and intervene on behalf of oneself if necessary. Recent research has shown that the feeling of personal value and self-esteem is linked to more efficient ways of managing one's life and frequently occurring preventive measures. (WHO according to Jesper Juul: Familien – det primære sundhedssystem (The Family – the primary health system). Kempler Institut 1989:30)

The question of health, or mental health, as the result of the organising of work has been the subject of many industrial psychological studies during the last thirty years. Agervold and Kristensen (1996:67) summarise the major psychosocial conditions important for mental health:

- to what extent does one have influence on and control over one's tasks and work situation?
- to what extent does one have the feeling of coherence in the task performed and the overall production?
- what does the job mean a) to me as a person, b) for the possibilities of using my qualifications, c) for learning something new and develop myself – and d) for co-operating horisontally and vertically?
- can I identify with the company or do I rather feel outside and alien to the company's objectives and values?

New learning and development seem here to be confined to the individual, and the relations mentioned are individual relations to the company. However in most contexts focus is on the social or group exposed individual – in other words the relation individual-group. This is also the relation underlying most of the new concepts of organisational learning.

Coping – Necessary New Learning via the Social Buffer

Karasek and Theorell (1990 – according to Agervold & Kristensen 1996) have developed a so-called demand-control model and point out that when demand and (self) control coincide in work *the result is learning, personal growth and greater resistance to strains.* And vice versa: if this is not the case, the risk is stress and illness.

This makes the concept of coping[31] central as it entails that the demands for employee competence might very well exceed the employee's "pain threshold" in terms of self-controlled planning of his or her work, etc. Such situations will require problem solutions different from how one usually copes with problems – "demands that are assessed to exhaust or exceed the individual's resources" (Lazarus & Folkman according to Agervold & Kristensen 1996: 73).

In this context learning organisation researchers are talking about so-called double-loop learning, the type of learning that requires conscious transformation of or reflection on the new conditions for problem solution. In the case of "periodic breakdowns" Winogad and Flores (according to Takeuchi & Nonaka 1995: 78 cont.) talk about a kind of temporary interruption of the habitual and normal way of perceiving the world/solving problems. According to Winograd and Flores such situations offer the opportunity for "creating" new order out of chaos' via social interaction and dialogue, or in the vein of Karasek and Theorell: social support can be said to constitute a buffer between strains and stress.

> "A breakdown refers to an interruption of our habitual, comfortable state of being. When we face such a breakdown, we have an opportunity to reconsider our fundamental thinking and perspective. In other words we begin to question the validity of our basic attitudes toward the world... A breakdown demands that we turn our attention to dialogue as a means of social interaction, thus helping us to create new concepts." (Takeuchi & Nonaka 1995: 79)

How can Individualistic Work Ethics be "Solidary"

It is evident that all this talk about self-realisation and self-responsibility is deeply rooted in liberalism and conservatism rather than socialism. However, one thing is to face the necessity of greater individual self-control because "the old walls have fallen" and the authority and community rules of the traditional society, which kept people in place, are gone. But how do we avoid the "ethics of

---

[31] Agervold & Kristensen (1996:73) in their book draw attention to the frequent misunderstanding of "coping" as being equivalent to tackle, master, handle problems. This use of the word is incorrect in connection with strenuous situations as coping here means the opposite of development. Coping shows that the person does not master the situation and ends up in a strenuous conflict – coping and development are opposites. On the other hand, coping may, if successful, lead the person back to the development situation, but in itself it signifies that development has come to a stand still.

personal utility", that is, unrestrained endeavours at the expense of others – is it at all possible to establish a "solidary individualism"?[32]

Sustainable Development: Idea Oriented Work Ethics

The concept derives from Hvid and Møller (1992: 124 cont.) who claim that the current struggle to gain power over the shaping of the new individualistic work ethics is enacted between two poles. On the one hand, there is a break with authorities and duties, which entails distance to both traditional management forms and unions. On the other hand work must be meaningful and developing for the individual. Competition mentality and career orientation seem to be natural concomitant phenomena with all what they entail in terms of holding one's own at the expense of others, using one's elbows, letting go of what is not profitable, and only caring for one self and one's own opportunities. Faced with this dystopia, the authors present their utopia for a new "idea oriented work ethics" that can combine the individual perspective with a sustainable and environment-friendly production and consumption. They advocate self-realisation in collaboration with others and based on democracy, equality and equal opportunities... in a (global, *the author*)[33] community in which the individual's free development is the precondition for the free development of everybody (in the vein of the Marx/Engels the Communist Manifesto).

Were the Theories of Herzberg premature or has Society not reached the right state until now?

It is possible that the theories advocated by humanistic oriented psychologists (Lewin, Maslow, Herzberg, McClelland/Atkinson, J.A.C. Brown and others) in the U.S.A. in the 1950s and the 1960s were in advance of the time? Or perhaps their concepts merely predicted a later general tendency to turn common workers into salaried employees in the knowledge and information society? Viewed in isolation I do not think either is the case – or at least I only believe in something one could call a theory of "the converging point". For various reasons, and in particular after the fall of the wall in 1989, the old individual-thinking of the free market ideology and a certain problem solution began to converge toward

---

[32] It is difficult not to see the problem as a paradox and it does not become less of a paradox when one of the Danish unions runs a youth campaign under the motto: "Be solidary with yourself".

[33] I have earlier touched upon similar ideas in the article: New Irrationalism, new Nihilism and the Need for a Strategy of Relearning Democratic Values and Peaceful Co-Existence. Canadian Journal of Peace Research 1997.

"a societal necessity". This necessity was brought about by the need of the post- and late-industrial society for flexible and competent labour in view of the increasing competition from the NEC countries in terms of cheap labour and quality. In other words, the societal development has drawn out a "combination" which – perhaps in need of better alternatives and not at least due the fall of the world socialism – is now in a position to refer to problems solutions stocked years back? Human Resource Management, Developing Work, Learning Organisation, Total Quality Management, etc. are concepts that connote the basic issue that "something is happening". And psychology is not longer reserved for experts.

The youth revolution in the 1970s, the women's liberation to enter the labour market, unemployment especially within office work, and the old, heavy and poorly paid industrial work all add to set the "good meaningful work" off. The popular mind consolidated during the 1980s through courses for unemployed, day high schools, and further training – activities that have appealed to self-realisation as the solution to all problems. The development in the family and leisure sphere complements this picture. It has never been more important to socialise coming generations into independence and self-control, to being able to stand alone without breaking down. Mummy is not at home so stop crying over being mobbed, suffer the noise from the others and forget about your other needs until you get home between five and six p.m.!

> "The children and young persons of today are marked by the rapid changes in society, which we are currently witnessing. First and foremost this means that the old power structures and hierarchies are no longer fixed – at least not at the personal level. The children and young people of today are much less orthodox than their parents and grandparents. Also, because their parents recognising that they do not know what the future will bring, raise their children to greater independence and to being able themselves to search for and find the answers to the great questions in life.
> If independence and self-administration are important properties in the future society, being able to co-operate and form part of communities will become even more important. Therefore, parents must teach their children to be active together with other, to show empathy and to find solutions to problems jointly in the community."
> (Jesper Jerlang. Fra Straf til omsorg. I: Samvirke. April 1997:68 cont.)

References

Agervold, Mogens og Kristensen, Ole Steen (1996): *Det udviklende arbejde.* Århus: Aarhus Universitetsforlag.

Argyris, Chris. (1993): *On organisational learning.* Cambridge, MA: Blackwell.

Bergman, Paavo (1997): *Moderna lagarbeten,* Lund: Arkiv förlag.

Bion, Wilfred Ruprecht (1993): *Erfaring i grupper,* Kbvn: Reitzel.

Christiansson m.fl. (1971): *Konsten att dressera människor,* Stockholm.

Doehlemann, Martin (1992): *Kedsomhed,* Kbvn: Reitzel.

Fibæk Laursen, Per (1996): Howard Gardner - en introduktion. I: *Dansk Pæd. Tidsskrift,* 4/96, s.44-54.

Goleman, Daniel. (1995): Emotional Intelligence. New York: Bantam Books.

Gøtz, Klaus. (1994): Führung und Persönlichkeit, In: *Zeitschrift für Personalforschung* 4/94, s. 446-61. München: Rainer Hampp Verlag.

Haire, Mason (1960): *Psykologi for virksomhedsledere,* Khvn: Nyt Nordisk.

Harrison, Albert A. (1976): *Individuals and Groups,* California: Wadworth.

Herzberg, Mausner & Snyderman (1974): *Arbejde og Motivation,* Kbvn: Gyldendal.

Holt Larsen, Henrik (1996): Det udviklende arbejde - et debatoplæg. I: *11 bud på Det udviklende arbejde,* Kbvn: Centralrådet for Statens Samarbejdsudvalg.

Hosking, Dian-Marie & Morley, Ian E. (1991): *A Social Psychology of Organising. People, Processes and Context.* N.Y.: Simon & Shuster.

Hvid, Helge & Møller, Niels (1992): *Det udviklende arbejde.* Kbvn: Fremad.

Israel, Joachim (1970): *Fremmedgørelse fra Marx til moderne sociologi,* Kbvn: Gyldendal.

Jørgensen, Bent (1977): *Taylor og Ford - til beskrivelse af arbejdspsykologiens opståen* I. I: Udkast. Dansk tidsskrift for samfundsvidenskab, 3/1977, s.275-298.

Keldorff, Søren (1986): Freds-troubadurerne, Valkyrien og ikkevolds-bureaukraterne. I: Keldorff. *Hvorfor krig? Kommentarer til en ny kold krig.* Aalborg: Aalborg Universitetsforlag, pp.79-124

Keldorff, Søren (1989): *Holdninger til kaprustning og Bekymring for atomkrig.* Gistrup: Edupax.

Keldorff, Søren (1996): *Tæt på en gruppe - en projektgruppes besvær og succés.* Gistrup: Edupax.

Keldorff, Søren (1997): *New Irrationalism, new Nihilism and the Need for relearning Democratic Values.* IPRAs XV conference, Valetta University, Malta, 1994 - in: Canadian Journal of Peace Research.

Langager, Søren Chr. (1994): *Kaospiloterne - afsluttende rapport.* Danmarks Lærerhøjskole. Pædagogisk-psykologisk publikationsserie. Kbvn: PPP 89.

Laursen, Erik. (1993): Den geniale fusker. I: *Dansk Pædagogisk Tidsskrift* 2/93.

Learning Organisation Homepage på browseren, "Webcrawler", især http://www.edison.albany.edu/-klarsen/learnorg/argyr2.html

Legge, Karen (1992): Human Resource Management: a critical analysis. In: Storey, John (Ed.) *New Perspectives on Human Resource Management*, London & N.Y.: Routledge, pp. 19-41.

Lysgård, Sverre (1976): *Arbeiderkollektivet - en studie i de underordnedes sociologi.* Oslo.

Madsen, K.B. (1968): *Motivation. Drivkræfterne bag vore handlinger*, Kbvn: Munksgaard.

Madsen, K.B. (1986): *Psykologi 2. Psykologiens historie efter 1945*, Kbvn: Gyldendal.

Maslow, Abraham H. A. (1974): Theory of Human Motivation, In: Vroom & Deci. *Management & Motivation.* London & N.Y.: Penquin, pp.27-41.

Marx/Engels (1968): Den Tyske Ideologi - I: Marx. *Økonomi og Filosofi,* Kbvn: Gyldendal.

Naisbitt, John (1997): I: TV-udsendelse i TV2 d. 27.2.97 (udsendelsen, som jeg tilfældig så var en billedlig repræsentation af Naisbitt & Aburdene´s argumenter i bogen "Megatrends 2000 - tendenser i 90'erne", Bonniers bøger.

Naisbitt, J. & Aburdene, P. (1989): Megatrends 2000. Tendenser i 90'erne. Bonniers bøger.

Nonaka, Ikujiro & Takeuchi, Hirotaka (1995): *The Knowledge-Creating Company,* N.Y. & Oxford: Oxford University Press.

Ouchi, William (1981): *Tvang eller tillid? Teori Z - management på japansk,* Kbvn: Borgen.

Petersen, Eggert m.fl. (1996): *Danskernes trivsel, holdninger og selvansvarlighed under "opsvinget".* Publ. nr. 14. Århus: Psykologisk Inst. ÅU.

Rasmussen, Jens (1997): *Socialisering og læring i det refleksivt moderne.* Kbhvn: Unge Pædagoger nr. B62.

Roethlisberger, F.J. & Dickson, W.J. (1939): *Management and the worker,* Harvard Univ. Press.

Schein, Edgar H. (1980): *Organisational Psykology,* Prentice-Hal.

Senge, Peter (1990): *The Fifth Discipline,* London: Random House.

Siggård Jensen, Hans (1995): De menneskelige ressourcer. I: *Dansk Pædagogisk Tidsskrift,* 5/95, pp. 282-286.

Sjølund, Arne (1965): *Gruppepsykologi,* Kbvn: Gyldendal.

Storey, John (1991): *New Perspectives on Human Resource Management* London/New York: Routledge.

Strasser, Johano (1993): Individualisierung - eine Bedrohung des Grundwertes Solidarität? - In: *Individualisierung und Solidarität - über die Gefährdung eines Grundwertes*, Bonn: Fr. Ebert Stiftung.

Taylor, F.W. (1967 reprint) *The Principles of Scientific Management*. New York: W.W. Norton & Co.

Trangbæk m.fl. (1996): *Kvalifikationskrav og -potentiale i voksenerhvervsuddannelserne*, Kbvn: Undervisningsministeriet.

Villemoes, Nils (1991): *Paradoksernes Paradis - om udvikling, omstilling, forandring og bøvl.* Århus: GAD/systime.

Vroom, V.H. & Deci, E.L. (1974): *Management and Motivation*, Penquin.

Wilhelm-Hansen, Henning (1992): *Arbejdspsykologi*, Odense.

Chapter 5

The Learning Organisation and the Labour Market

By Jens Lind

The Reflexive Trend and Working Life

The recent interest in "the learning organisation" is both novel and not novel. The modern society (or the modernised society) that has emerged over the last three hundred years along with capitalist production methods gaining ground has implied permanent changes in social relations and the realisation of the necessity of continuous organisational restructuring. In that sense the learning organisation is not a new concept. The novelty of the concept is the rapidity of change. And change has always meant something new in the sense that man has always perceived changes in his period as accelerating compared to previous periods in history. The novel aspect primarily concerns the understanding of the relationship between the individual and institutions and organisations. The current discourse on the learning organisations strongly builds on ideas in the 1970s and 1980s about communicative action and reflexiveness. Ideologically it rests on the renaissance of liberalism and focuses on the sovereignty of the individual, politically on participatory democracy, and in economics on the advance of capitalism and new forms of exploitation.

The novel requirements are for institutions and organisations to change their legitimisation rationale toward external stakeholders and achieve greater productive rationality internally. The latter is probably most decisive for the success of the current gospel of reflexiveness. It is impossible to decide whether this is due to a real material need for the contents of the gospel or simply because a new gospel is required to stir organisations. And it does not really matter. But it is important that we realise the limits and potentials of the current ideas and processes. And the reflexive trend has both limits and potentials. First and foremost the possibilities of realising reflexive processes in the capitalist society set limits, because freedom, equality, and participatory democracy will always be relative concepts. The potentials are in the relativity: If the limits for other's determination are alterable, and the individual gains increased autonomy, learning processes have the potential of being emancipative.

Traditionally workplaces and working life are perceived as having emancipative potentials. The learning organisation, the developing work, and the new forms of human resource management attempt programmatically to develop reflexivity in the organisation. The individual is in focus as employee and producer. The human resources must be emancipated from the tight organisational fabric, and creativity must ensure increased productive rationality.

The learning organisation is an organisation characterised by the individual actor participating actively in the survival of the organisation by communicating, processing and applying experience. The individual actor must participate actively in the organisational learning process in order for the organisation to be learning (internal reflexiveness). It does not suffice that only an elite participates in this process. Ideally, but quite unrealistically – the precondition is that everybody participates. The individual actor is part of a communicative community in which s/he must be able to act autonomously and not be subject to other's determination though s/he is accountable to the community - the organisation.

In working life these criteria for the learning organisation are only met in exceptional cases. In this article the learning organisation will be discussed mainly as what could be termed "companies with a personnel strategy that is focused on functional flexibility", and the main focus of the article will be to discuss how the labour market and labour market regulation affect the development of functional flexibility in companies.

The Learning Organisation and Flexibility

Like other qualitative concepts, such as "human resource management" and "developing work", ideas about the learning organisation have had strong impact on the discussions of working life in the 1990s. Common to these concepts is that they focus on the qualifications of the labour force in a wider sense and on a specific way of managing manpower in the organisation. Labour is often ascribed decisive importance for the development of the organisation and focus is on the qualitative aspects of labour.

And like many other concepts and theories, "the learning organisation" and related phenomena are influenced by various perceptions and definitions of what they entail. Emphasis can be placed on the strategic, managerial potentials, on organisational principles, on the concept of learning, etc. In this context the detailed aspects of the various understandings are relatively insignificant in that the focal point lies outside the individual organisation when investigating conditions in the labour market.

The learning organisation is here defined as the organisation that emphasises functional flexibility in the management of manpower. In a narrow sense this may simply mean that the organisation, depending on changing demands of production, uses its labour to perform varying and simple functions that require no specific qualifications. But in a wider sense functional flexibility implies that the organisation gives priority to developing employee qualifications. This will enable the employees to alternate between various functions, participate actively in the planning of production, and possibly possess collectively a high degree of autonomy in relation to higher hierarchical managerial levels. The functionally flexible organisation thus gives high priority to the development of employee qualifications, which is often combined with stable employment.

Ideally, managing labour in a functionally flexible way contrasts with numerical flexibility. The latter implies that the organisation replaces existing labour with new labour concurrently with changes in qualification requirements. If the production requires different qualifications, the organisation can fire the workers and hire new ones with the desired qualifications provided that they are available in the labour market. In using numerical flexibility to cover the need for labour, the organisation will not give much priority to develop employee qualifications and will not to a very large extent delegate responsibility and autonomy to numerically flexible workers.

In the debate on the learning organisation attention is usually directed toward what the organisation itself can do in terms of personnel policy and organisational restructuring. And rightly so. To realise the ideas of managing labour in a qualitatively new way requires the individual organisation or workplace to interfere actively. But the organisation acts on the basis of the conditions and relations governing the externality in which it is embedded.

In this chapter we shall investigate a small part of this "externality". External to the individual organisation is the supply and demand of labour and the agreements regulating the buying and selling of labour. In using labour the organisation is subject to certain societal conditions that must be assumed to be important for its development into the "learning organisation". Therefore, we shall attempt to elucidate if the development and regulation of the Danish labour market pushes or pulls the diffusion of new qualitatively oriented ways of managing manpower.

Flexibility and Work

In the 1970s, discussions on the new work were primarily based on the traditional ideas of industrial sociology. The main concepts were the rationality of capitalism and the alienating work (Braverman 1974; Mendner 1975). The intention was to call attention to the disqualification, attrition, and one-sided way of using labour in capitalist societies based on the principles of Taylorism and mass production. One outcome of the discussions would be that work had to be changed, another one was Gorz' recommendation that man should liberate himself *from* work (Gortz 1981) and not *in* work. Early in the discussions Bell pointed out the emergence of the post-industrial society (Bell 1973), which heralded a settlement with the social relations characterising the industrial society. Combined with the theses about post-Fordism and new production concepts in the early 1980s (Aglietta 1979; Piore & Sabel 1984; Kern & Schumann 1984) the possibilities of liberating man *in* work looked promising in that emphasis was on the possibilities for realising human creativity in working life. Small batches of tailor made products in the production of goods and services require flexibility in production and a well qualified, functionally flexible labour force.

The functional flexibility presupposed that the workers possessed new and additional specific qualifications and other general qualifications. The labour force should be employable in changing work processes and should be ready to accept these conditions. According to the theses, the hierarchical lines of command would be replaced by democratic work organisation. During this process, much attention was directed toward the introduction of new technology and the qualifications required to managing this technology (Gjerding et al. 1990), and management strategy increasingly emphasised the necessity of developing trust relations between management and employees. The latter because employee commitment to and identification with the organisation became increasingly important for the organisation. This implied a new and strategic attitude toward human resources (Beer et al. 1984; Fombrun et al. 1984).

The thesis about the new work and the new management strategies contain elements from segmentation theories. Originally, these theories emerged in contrast to or were modifications of the neo-classical macro-oriented understanding of the dynamics in the labour market. The diverse variations of the Dual Labour Market Theory (DLMT) took as their point of departure the categorisation of labour supply into primary and secondary labour markets. The primary labour market exists in the large organisations offering good, well-paid, stable jobs with internal career ladders and stable markets (monopolies, oligopolies, industries producing capital goods, etc.). The secondary labour market with poor, ill-paid, and unstable jobs exists in small companies liable to competition (Doeringer & Piore 1971; Reich et al. 1973).

In *Model des segmentierten Arbeitsmarkts* (MSAM), Lutz and Sengenberger (1974) recommend to operate with three segments of labour supply. The market for non-specific qualification is liable to competition in the traditional neo-classical sense, the market for specific qualifications is liable to competition within the sub-market, and the market for company specific qualifications is not liable to competition beyond the boundaries of the company. Lutz and Sengenberger (ibid.) start from Human Capital Theory that assumes investments in qualifications employable in the market for specific qualifications to be carried by the workers, and by the companies in the market for company specific qualifications.

The synthesis of the theories of segmentation is the theory of "the flexible firm" emerging in the 1980s. This theory stresses that the individual company segments the labour force in core and periphery labour. Functional flexibility characterises the former and numerical flexibility the latter (Atkinson 1984). Especially DLMT and the flexible firm, but also to a certain extent MSAM, are proposing the interpretation that it is the behaviour of the individual firm in connection with optimising the management of manpower which leads to segmentation of the labour market into two categories. One of stable, functionally flexible employment, which is an object for investing in qualifications, and another of unstable employment (numerical flexible) and non-developed qualifications.

The theories of the new work, and perhaps the new management strategies of the 1980s, assume that work will develop toward greater functional flexibility. However, the theories of segmentation are not as clear on that issue, but the flexible firm could be interpreted as strongly normative (Pollert 1988), and segmentation of the labour market may well be explained as a consequence of a strategic personnel political action (Gordon et al. 1982).

Combined the theses about the post-industrial society, post-Fordism, and new production concepts are clear propositions about the changed nature of work. First, the shift from the secondary to the tertiary sector in result of which work and hence also the demands for qualifications change. Second, a new production and accumulation paradigm leading to qualitative changes in the management of labour, also in production companies. This is supplemented with segmentation theories emphasising that these changes need not affect all workers in the same way. If so the qualitatively new rationales in the management of labour would first and foremost concern the core staff in the primary or the internal labour market.

It is undisputed that the industrial structure in the western capitalist societies has changed. Today, fewer people are working within the primary and the secondary sector (in countries like Denmark the percentage working in the secondary sector has not declined significantly), and more people are working within the tertiary sector, in the service industries. In consequence the nature of qualifications in demand has changed, but it is still an open question whether this will also imply a qualitatively different management of manpower toward increased functional flexibility. Many services are produced in the same Fordist and repetitive way as much production of goods. In addition it is yet to be demonstrated that post-Fordist and new production concepts have become prevalent in the production sector and that work and the relations between management and employees are dominated by the new trends. Quite the contrary much has been said against these prophecies that are accused of building on the best case argumentation or they are merely new interpretations of by and large unchanged structures (Hyman 1990).

The deficient documentation and the widespread tendency to accept new fashions in the interpretation of the world also exist in Denmark. In the next section, we shall discuss the dissemination of new wok methods of functional flexibility in Danish companies, and whether or not service companies differ from other companies in this sense.

The Relationship between Supply and Demand

The relationship between the supply and the demand of labour must be assumed to affect the ability or incentives of organisations to develop toward managing labour in functionally flexible ways. In case employers are unable to recruit employees possessing the required qualifications, measures can be introduced to encourage people to acquire such qualifications or, in case of unemployment, discourage people from acquiring specific qualification because employers will be able to satisfy their need for labour by numerical flexibility.

The high rate of unemployment that characterised the labour market since the early 1970s meant that employers should have been able to recruit the manpower that they needed. Thus there was really no incentive for staking on functional flexible management of manpower in the 1980s and the first half of the 1990s in Denmark with continuously increasing unemployment. However, if we assume that companies during this period developed toward functionally flexible management of labour then there may be all kinds of more important reasons for this than the plethora of vacant labour.

But if we only focus on the possible importance of the relationship between supply and demand, we can assume competition among companies over labour to be intensive, even in periods of high unemployment. The individual company needs to recruit the best manpower in the market in order to hold their own against competition, and the competitors will do the same. Therefore in situations of high unemployment the demands for appropriate specific and general qualifications among workers are high, because the companies think that there will be an abundance to choose from. And if the companies want to optimise their usage of this labour, they must stake on functional flexibility. Whether the recurrent assertions of paradox-, bottleneck-, or structural problems since the 1970s were caused by a genuinely felt lack of labour or by the belief in a shortage of labour does not matter. The outcome is the same – the companies' stake on being able to use the labour in functionally flexible ways.

Second, we can assume that in spite of high unemployment there may be a deficient supply of certain types of labour. This will typically concern certain specific qualifications for which demand tends to be increasing such as IT, seasonal production, blooming industries or industries characterised by special conditions. During a short period in the mid-1980s, the Danish building and construction industries were short of workers and since the 1990s there has been a shortage of nurses and certain types of public employees (high rates of permanent or temporary exits from the profession). This shortage has spread to a number of other occupations when unemployment further decreased to around 4 per cent during 2006.

In theory, this tight labour market could have the effect that companies relied more on applying functional flexibility instead of numerical flexibility. At any rate the advantageous market situation of workers may put them in a situation where they can claim better working conditions and succeed in their demands for functionally flexible employment patterns.

Flexibility and Regulation

Regulation is here defined as the societal or collective regulation of certain relations governing the buying, selling and management of labour. An act performed (by representatives of) the many actors as opposed to the "market" that constitutes the actions and arrangements of the individual actors. The market can also be conceived as a form of regulation or rationale, but this is not what is implied here. In the labour market, which, admittedly, is not the right concept here (working life would be better) regulation includes political intervention through legislation and collectively negotiated intervention through collective bargaining.

In relation to the regulation of the labour market, the overall question is whether and to what extent the labour market must be regulated. In theory labour market relations could be based on "pure market conditions" where buying, selling, and management of labour would be a relationship between the individual employer and employee. Under these conditions, functional flexibility would be the outcome of (in theory) isolated negotiations between the two parties. The specific features of the Danish regulation model (Lind 1995) are fundamentally based on voluntarism in the shape of collective agreements that regulate the conditions for buying and selling labour. However, the state monitors these processes closely, determines the framework and interferes if assessing that a conflict may have serious socio-economic consequences. Likewise the procedure for solving conflicts is agreed upon by the two sides of industry, guaranteed and supplemented by legislation. The major area of state regulation, the relationships between supply and demand of labour, is subject to strong pressure from the labour market organisations both in terms of policies and implementation. This also applies to the management of labour (occupational safety and health) which is regulated by law, but strongly influenced by the two sides of industry.

The labour market policy concerns employers' liability, regulation of conflicts, supply, and demand by virtue of measures promoting employment, allocation, qualification, and provision. All three elements of the labour market policy affect how companies manage labour. Potentially, the three elements can stimulate or obstruct managing labour functionally flexibly. Protection of the worker by reducing physical and mental attrition and perhaps downright stimulate employers to replace one-sided jobs with functionally flexible ones. Conflict regulation by promoting the solution of conflicts and establish co-operation procedures of trust in the company.

Regulation of supply and demand in the labour market has indirect effects in that it attempts to reach approximated equilibrium on supply and demand, partly within the total labour market, and partly within the individual labour markets. In case of high unemployment, companies will find it less attractive to develop jobs requiring functional flexibility, whereas efforts of allocation (employment service) encourage numerical flexibility. Further training of the labour force promotes functional flexibility, because the companies are offered resources for further training of labour. However, such measures could also promote numerical flexibility if the unemployed during unemployment have upgraded their qualifications thus becoming more attractive for the companies to employ.

Social security provisions for the unemployed have also ambiguous consequences. If the level of unemployment benefit recovers a large share of loss of income in case of unemployment, the unemployed will make greater demands on work than would be the case if the recovery were lower. Conversely, a high level of compensation will offer the companies the opportunity of numerical flexibility because workers are more willing to accept lay-offs. Workers and trade unions are less hostile to redundancies in case of high unemployment benefit compensation rates.

In fact, this is exactly the argumentation behind the heavily praised "flexicurity" model which often is seen as an important reason for the economic and employment growth in Denmark since the mid-1990s (Bredgaard et al 2006). If this line of argumentation is correct the economic and employment success story is mainly due to a high level of numerical flexibility and not functional flexibility (for a critical assessment, see Lind 2004).

The collective agreements to a large extent contain elements identical with those of political regulation, but the core elements are determining the minimum conditions for the buying and selling of labour. These elements include a series of conditions for the management of labour, both quantitatively (the scope and amount of work) and qualitatively (contents of work). Especially in the case of the latter, the management's prerogative prevails. However, also in Denmark this managerial right has been reduced through collective agreements, and despite the fact that the unions recognise the principle (the General Agreement §4) they continuously attempt to push the boundary towards greater co-determination or workplace democracy.

As argued above, presumably the conditions for buying and selling labour will affect the management's human resource strategy in the deployment of functional and numerical flexibility. In terms of the former, the means will be wage level and wage structure and for the latter it will be hiring and firing. Wage is always relative. Relative compared to other groups of workers, relative to unemployment benefit, and relative to the wage offered by competitors. According to the theory of economics, low wages and high wage differentiation will always lead to lower rates of unemployment, which will function as an impetus to manage highly paid labour in functionally flexible ways and the low paid deploying numerical flexibility. High wage differentiation will enable companies to realise the idea of functionally flexible management of labour, at least for certain types of labour. The same applies to hiring and firing as regulation mechanisms. Increasing transaction costs caused by reduced possibilities for managing labour numerically flexibly, e.g. due to long terms of notice will encourage functional flexibility. And if the regulation of hiring and firing becomes more differentiated so will the management of labour become more differentiated.

When the management of labour is primarily synonymous with exercising managerial power, and when this power essentially rests with the buyers of labour, regulation in the form of collective agreements will have a limited effect on the furthering of functional flexibility.

Selected Themes in the Regulation of the Labour Market

It is not possible here to review systematically all type of regulations of the labour market and their importance for the development of functionally flexible management of labour. However, below we shall discuss three important themes. First, the current trends in the political regulation of the supply of and demand for labour. Here the so-called active labour market policy is seen as an alternative to the neo-liberal policy. Second we shall discuss the decentralisation of the collective agreement system, and third we will scrutinise the concept of "the developing work" that contains both legal and contractual dimensions.

Labour Market Policy

The underlying rationale of the political regulation of the supply of and demand for labour is still the so-called active labour market policy that aims to increase the geographical and qualificatory flexibility of labour among sub-markets and in general to further the allocation process. This institutional interference in the market forces at first promotes numerically flexible manpower management.

This is most conspicuous from the fact that employment agencies function as staffing firms for that segment of the labour market that requires no specific qualifications. The fact that employment agencies (Jørgensen et al. 1990) primarily support the allocation processes in segments of the labour market characterised by low wages and insignificant qualification requirements impedes functionally flexible manpower management.

This should be seen in a broader context. A major condition for being able to maintain a relatively high degree of compensation for loss of income in case of unemployment is that the unemployed are available for work by being registered with the employment service as job-seeking and accept offered work. The deficient incentive for unemployed to accept less attractive jobs caused by a high level of unemployment benefit will be discouraged by the employment service de facto monitors that unemployed fulfil the obligation to be actively seeking jobs. In order to meet employers' demand for labour and maintain a relative high degree of compensation for unemployment, the market constraints have been replaced by institutional constraints. It is impossible to say whether the result is the same in regard to the (lacking) incentives for companies to develop into functionally flexible manpower management.

Another and related trend is that the compensation rate of unemployment benefits has been reduced since the early 1980s. The main reason for this is to improve the incentive among unemployed to accept a vacant job, and it also means that competition for jobs has been increased with the result that wage competition has become more effective. The outcome is lower wages and improved competitiveness of the entire economy followed by employment growth.

Figure 5.1: Unemployment benefit compensation rates for various groups of LO-members, Denmark.

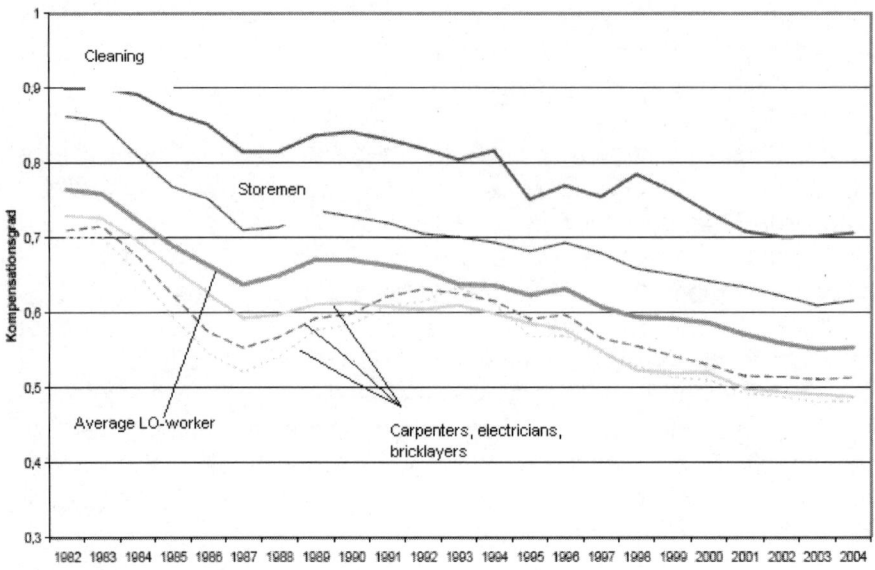

Source: LO 2006.

In sum, the obligation of unemployed to be available for work has been gradually tightened, unemployment benefits have been reduced and the period for which unemployed can receive unemployment benefit has been shortened since 1979. Combined the conclusion must be that this part of the labour market policy does not promote functionally flexible labour management. Rather the opposite. Employers tend to apply a hire-and-fire policy, and the weakened market situation of the employees tends to restrain them in their claims for better (functionally flexible) working conditions.

The same trend also applies to that part of the unemployment policy that is intended to have disciplining effects – the so-called activation policy. The obligation to accept activation has increasingly been imposed upon unemployed people, activation either in the form of education or employment in particular jobs established for the purpose and often of relatively little job contents and of limited duration. Despite this activation policy originally was developed as aiming at improving the employment opportunities of the unemployed their main function is now to "motivate" unemployed to find an ordinary job instead of being activated in some activation scheme (Møller & Lind 2004).

However, efforts of activation also contain elements that improve the qualifications of unemployed thus improving their chances of getting proper jobs. Ideally this would mean that the competition for work will intensify if unemployed become more attractive for employers. Therefore this policy is not in general promoting functional flexibility. But another effect of the policy is that it improves the access of unemployed to jobs with functional flexible contents. To the extent that activation efforts improve the qualifications of unemployed, the possibilities of numerical flexibility increase among labour in general, but functional flexibility among the activated.

The need for qualifying the labour force is increasingly reflected in the labour market policy. It has always been a key element in the active labour market policy to support objectives of growth, structure, and allocation, but during recent years efforts of strengthening the qualifications of labour have played an important role as a political reaction to the deregulation strategy of neo-liberalism. The state, the employers' associations, and the trade unions actively support qualifying the labour force. And despite the fact that companies are most often of the opinion that on-the-job training is the most important tool for qualifying employees (Eriksen & Lind 1989; Erhvervsredegørelse 1996), improving the qualifications of the labour force through labour market policies must be assumed to be an important factor in the development of functionally flexible manpower management. Both because qualifications facilitate this development, and because workers often expect functionally flexible jobs in return for their educational efforts.

The last salient trend in the Danish labour market policies regulating the supply and demand of labour are efforts to encourage retirement from the labour market or reduce the labour force. Apart from the social-political schemes for early retirement, disability pension, etc., many of which are schemes for permanent support of people that under different market conditions would be able to find employment, schemes for early retirement and leave-of-absence contribute to reduce competition in the labour market. They may promote the development of functional flexibility, because in periods of high unemployment these schemes will have little effect on competitive conditions. Until 1995 the permanent (early retirement and transitional allowance) and temporary (leave-of-absence) schemes were continuously expanded, but they have since been limited - most drastically in 1999 and 2006. The major arguments have been that societal obligations to support a growing number of people were becoming too heavy and that the scope of the schemes might lead to shortage of labour.

These restraints on the schemes must be assumed to limit the incentives on applying functional flexibility in HRM.

Collective Agreements

The collective agreements only regulate approximately 60% of the private labour market, meaning that at the most 80% of the total number of employees (including the public sector) is regulated directly by a collective agreement (Scheuer & Madsen 2000). Nevertheless, collective agreements have decisive importance for the creation of norms for regulating the relationship between capital and workers. The most important issues are the managerial right, wages, and management of labour.

In principle the managerial right has remained unchanged for more than a hundred years. The unions have long wanted to limit the employers' right to manage and distribute work, but the employers have rejected all attempts of establishing workplace democracy (Dalgaard 1995; Knudsen 1995). Today, the employers are formally still in a position to decide almost unrestricted on the management of manpower, but the regulations that promote information and dialogue between management and the employees (the system of shop stewards and co-operation committees) often support the developing relations of trust between management and the employees rather than relations of distrust and conflict (Navrbjerg 1999). Compared with other European countries the chances of establishing good relations between management and employees are good in Denmark.

The good collaborative relations between management and employees yield good possibilities for developing functionally flexible manpower management. On the other hand, the reluctance of employers to discuss their managerial rights significantly contributes to the recurrent conflicts over the limits of manpower flexibility. The employers want to have the best possible options for managing manpower according to production requirements. Viewed from the perspective of the individual company this means to obtain the greatest possible advantages compared to those of competitors by virtue of being able to manage manpower flexibly, that is, optimise the performance of the individual employee during working hours. This struggle over competitive advantages involves all types of flexibility, i.e., numerical, temporal, intensity, and thus also functional flexibility. This is reflected in the employers' desire to curb or eliminate traditional boundaries between trades and professions in order to implement more functional flexibility, and many consider the unions as being in opposition to such a strategy and thus main responsible for the difficulties of being able to plan manpower management sufficiently flexibly.

This critique of the unions is well-deserved if one takes competition and market forces to be the ultimate rationale underlying society, but unwarranted when recognising that the very task of the unions is to secure employees against the worst sorts of exploitation. If it is possible to create common conditions for manpower management in the companies, these will be the collective conditions underlying competition. But if competition among companies is not restrained there will be no limits for the flexible management of manpower.

Crudely speaking this is what is happening with the increasingly decentralised bargaining system since the 1980s (Due et al. 1996; Lind 1995). Increasingly fewer issues are being regulated identically for the whole labour market, and during the last bargaining rounds since 2000 this decentralisation has been supplemented by a more individualised choice between various elements of the collective agreement. In principle, the employers are in favour of decentralisation in order to be able to adjust agreements to the needs and possibilities of the single company that is to approximate a deregulated labour market. Adjusting the agreements to the companies implies that companies also compete over flexible management of manpower, that is, compete over optimisation of the flexible management of manpower in order to obtain competitive advantages. A common regulation by virtue of uniform agreements or legislation that comprises the entire labour market would function to counteract such attempts.

It is most likely that this development will lead to greater diversity in the management of manpower. Within certain industries characterised by limited resistance among employees and unions, the companies will possess greater opportunities for realising numerical, temporal (which actually has been most in focus since the early 1990s) and intensive flexibility. And naturally also functional flexibility if this is what the management wants. But since the unions give high priority to functional flexibility this will probably spread among industries where the unions have gained a relatively strong foothold – if they are not staking on maintaining traditional work routines and boundaries between occupational groups.

Developing work and other ideas

The learning organisation or functionally flexible management of manpower shares a series of features with the ideas about "the developing work" launched by the Danish Federation of Trade Unions, the LO, and many unions during the 1990s. The ideas are strongly inspired by the thesis about the changed nature of work in the post-industrial society (Hvid 1990). The intentions of the unions have been to supplement managerial "concepts" and to suggest "how we meet the growing demands from members to support the development in workplaces" (LO 1996).

The fundamental elements in the union strategies for the developing work were adopted at the Danish Federation of Trade Unions Congress in 1991. Essential to the understanding of the concept of developing work is that it implies "work that continuously contributes to the positive development of the individual, the workplace, and the society in which we live. An industrial policy for the developing work encompasses the development of work, product, environment, and "the holistic life". In consequence the developing work is not a state that can be achieved, but a goal toward which we continuously must strive" (LO 1991:3). Spelled out this means that:

- "the work must be neither physically nor mentally attritive, offer the possibilities of applying and developing capabilities and knowledge, and of continuous further training;
- the employees have influence in work and on the future development of work;
- the possibilities for social contact and collaboration in work;
- the workplace is secure and well-functioning;
- the individual can see the meaning with what she or he is producing. The product must contribute to the positive development of society, including to avoid damaging effects on the environment;
- the employees have influence on the placing of working hours" (LO 1991:18-19).

The LO has been very active in realising these ideas, but inertness has characterised both the unions internally and the Danish Employers' Association (LO 1996). On the other hand, since 1993 the social democratic government strongly favoured the idea, and implemented a series of initiatives. First, a program under the Ministry of Labour, in promotion of a better working life and increased growth (DKK 105 million). The purpose is to improve the working conditions of employees simultaneously with strengthening the flexibility and competitiveness of companies. Second, a commerce promoting program under the Ministry of Trade targeted at small and medium-sized companies (DKK 216 million). Third, a program under the Ministry of Research comprising research into and elucidation of "the development of human resources in working life" (DKK 55 million). Forth, a campaign targeted at limiting one-sided, repetitious work. So with the LO we can conclude that "the developing work as a political strategy has had great effect" (LO 1996), but it soon became uncertain whether the strategy did yield any significant results.

During the first years of the new millennium the strategy of the "developing work" gradually lost impetus in the LO. The results seemed to be meager and the liberal-conservative government that took office in 2001 was not as dedicated as the social democrats to promote the strategy.

Some early and recent evidence

What is really required in the promotion of functionally flexible manpower management is that employers realise that it could be to their benefit. Some do (Erhvervsministeriet 1996), but whether they represent isolated cases is impossible to say. Some early findings indicate that many companies did not find this trajectory very attracting.

The so-called VPL (manpower planning in companies) study from 1989 divides companies into four categories based on numerical and functionally flexibly manpower management:

1. Companies characterised by a mixture of numerical and functional flexibility. They represent 33% of all companies and are primarily located within the foodstuff and beverage industry, the textile and clothing industry, and the building and construction industry.
2. Numerically flexible companies of great numerical and little functional flexibility. They represent 17% of all companies and are primarily located within the building and construction industry and the hotel and catering industry.
3. Functionally flexible companies of little numerical and great functional flexibility. They represent 32% of all companies and are typically located within the textile and clothing industry, retailing, banking and insurance, and other service industries.
4. Non-flexible companies of little numerical and functional flexibility. They represent 18% of the companies and are primarily located within the wood and furniture industry, wholesale, carrying trade and other business services (Eriksen & Lind 1989).

Based on a somewhat different categorisation and including somewhat different variables, findings from the subsequent DISKO project were fairly similar and comparable. The DISKO project operates with four criteria for categorising companies (implemented changes in the internal organisation, scope of strategic priority to learning-on-the-job and further training, involvement of employees in the planning of work, and scope of collaboration with customers and suppliers):

1. Companies of flexible organisation (FLO) that meet all four criteria. They represent 20% of all companies and are relatively most common within industry, wholesale, and business service.
2. Companies that are partly FLO and meeting two-three criteria. They represent 53% of all companies and operate within the same industries as in (1).
3. Companies without FLO that meet 0-1 criteria. They represent 28% and are most common within the building and construction industry and other services (Erhvervsministeriet 1996).

Functionally flexible companies and companies of flexible organisation share certain features which support the assumption that staking on managing manpower in a functional flexibly way is part of the same pattern that characterises companies of flexible organisation, cf. Table 5.1.

Table 5.1: Comparison of functionally flexible companies and companies of flexible organisation

Functionally flexible companies are characterised by	Companies of flexible organisation are characterised by
Advanced manpower planning	
Decentralised decision processes	Greater autonomy in work
High degree of employee participation in decision processes	Greater emphasis on collaborative abilities and communication. More collaboration with colleagues and management
Advanced relations of collaboration with public labour market institutions	
Strong emphasis on the development of employee qualifications	Work characterised by less routine
Small batch production, larger individual products, standard service	Stronger emphasis on awareness of responsibility and quality

Source: Eriksen & Lind 1989; Erhvervsministeriet 1996.

Functionally flexible companies (or flexible organisations) must, based on the above, be assumed to represent between 20% and 30% of all companies depending on the criteria applied. Thus, much seems to indicate that the post-industrial or post-Fordist production concept to a certain extent has gained ground in Denmark though it is not the predominant concept. Functionally flexible companies exist within all industries, but they are represented above average within the service sector though with great variations. For example companies of very little functionally flexible manpower management characterise the hotel and catering industry. However, there are no clear indications of the current trends in industrial structure furthering the possibilities of the diffusion of functionally flexible manpower management.

Differences in manpower management among the companies and their different usage of categories of employees are indications of segmentation of the labour market. The "flexible firm" a la Atkinson could be identified in Denmark in the late 1980s in the sense that there was a clear distinction between core and periphery staff with functional flexibility applied to the core and numerical flexibility to the periphery (Jørgensen et al. 1990). This is also evident from the fact that the developing work is more prevalent among employees of high education (44%) than among employees of no education (12%). The difference is even greater between top management (42%) and unskilled workers (5%) (Thaulow 1994).

At the turn of the century this seemed to be almost unchanged. According to the results from a research project on innovative and knowledge based companies with characteristics that match the "learning organisation" the proportion of such companies had not increased during the 1990s (Nielsen 2004). Those companies with a high level of development towards a knowledge organisation comprised approximately 30 per cent of all companies, and the deployment of such strategies among the various categories of employees seemed still to be heavily segmented according to the level of education.

Concluding remarks

Whether the current trends in the labour market push or pull the development of the learning organisation is hard to say. And certainly not, if it implies that the learning organisation must include the entire staff in a company. Segmentation will continue to be the great problem in the labour market, meaning that some get good, developing jobs and work in functionally flexible ways while others get poor jobs of unstable employment and fewer possibilities for developing their professional and personal qualifications.

Employment and industrial policy is very much in favour of strengthening innovation in companies based upon a highly educated work force. And with the decline in unemployment rates since 1994 there should be good opportunities for developing more functionally flexible patterns of labour deployment. The present liberal-conservative government seems, however, to emphasise numerical flexibility in the so-called and highly praised flexicurity model. So, at the end of the day the responsibility for developing patterns of functional flexibility in the deployment of labour it is entirely up to management preferences. Under the pressure of increasing competition following the globalisation of the economy it seems that most employers choose to rely on traditional concepts. To develop the core of the staff and to economise the periphery by means of numerical flexibility.

Therefore, if realised the learning organisation will only comprise certain types of manpower that is people in challenging and well-paid jobs where the employer is also willing to invest in further training. The campaigns launched by the trade unions and other dedicated institutions and persons to improve the working conditions of labour emphasised that improvements were meant for all kinds of staff, but it was always uncertain if the good intentions were sufficient to avoid segmentation, as the strategy contained no explicit considerations of how to avoid the supremacy of management.

References

Aglietta, M. (1979): *A Theory of Capitalist Regulation.* London.

Atkinson, J. (1984): *Flexibility, Uncertainty and Manpower Management.* Brighton.

Beer, M., Spector, B., Lawrence, P. R., Mills, Q. D., Walton, R. E. (1984): *Managing Human Asset.* New York.

Bell, D. (1973): *The Coming of Post-industrial Society.* New York.

Braverman, H. (1974): *Labour and Monopoly Capital, Monthly Review Press.* New York.

Bredgaard, T., Larsen, F., Madsen, P.K. (2006): *Opportunities and challenges for flexicurity – the Danish example*, pp.61-82 in Transfer, vol. 12, No. 1. Brussels.

Dalgaard, N. (1995): *Ved demokratiets grænse*. SFAH, København.

Doeringer, P., Piore, M. (1971): *Internal Labour Markets and Manpower Analysis*. Lexington Mass.

Due, J., Madsen, J. S., Jensen, C. S., Petersen, L. K. (1994): *The survival of the Danish model*. København.

Erhvervsministeriet (1996): *Erhvervsredegørelse 1996*. København.

Eriksen, J., Lind, J. (1989): *Virksomhedernes vurdering af personaleplanlægningen og samspillet med de offentlige myndigheder*. Aalborg.

Fombrun, C., Tichy, N. M., Devanna, M. A. (1984): *Strategic Human Ressource Management*. New York.

Gjerding, A. N., Johnson, B., Kallehauge, L., Lundvall, B.-Å., Madsen P. T. (1990): *Den forsvundne produktivitet*. København.

Gordon, D. M., Edwards, R., Reich, M. (1982): *Segmented work, divided workers*. New York.

Gorz, A. (1981): *Farvel til proletariatet*. Viborg.

Hvid, H. (1990): *Det gode arbejde*. København.

Hyman, R. (1990): Plus ca change? *The Theory of Production and the Production of Theory*. Årbog for arbejdsmarkedsforskning, pp.89-110. Aalborg

Jørgensen, H., Lind, J., Nielsen, P. (1990): *Personale, Planlægning og Politik*. ATA-Forlaget, Rapport nr. 23, Aalborg.

Kern, H., Schumann, M. (1984): *Das Ende der Arbeitsteilung?* München.

Knudsen, H. (1995): *Employee participation in Europe*. London.

Lind, J. (1995): *The modernisation of trade unions in Denmark*, pp.44-63 in Transfer vol. 1 no. 1, Brussels.

Lind, J. (2004): *Labour market policy in Denmark – A European success story?*, pp. 307-328 in Lind, J., Knudsen, H., Jørgensen. H.: Labour and employment regulation in Europe, P.I.E.-Peter Lang, Brussels.

LO (1991): *Det udviklende arbejde.* København.

LO (1996): *Ekstraordinær Kongres.* København. (http://home.lo.dk/lo/kongres.htm).

LO (2006), *Dagpengesystemet. En analyse af dagpengesystemets dækning,* København.

Lutz, B., Sengenberger, W. (1974): *Arbeitsmarkstrukturen und öffentliche Arbeitsmarktpolitik.* Göttingen.

Mendner, J. H. (1975): *Technologische Entwicklung und Arbeitsprozess.* Frankfurt a.M.

Møller, I.H., Lind, J. (2004): *The Danish experience of labour market policy and activation of the unemployed,* pp. 163-196 in Serrano, A.: Are Activation Policies Converging in Europe, ETUI, Brussels.

Navrbjerg, S. (1999): *Nye arbejdsorganiseringer, fleksibilitet og decentralisering,* Jurist- og Økonomforbundets Forlag, København.

Nielsen, P. (2004): *Personale I vidensøkonomien,* Aalborg Universitetsforlag, Aalborg.

Piore, M. J., Sabel, C. F. (1984): *The second industrial divide.* Basic Books.

Pollert, A. (1988): *The "flexible firm": Fixation or fact?* In Work, Employment & Society, Vol. 2, No. 3, pp.281-316.

Reich, M., Gordon, D. M., Edwards, R. C. (1973): *A Theory of Labour Market Segmentation.* American Economic Review, vol.62, pp. 359-365.

Scheuer, S., Madsen, M. (2000): *Mod en ny balance mellem kollektivisme og individualisme*, pp.5-54 in LO-dokumentation 2/2000, København.

Thaulow, I. (1994): *At måle det udviklende lønarbejde.* SFI, København.

Chapter 6

Learning Environment in the Process Industry – Method and Results

By Kjeld Nielsen and Ove Mølvadgaard

> "What actually happens in learning and development (L&D) is a matter of choice in conditions of uncertainty, influenced by power and politics rather than the objective application of an L&D process." (Stephen Gibb 2002: 10)

Introduction

A Danish company within the process industry implemented a further training program in 1997-1998. The purpose was to enable the labour force to operate two new production technologies that had recently been installed (equipment A and B). In collaboration with the local technical and vocational school the company designed a training model for teaching the workers to operate the new technology. A research team from Aalborg University followed and evaluated the effects and the processes resulting from this model.

In this chapter we shall:

1. describe the evaluation method developed during the project
2. present qualitative and quantitative findings from the study
3. discuss the results in view of what kind of organisational and environmental factors that push and pull the development of a stable and learning environment of quality

First we shall present the training model and then describe our evaluation method and results from the project.

Further Training – the Model and the Evaluation Study

The further training project was designed before the introduction of the new technology. The management opted for a training model the core of which was *mediator groups*. The groups were recruited internally.

Each group consisted of representatives of the production and of the production management. The task was to collect, disseminate, and implement knowledge of production technology to those employees who would have to learn to operate the new technology. Two mediator groups were established, one for each of the two pieces of equipment. The primarily task of the groups was to collect and communicate technical knowledge internally within the framework of the training model's practice and pedagogy. The group would gather information from the supplier of the two pieces of equipment, the machine fitters, and the production technicians. This information was complex and extremely technical implying that the groups had to process the information prior to mediating it to their colleagues in the production who would be working with the new equipment.

Viewed in a broader perspective, the establishment of mediator groups for managing in-house learning and training processes in relation to the other groups in the new way of organising work is a novelty compared to traditional in-house training of managers and employees in managing new technology.

Traditionally, employees will learn to operate new technology at supplier courses. Here representatives of the managerial staff and machine operators participate to a varying extent and acquire limited theoretical and practical knowledge about new machines. In most cases the courses include various forms of follow-up courses in the shape of "on-the-job training", possibly supplemented with external courses developed by local training and vocational schools (Nielsen 1987:111; Nielsen 1997:143). The pattern of this traditional way of learning new technology is often individualised and unsystematic, and a number of social conditions will determine who is learning the new technology and to what extent. In consequence, the dissemination of the knowledge required to manage in new forms of work organisation becomes contingent.

The training model designed for this project is also a novelty within in-house learning practice in that its basic idea is planned training in a holistic learning perspective. One view in support of this practice is that in-house training may contribute to facilitate the creation of efficient teams (see DTI Arbejdsliv 1997). In our evaluation study we have attempted to elucidate such interrelationships.

In other words the training model was to contribute to the development of professional and personal qualifications and to build up qualifications in support of management's desire to introduce teamwork and cross-boundary collaboration.

The in-house training was organised along the following principles:

- teamwork
- cross-boundary collaboration
- delegating responsibility
- holistic learning process

The target group was various groups of employees working in workshop, two mediator groups, fiber workers and spun bonded workers who would be operating with the new technology.

Our evaluation study only included the two mediator groups and a number of production teams were recruited internally to operate the new machines – in total fifty persons. Data was generated during the training process by means of questionnaires, group and individual interviews, and observations. Thus following the process closely enabled us to observe the effects of processes initiated at both individual and group level. On the other hand, we have only collected scattered information on the processes at and effects on the organisational level. We have defined the study as a combined process and effect evaluation.

Evaluation Method

We developed the evaluation model in collaboration with the company, but are sole responsible for the method and measurement criteria.

Objectives

Early in the project we formulated three objectives within the framework of the training project:

1. to evaluate whether the transfer of new technological knowledge from machine supplier via mediator groups to production teams was optimal
2. to evaluate the qualification process with a view to establishing production teams of individuals of different vocational background, such as unskilled textile workers, blacksmiths or former principals
3. to contribute to document future training efforts of the company

Figure 6.1.

Machine supplier knowledge

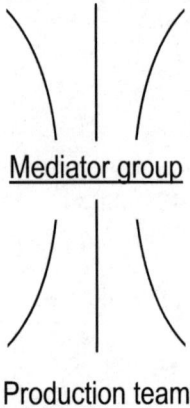

Mediator group

Production team

In collaboration with the management, shop stewards and the participating vocational school we decided that the evaluation task required us to develop a method that would both capture effects of and processes in the implemented training model. The management and the school were especially interested in a method that would capture the processes. Therefore, to start with we opted for developing a method based on studies within evaluation research. Once the method was decided we could start our data collection. This did not imply, however, that we a priori excluded to investigate specific courses in the process.

The evaluation model

Based on studies within working life and evaluation research we developed the model illustrated below in which the training activity was pre-determined exogenously.

Figure 6.2

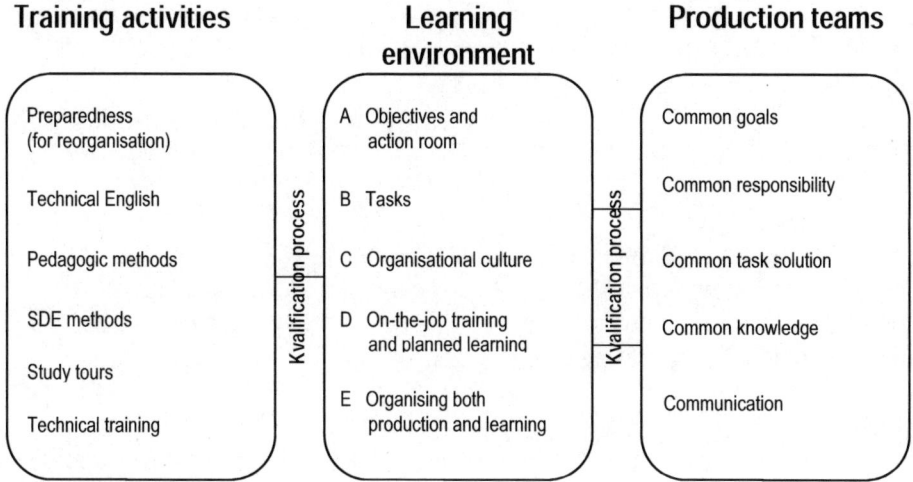

Training activities

Training activities included introductory courses, training courses, and study tours primarily developed by the production management and the vocational school. The latter was supplying the major part of the training input. The mediators participated in all the training activities due to their key role in the program. The production staff, on the other hand, participated in certain defined parts of the program, such as courses in preparedness for reorganisation, the SDE-method (Strategic Development of Employees), and technical training.

In the model, we perceive the learning environment as a significant factor in establishing qualification processes that lead to the creation of (efficient) production teams.

In relation to the contents and didactic aspects of the courses, we wish to emphasise:

Technical English: The purpose was to enable the participants to discuss in English relevant subjects with the supplier technicians. Pedagogics: The participants worked with the supplier's technical documentation and description of the machines. In practice this meant that the participants translated the English manuals into Danish. Duration: one week. The idea was that the mediators should use the "translated" material in the training of production staff.

Pedagogic methods: The idea was to work with communication and motivation methods when having to communicate technical knowledge to the production staff.

SDE-methods: The Confederation of Danish Industries and the Central Organisation of Industrial Employees in Denmark developed this method in the 1980s and the 1990s. The training program included a course in job and qualification descriptions related to the new technology. The purpose was to teach the participants a method for mapping out tasks and qualification requirements related to the new technology and currently register and assess needs for further training. Duration: one week.

At the course *preparedness for reorganisation* the participants learned to be part of collaborative relations, including themes such as team building and problem solving. The course included the following themes: communication, collaboration, assertion, motivation, group structure, and a course in Fibertex. Duration: two weeks. Teaching method: input from teachers in plenary, group sessions, dialogues, etc. The purpose was to make the participants better at handling and solving problems of collaboration in groups and in the organisation.

Study tours: The mediator groups planned and effected visits to the machine suppliers. At these visits the participants were expected to acquire new technical knowledge by applying the methodologies and pedagogical principles they had become familiar with at the other courses. Furthermore representatives of the management and the vocational school involved in the program participated. One of the mediator groups organised a study tour to an Italian machine supplier for two days in the spring of 1997. Eighteen persons participated, ten of whom would be mediating the new knowledge to the production staff. The other mediator group went twice to Germany. On the first visit to the machine supplier nine persons participated, including five former principals, one head of department, one technical manager, one production manager and two representatives of the schools. On the second visit to the German supplier ten employees from the production participated, five of whom had also participated in the first visit and five new ones, the senior ship steward, one technical consultant, one head of department, and one teacher from the vocational school. The visit lasted two weeks.

Training in production technique: According to the plan, production staff training would be based on the mediator groups' knowledge about the machines supplemented with instruction by staff from the machine suppliers. The suppliers should furnish the mediators with knowledge sufficient to run the equipment optimally. This requirement was referred to as "acceptance runs" and was something that the company had demanded from the suppliers. The company had not required that the machine suppliers should coach the production staff in learning how to operate the equipment. This role was more or less deliberately allocated to the mediator groups in their dissemination of knowledge to the production teams. In practice especially the German instructors were involved in on-the-job training during which the mediators functioned as links.

The evaluation criteria for learning environment, production team, and qualification process are described in detail below.

Choice of evaluation method

Within evaluation research scholars in general distinguish between goal-based and goal-free evaluation methods (Scriven 1972; Dylander & Olsen 1975; Vedung 1991; Asmussen 1996; Krogstrup 1997, Gibb 2002).

Within the goal-based evaluation research on further training activities, the researcher/evaluator describes and assesses the connection between activities and their expected effects on the participants' professional and personal qualifications. The effects are then compared with the formulated goals of the activities. Here the task is to demonstrate a relationship between a given course and changes in the participants' performances and qualifications after the course. The method is called effect or result oriented evaluation. The evaluator asks: do the training activities satisfy the expected goals? In its pure form the researcher distinguishes between initial behaviour, i.e. behaviour prior to the training course, and terminal behaviour, i.e. behaviour after the training course. The two measurements are compared on selected performance criteria and based on this it is possible to describe the effect of the training activity and evaluate this effect in relation to the training objectives.

However, this type of studies only seems to be sufficiently valid if measurements are confined to delimited and formal, technical qualifications. One example is technical certification courses where the participants are required to learn to operate a piece of equipment or drive a truck. However, when measuring the effects of training activities aimed at improving general and personal qualifications, the goal-oriented method is not particularly applicable. One problem is that it is difficult to isolate the effects of the training activity itself from the effects of, for instance, the training environment. Simultaneously the individual is subject to other types of socialisation that cannot be referred to the specific training activity, but which adds to constitute a learning environment.

In our view an evaluation of the effects of training activities can function to support the ongoing development of the participants' professional and personal qualifications that might facilitate the establishment of production teams. Group exercises, for instance, may help improve interpersonal skills and thus contribute to conflict solution in a production team.

However, the method does not meet traditional scientific criteria of validity adequately when evaluating the effects of training designed to give the participants knowledge about and attitudes toward interpersonal issues. This also applies to much of the evaluated training program.

Instead our evaluation attempts to "open" up individual and group processes, an idea that was supported by the project management. We became interested in focusing on the processes of learning within the learning environment that would support the learning of personal and professional qualifications. And in the end we chose to focus on group processes rather than individual learning processes.

Summarising the goal-oriented method it can be concluded that it defines a priori certain criteria for relevant measurable effects of a given training activity. The methodological requirements are that the goals of the given activity must be clear and consistent in order to manage the evaluation rationally through a series of effect measurements at given points in the process. The basic requirement is that the evaluator in collaboration with the customer specifies goals that can be operationalised as measurable variables prior to the start of the project. In other words, measurements that can uncover the effects of a given activity over a given period attended by the same persons. Activity goals and procedures will thus govern data collection and processing.

Evaluation Results

The effect of the program on the mediators

A questionnaire survey was conducted among the members of the two mediator groups responsible for disseminating knowledge about the two new machines. The questionnaire was mailed to twenty persons of whom sixteen responded. The results showed the mediators to have acquired a high/certain degree of:

- professional conditions for training production teams in the new technology
- knowledge that facilitated cross-boundary collaboration in the organisation
- knowledge that contributed to create greater job satisfaction in the group

and the courses had

- contributed to create commitment and responsibility for being able to manage and use new technology
- contributed to a lesser degree to break down occupational boundaries
- to a high/certain degree increased their personal qualifications
- to a high/certain degree enabled them to train and form part of production teams

The aggregate effects of the courses were that the mediators had acquired qualifications that to a high/certain degree satisfied the goals. The courses have thus enabled the participants to build up cross-boundary collaboration, and in practice helped furthering the company's desire for organising work in teams across internal organisational boundaries.

Effects of the courses on the production staff

We distributed thirty-two questionnaires among the production teams and thirty responded. The population covered both of the two new technologies.

Results from this part of the study shows:

- The production staff assessed the training activities to have resulted in a high/certain degree of new knowledge. However several of the respondents did not find the training activities to have included sufficient information and knowledge about the entire B equipment. In relation to

equipment A half of the respondents said that the courses had not added new knowledge about the machine
- The production staff operating machine A assessed the training activities to have given them some insight into cross-boundary collaboration. Several of the respondents stated that they were fully capable of managing cross-boundary collaboration. That capability could not be acquired at courses
- The production staff at machine B assessed the training activities to have strengthened, to some extent, cross-boundary collaboration, and to a higher degree to have strengthened the creation of teams among the production groups
- The production staff at both machines assessed the activities to have contributed, to some extent, to improve professional and personal qualifications
- The production staff found that the mediators only to some degree had succeeded in meeting the objectives of the training project
- The production staff stated that they independently had acquired new knowledge about the production technology that they used when operating the equipment
- The production staff, however, assessed the mediators to be somewhat more successful in communicating knowledge about individual operations related to the equipment

Overall the production staff assessed the training activities to have had a positive effect on their personal development and the creation of production teams. On the other hand, they did not find the activities to have resulted in sufficient knowledge about the machines. The individual teams had found it necessary to acquire additional knowledge in order to operate the equipment. One of the goals of the courses was to strengthen the participants' capabilities for individual learning, and our observations seem to confirm the success of these efforts.

The Process Oriented Evaluation

The management and the participating vocational school had also required that the evaluation model included a method for process evaluation, including potential unintended effects.

However, many evaluation researchers have pointed out that the goal-based method (discussed above) does not allow for the measuring of non-intended, non-planned and non-expected effects of a given activity on the participants. These are the effects that process-oriented evaluation measures. In principle this type of evaluation aims to include all variables that must be assumed to have an impact on the effects of a given activity (Asmussen 1996:36). Registering the unintended effects of a given training activity is important in a learning environment within production for the practical consequences to be deduced from the evaluation results. This might be the consequence of experiences during the training project. However, including the entire effect of the training project in the goal-free evaluation is quite resource demanding. For instance, certain effects of courses will, ceteris paribus, have greater impact on the creation of production teams. We are of the opinion that the organising of work, management conditions, and learning environment are factors that combined should be taken into consideration when evaluating the process started by the training activity. By operating with several variables, the process evaluation will become more varied, but also more complex to manage in the data analysis phase.

The connection between process and effect evaluation

Based on the process-oriented model we chose to evaluate the results of the implemented training project compared with the original project. We focused on the participants' experiences of the processes leading to the realised effects and compared these with the original objectives of the training project.

The original project contained several objectives one of which was organisational change. The management wanted to introduce "a flat and more dynamic organisational structure characterised by teamwork, cross-boundary collaboration, and delegation of responsibility". This element in the program entailed training a confined group of employees (the mediator groups) that would be allocated the task of translating supplier knowledge into a training program for the five production teams in charge of operating the two new machines.

We developed a method for uncovering and evaluating both the processes started by the training program and their effects on the involved groups and persons within the social room, which we termed the participants' action and learning space in "the class room" and in "the production room". That is the participants' organising of learning and work processes tied to the use of new technology.

Within the terminology of the social sciences processes are individual or group behaviour in concrete rooms of action, such as those within which the individual acquires knowledge and skills. From earlier studies we knew that employees are not necessarily learning to meet changing demands introduced by new technology and management in stable environments. Technical production problems or changing customer demands often influence the learning environment and the action rooms established in the environment (Nielsen 1987). In consequence, processes cannot be evaluated without describing and assessing the action rooms within which the participants experience learning to take place. The learning environment in the company is confined to cover relevant participants in a given period (individuals and groups).

Process evaluation – criteria

We decided that the process evaluation would focus on three criteria (see the above model), which we viewed as central to measure in relation to the processes and effects experienced by the participants in the training project.

- Learning environment
- Development of qualifications
- Production teams

In the remaining part of this chapter we shall discuss the first criterion – learning environment – and present the results of the process evaluation.

What is a rich learning environment?

The learning environment of the individual workplace plays a significant role in the success or failure of a given training program. In order to achieve the stipulated objectives, the learning environment must be organised in such a way that it enhances the employees' employability either as a result of informal on-the-job learning and/or of participating in formal training programs.

Scholars within working life research agree on a series of principles for organising learning environments that strengthen employee qualifications combining on-the-job training and formal training programs (Rönnqvist & Ellström 1992). The principles (A-E) are summarised below followed by sub-results from the process evaluation.

A. The necessity of not only objectives but also of action room in order to reflect upon and test critically the objectives

Two major viewpoints are prevalent within research:

1. The objectives of learning must be clear and consistent and rest on consensus among management and employees. The formulation of and consensus on the objectives are important preconditions for instrumental action in work and constitute an adapted form of learning the requirements of the new technology. This means that employees are motivated for further learning if the objectives are clearly formulated. This especially applies to production processes that make relatively simple demands on the employees, and when the company operates in stable environments.
2. Clear objectives for learning may prove counterproductive or impede learning if these objectives are not currently discussed, tested or re-tested. This type of development-oriented learning takes place where the technology is unknown, the production process complex, and the company operates in rapidly changing and turbulent environments.

Both approaches are adequate in relation to the conditions for learning processes that we as evaluators experienced at Fibertex. The company included both production processes that required relatively simple qualifications and processes that required learning about a new technology unknown to both the management and the employees.

Ellström et al. draw the conclusion from results of working life research that a major condition for strengthening the staff's motivation and possibility for learning is that objectives are formulated clearly and unambiguously, and are communicated to the staff.

It is important that the learners understand and accept the objectives to be realised and have participated in the formulation and discussion of the objectives. Furthermore, participants must be given the opportunity to reflect upon the objectives in relation to working methods and results required. In other words the participants must be allowed room of action and learning in order to think the series of tasks over and to test whether the objectives are realisable, relevant and consistent with the tasks.

The creation of a learning room requires that the participants themselves begin to collect and structure knowledge at a given level in the learning processes. The processing and transformation of this knowledge into other practical contexts are important for the participants' motivation for learning and for teaching others what they have learned.

The creation of action and learning room– an example from the production technical learning at the machine supplier

Equipment A. The visit to the machine supplier was not properly planned because it took place ten days earlier than originally scheduled. On the first day the group was given a guided tour of a demonstration machine and was given the possibility of testing stop and start functions. The group was dissatisfied with the introduction. The supplier did not furnish them with a general view of all the functions of the machine and the participants felt that "they were falling over each other" during the guided tour. In consequence it was fairly contingent who learned what about the functions of the machine. Due to the general dissatisfaction with the introduction on the first day, the group decided to go for more targeted knowledge on the second day. They split into two smaller groups that each worked out a list of the technical information they wanted from the supplier. This process resulted in a functional description of the machine. The participants took as their point of departure the SDE-method that they had become familiar with at in-house courses. This technical knowledge was later on transformed into documentary teaching material that was subsequently used to disseminate the knowledge in the factory. The latter two issues are examples of how the participants expanded the learning room for communication of knowledge.

Reflecting on the visit, one of the participants said "...before going to Italy we should have made up our mind about why we wanted to go to Italy ... you need not go to Italy for that..." Another participant said that "...there was too little time to process the impressions..."

Nevertheless the participants did, taking the premises into consideration, establish some kind of a learning room.

The example demonstrates the initial creation of a learning room during the visit to the Italian manufacturer. Some of the knowledge acquired during the visit was transformed into technical knowledge to be communicated to the production teams. Before going to Italy the group had decided to videotape the instructions.

This decision later helped facilitate dissemination of knowledge in the factory. It was used as input on the courses for production staff that had not participated in the visit to the manufacturer.

Equipment B. The mediator group had no influence on the program planned by the machine supplier. The group spent one and a half-day of the two-week study tour, inspecting the test equipment. The remaining days they visited subcontractors. The experience with the main supplier was described as follows: "...We thought we were going to work the machine, start it and stop it ... but we were disappointed. We would have preferred to see the real technological novelty – the melt blown machine working, but that was not possible either..."

The example illustrates that the mediator group was cut off from creating a learning room around job-relevant learning of the new production technology – a learning room in which they actively could have been working the equipment. The supplier sat the agenda for learning.

In view of the criterion that learning participants must contribute to formulate the objectives of the learning process, it is evident that none of the supplier visits met this criterion. In consequence the participants were not sufficiently motivated for creating a learning room. This may have had consequences for the practical learning process in the factory.

The training model's criterion "holistic learning", important for the organising of the learning environment at the suppliers, is partly undermined. The instructions did not provide the mediator group of equipment A with an adequate overview of the process. Likewise, the mediator group of equipment B was also given an inadequate overview of the equipment, given that most of the time was spent with subcontractors. This part of the learning process can be characterised as "piecemeal" learning which renders difficult the creation of a "holistic learning process".

The process of creating a learning room differs between the two mediator groups during their visits to the suppliers. During the visits, the mediator group of equipment A created a learning room around job description. On the other hand, the conditions under which the other mediator group had to work excluded the creation of a learning room. The supplier did not allow the group to operate the equipment and much of the time they spent on fairly irrelevant visits to subcontractors of components for the machine.

However, both study tours started social processes in the creation of learning rooms. In the subsequent interviews both groups expressed that the visits to the suppliers had help demystifying the new technology, resulted in less fear of the unknown technology, and positively effected the social climate in the groups.

Consequently, the study tours may have strengthened trust relation among the group members, which may have helped facilitate their task of communicating knowledge about the new technology.

B. The necessity of tasks of high learning potential

It is important for the quality of the learning environment that qualification requirements are sufficiently high to allow the employee to develop their competencies on the job. By qualification requirements we refer to the complexity of tasks and the degree of autonomy in the job in terms of being able to influence the details of the tasks, the method of work, and to assess the outcome. Scholars within the field widely disagree on which individual and organisational factors that help further the development of competencies. But one thing that they agree on is that the autonomy and complexity characterising work are decisive factors in individual competence development. If the job is too simple the individual will experience it as routine, lacking potentials for learning, and reducing intellectual capabilities. On the other hand, if the work is too complex it will lead to poor performance and stress. A maximum degree of autonomy and an optimal degree of complexity are thought to create the best conditions for competence learning and personal development.

The findings of Volpert and Oesterreich (here quotet from Rönnqvist and Ellström 1992:25-26) show that in order for work to support learning it must:

- contain a high degree of autonomy in relation to decisions on means-ends, i.e. the tasks must involve high competence requirements in terms of action regulation
- allow for a high degree of autonomy as to temporal aspects (e.g. rate of work and planning of working hours)
- allow for knowledge development and a holistic understanding of the technical and social-organisational aspects of the tasks
- to as large a degree as possible free the employee from technical and social-organisational impediments for exploiting the action room potentially embedded in the tasks

- offer experience based competencies based on appropriate and varied physical activity, different sense impressions and actual handling of the object of work
- offer the possibilities of performing tasks under varied conditions
- offer the possibilities of and encouraging collaboration and interaction with others

The organising of work, work methods, and utilization of the technical system are decisive factors in determining whether or not the company will succeed in establishing a good learning environment. Among other things it is necessary to monitor the distribution of tasks among various areas/departments in the organisation. Designing the organising of work to allow for these requirements can be said to be a *necessary* but not sufficient precondition for the employee being able to exploit his or her opportunities for on-the-job learning.

Do production line tasks contain high potential for learning – what is the opinion of the mediators?

The mediators experienced several problems implying that the production line tasks did not contain much learning potential – neither with regard to job requirements nor autonomy. It is our impression from the group interviews that certain tasks were confined to simple monitor functions whereas requirements increased considerably in other situations, such as in the case of unanticipated production stops.

An example of limited job requirements is:
"...for a period one man was placed in a monitor function - just sitting there looking at the roles ... if you looked away for five seconds some problem might occur that job did not involve much learning..."

Examples of limited autonomy and job requirements:
"...one of our functions involved taking out bales... it is a boring job ... they come back and say ... we won't do it anymore..."

This is a routine task governed by the fiber flow and various types of technical facilities are used in packing and transporting the fiber material.

"...in addition people are checking us all the time... now we cannot be bothered to work on the old machine..." (they are organised in teams that must also be able to work on the new machine).

"... and then a third person comes who also wants to try the new equipment."

The quotations from the mediator groups underline that the new machines involve tasks and processes which require very little training and where the demands for learning something new and perform autonomously are modest (bale and monitoring functions). The technological content of certain jobs is not very motivating for learning the new technology.

However, other jobs involving the new technology are very challenging:
"... the greatest problems that I have experiences as a mediator is the conflicts among workers caused by the technology... a lot of them don't want to take out the bales when there is something more exciting going on in the other end of the workshop..."

Something seems to indicate that the modest learning potential inherent in several of the tasks raised the expectations of and demands from the productions staff toward the mediators to learning something new elsewhere in the line – e.g. at the desk. This function was new and hence interesting for the production staff. Therefore, the interviewed productions team decided on extensive job rotation in order to enable all members of the team to learn the more demanding tasks on the line – e.g. desk management. Jointly the team has developed a learning room, which allows each member to perform tasks different from those allocated to the individual during the training period. At the same time the demands on the individual and the "team" have increased which has led to greater motivation to learn. Organising of the learning process has strengthened the teams in that they feel mutually responsibility for knowledge communication and training. In consequence they have acquired a shared knowledge about the production line functions. This has further helped establishing general knowledge about the new technology, which is vital when something goes wrong.

What is the attitude of the production team toward line tasks?
The demands for qualifications are sometimes high, but the teams can solve problems autonomously when they occur.

"...trouble-shooting is what we really learn from ... the next time the problem occurs we know how to solve it... this is how we learn to solve most problem... we gain experience ... for instance, we have learned to keep an eye on the nozzles becoming clogged – they must be cleaned regularly ..." (see the example below).

"... and we use our experiences pro-actively..."

The learning potential is high in situations of technical problems. Simultaneously, the demands (professional and personal) on the individual and the team increase. On other hand, several line tasks, such as monitoring and bale handling contain little learning potential and are not experience as requiring particular qualifications. They are routine tasks primarily involving the operation of lifting gear, internal transportation systems, computers, etc. Those on the team that perform routine tasks will, ceteris paribus, be much more motivated for learning more demanding tasks. This situation has occasionally caused severe headaches for the mediator on the team.

C. The necessity of an organisational culture that supports and encourages learning

In analysing the possibilities of motivating employee commitment to work, we must distinguish between objective and subjective room of action. In general, it is assumed within working life research that the individual possesses an objective room of action (degree of freedom). This concerns the approach to the given task, choice of methods/means for solving tasks, and to a certain degree the possibility of affecting and assessing the outcome (Ellstöm et al. op.cit; Nielsen 1997). Simultaneously, various studies show that employees may, objectively seen, have an action room, but subjectively, this is not their experience or they do not utilize it. On the other hand employees may think that they have action room, which is not the case objectively seen.

To what extent employees are able to exploit their action room depends on their self-perception. Studies point to factors such as self-confidence, self-control, and ability to master the situation. These are capabilities that the individual has been socialised into mastering through previous work experience, education and assumptions about how others have approached the task.

In this context it is important that the organisational culture affects positively the subjective action room of the employees and hence the potential for learning. Culture can emphasise the employees' freedom to act, commitment toward work, but it can also have the opposite effect – employees that are self-sufficient, demonstrate fear or indifference. So culture can affect the learning environment positively and negatively.

The culture that supports development oriented learning is characterised by:

- emphasising action, initiative, and risk taking
- tolerance toward different perceptions, uncertainty and error
- emphasising and encouraging reflection upon and critical testing of diverse aspects of the company – especially the established "truths" about what is natural, desirable and possible

In general the company in our study must be characterised as having a development oriented organisational culture. Since the early 1990s the management and the employees have jointly designed and implemented a wide range of in-house training activities targeted at hourly-paid workers. These activities have had a spill over effect on the employees' work commitment, resulting in team spirit and great commitment among managers, mediators and production staff.

When we interviewed the mediator groups about the problem of melted fiber on the production line, they said: "... yes, it happens, but we act as quickly as possible. Nobody is interested in destroying anything, we do whatever we can and then the company must bear the costs if anything is destroyed."

The quotation reflects a positive organisational culture characterised by the attitude that the employees do their best and look after the production equipment without fearing that they might ruin something.

What is the attitude of the mediator group for equipment A toward the role of organisational culture for the learning of new requirements?

On returning from the visit to one of the machine suppliers, the mediator groups were strongly motivated and well knit. They had acquired the first tentative knowledge about the new production technology. One of the mediators expressed his attitude toward the new task as "... we felt that we had to join hands..." The visits to the suppliers had thus resulted in the creation of a group culture. However, when they on their return began to search for additional knowledge about the machine, the learning environment revealed several barriers.

Communication between the supplier's fitters and the mediators was deficient, especially during the installation of equipment A. The foreign fitters did not understand, or perhaps did not want to understand the mediators when they asked questions in English. The fitters would merely respond with gestures. In consequence, the mediators gained little knowledge from the fitters, which had a negative impact on the learning environment, and on the objectives of the training project.

Thus the mediators' room for learning and understanding the workings of the machine was confined by the fact that those supposed to be familiar with the machine were unable to communicate their knowledge.

Later on in the process the management and the production staff tightened the demands on the mediator group for equipment A:

"... the management has said that now it must run... as a mediator you just say ... well then we have to start the equipment... we press the necessary buttons and then... then the others come and say,,, you have not explained properly how.... what are we to do now?... and the management is after you... what the hell do you do? ... there have been too many problems of this kind..."

External demands for "something to happen" have constrained the mediators' learning room. The management and the colleagues did not support and encourage the mediators in the period when the learning environment was troubled and unstable. Different levels in the organisation had different expectations of the mediator groups that apparently could not be met. Considerations of production and learning appeared as a dilemma for the mediator group. Did the group solve this dilemma and how?

About managing their own development the mediator group says:

"The group has not really been responsible for managing the work... the group that participated in the visit to the supplier turned the mediators into being responsible... this has been a great disadvantage... if anything happened the mediators have been sole responsible for solving the problems... the mediator has been blamed if he had not given full information and that is not easy when there are four others managing the training... we have felt under pressure... we have argued with the production staff... patience has been the major ingredient..."

For lengthy periods during the training phase the mediators by no means functioned optimally. Both as individuals and as a loosely coupled group they were isolated from the rest of the organisation. They were unable to create and develop the necessary learning room both for themselves and for their target group. The mediators were facing different expectations that they did not met.

An important reason for the mediator group not functioning optimally in the first part of the training period was the turnover among mediators that were allocated other tasks in the organisation.

"Suddenly one of the mediators was elected senior shop steward and two others were allocated a different team... they lacked any kind of motivation...we were actually only three that took some interest in it... in addition we had a new man to train from scratch..."

"...After two of the mediators had been moved to the old machine we were three left that had to work like hell to make it run again..."

Those mediators that worked with the machine were under heavy pressure for solving production and training tasks simultaneously. The reduced number of mediators has not made the job of communicating knowledge easier in an unstable learning environment.

When we interviewed one of the mediators in November 1997 he summarised the state of affairs as "... the atmosphere has become calmer..."

What is the attitude of production team A toward the culture characterising learning in the organisation?

By and large all members of the team have participated in the learning process since the start up of the new equipment and they confirm the mediators' statements. One interpretation of the fact that the same individuals have made up the team despite poorer conditions in the learning environment is that the established group culture has succeeded in creating a rich learning room among participants for the informal learning of new job requirements.

One of the team members says about the first period "...for two-three months he was allowed to spend all his (the mediator) time at the desk and the line ... and we did the rest of the jobs... this enabled him to gather as much knowledge as possible before we started rotating... it has proved to be a good idea... if we are doubtful of something, we ask the mediator... there is no one else..."

About the established learning room in the group, the mediator says: "...we manage fairly well... there are certain things that still surprise us... that is unavoidable... we search for knowledge and attempt to solve the problem in collaboration with the department manager... we are not in a position to be pro-active... the day-to-day running functions well..."

In the interview the mediator states that combined they solve the problems, they accept each other and exchange knowledge and experience. One of the other team members says "...we ask the mediator and wait to see what he pulls out of his backpack..."

D. The necessity of integrating on-the-job training and planned learning

Within working life and evaluation research the integration of formal and informal training/learning is often referred to as the so-called *transfer problem*. In other words, knowledge acquired by an employee on a course is seldom translated into or applied to the work situation. Elsewhere the same phenomenon is referred to as the participants' "embedded knowledge" when they have to transfer newly acquired knowledge to the work organisation. It appears from working life research in general (Ellström and others) that informal learning is bound to take place in any organisation. However, this type of learning will rarely lead to new qualifications if not integrated into some kind of planned systematic training. There are various training models that take into consideration the application of informal learning. There are models that:

- start from a problem and the development needs of the organisation
- are based on the individuals' experiences of solving problems in practical situations
- function as a form of group studies allowing for dialogue among the groups and among the various groups of personnel and experts in various areas
- are designed and implemented in interaction with the persons that will be subject to the training

The mediator groups' experience of integration

The positive effect of designing the training project with mediator groups and of integrating the latter and the production teams was that informal learning ran parallel with the formal and was utilized, because the groups continuously discussed how to solve problems in practice. In consequence, informal knowledge did not remain "embedded" in the individual employee. All members of the group became more or less involved in communicating new knowledge. On the other hand, there was no transfer of knowledge between the mediator groups across production teams and technologies.

According to the mediator group of equipment B it has been very difficult to establish collaboration among production teams, either due to deficient time during the running-in period or lack of management initiative. However, the logbook of each machine has served to remedy the deficient collaboration combined with the fact that the teams are overlapping.

A major element in integrating informal and formal training was that the mediators, who participated in the courses and collected knowledge, were later on to be part of the teams. For equipment A the intention only proved successful in two of five cases due to personnel turnover in the mediator group early in the process. In general for equipment A, the integration of planned and informal learning was only partly successful.

However, our data show that there are examples of the learning environment having been strengthened by integrating formal and informal learning.

Example 1: The course in "technical English" illustrates how technical knowledge provided by the supplier of equipment A was transferred to informal on-the-job learning.

The manual was an English translation of the original Italian version, and it constituted the major input to the course in technical English. "We took our point of departure in the book, discussed some of the technical subjects and translated these into Danish... It (the English version manual) was a strange jumble... incoherent... so we had to find new words for "what they had translated" to use for our translation into Danish... it was a different kind of introduction to the machine... you had to think differently from what you were used to... It was a challenge as the desk had not yet been installed... we could not point to the button we were talking about... we had to go over drawings in order to figure out what it was all about... The terminology that we invented at that time for referring to various part of the machine we are still using."

Example 2: The course in the method "Strategic Development of Employees" (SDE) is another example of how planned training is transferable to informal on-the-job learning. The mediator group informed that it had no part in analysing the actual qualification requirements that is in formulating the qualifications that could be based on the SDE-method. But the group was introduced to the method. It was applied at the study tour probably because the group had no other "tool" on the second day. During the tour collaboration was established between the vocational school, responsible for teaching the SDE-method, and the mediator group. One of the participants tells about his experience with the process: ..."Before going on the tour we had learned the construction method. We worked out job descriptions for equipment A based on the SDE-method. We were divided into smaller groups... we wrote down what we needed... based on this we worked out job descriptions... we got an understanding of what a job description is... it says what is required to master this function... and we applied it on our return."

The group assessed the SDE-method to be a potential tool for working out job descriptions to be used for teaching new colleagues. On the other hand, the group was very doubtful of the method in relation to older fiber workers who knew what working on the process line implied.

The mediators might have been able to expand their learning room had they been more active in formulating the overall qualification requirements from a holistic perspective and targeted the entire equipment. This might have supported their efforts of acquiring process knowledge during the first phase of the learning period. On the other hand, the mediator group generated detailed knowledge about the individual processes (mixer and operation functions, etc.) With a view to the basic idea of the training program, the holistic form of learning would have been preferable.

Example 3: The course in *teaching methods* for mediators was also transformed into informal learning: "...You were given the task of explaining to the others in the group how to make a paper dart without showing them in practice ... It was a good exercise. Later on it was easier to explain something to somebody ... I recall the method when having to explain something..." "... there are people who are unfamiliar with having to explain something ... for that kind of people this course was especially important..."

At this point in the process evaluation it was evident that the participants applied several of the elements from the various courses to the exchange of knowledge and to training, thus meeting the definition of a good learning environment as one that integrates formal and informal learning.

According to the head of department, the employees were strongly motivated for participating in the courses. On the other hand, the courses seemed to have been of limited applicability.

"...I recall people being very impressed by the courses in technical English, preparedness for readjustment, and the SDE course ... however, only a few of the elements were applicable in other contexts of teaching and knowledge exchange ... the mediators and some of the other participants were, however, very keen on applying it..."

During the course in preparedness for readjustment we observed that several of the exercises required interpersonal skills, especially in situations where the participants had to make decisions under strong pressure. It is possible that these exercises have helped the participants function as teams, especially when having to solve new problems in the production process.

The total analysis shows that knowledge from the courses has been applied to the learning process and several of the mediators have drawn on this knowledge to fill a learning room.

What is the attitude of production team A toward the relationship between planned training and informal learning?
"It has been modest..."

"...The course in production technique was fairly thin (one week)... the teachers did not have much to offer... (the mediator)."

Apart from the course and training program included in our evaluation project, a start-up course was effectuated immediately after the equipment had been installed. An external supplier who knew the equipment thoroughly ran the course. The comments on this course were: "... it was the most informative course... it was the course that we learned most from... he returned later and did the up-start with us... and showed us how to do it..."

Other employee comments are: "...this is actually the only training that we have received, he showed us and explained... and we tried to start-up the machine... together with him... what we have learned aside from that we have picked up elsewhere together with the head of department and got from the mediator... and a lot of things we have figured out ourselves...aside from that we have not received any training... and then there was an Italian showing us how to run aspects of the machinery... apart from that we didn't received any training..."

About the mediators' retrieval of information from the fitters that installed equipment A, the comments are:

"...the mediators had been made responsible for talking with the Italian fitters... however when asking questions they would merely gesticulate... it was not easy to get information... or they would do some operation fast... nobody really saw what happened..."

E. The necessity of organising the company to serve both production and learning

It has often proved difficult to adapt a non-learning organisation in stable environments to changing environments. The organisational members are facing new demands for learning when the technology (process and product technology) and the organising of work change significantly. The basic assumption is that in order to meet this demand the functionality of the organisation will always depend on the employees' ability and will to learn. According to Ellström and others this applies to organisations such as hospitals and service companies that are in close interaction with patients/clients /custommers. It is necessary for this type of organisation continuously to adapt to internal and external changes. This requires learning at all levels of the organisation, which is why the organisation must be organised in a way that facilitates and stimulates learning.

In consequence, most companies will find it necessary, in the short and the long run, to organise e.g. new technology and tasks with a view to both production (action) and learning (reflection). This implies that the organisation must create the premises for enabling employees to act independently. This involves creating room for discussing objectives and planning, for testing different action alternatives, and for evaluation of and reflection on the organisation and its consequences. This can happen through the daily decision and change processses.

Organising the company to fit both production and learning

The major criterion for the good learning environment is that managers involve the employees in new ways of organising new tasks and simultaneously make it possible for them to learn and reflect on the positive and negative aspects of the outcome and to operate with action alternatives.

Against this view the mediators say:

"...one of the problems during the training course was that the machines were still wrapped up in plastic... we could walk around them and look at them... we only had copies of screen prints to look at..."

Learning at the equipment during the installation phase

The above quotation from an interview with one of the mediators of equipment A demonstrates that when the need for learning and the motivation were greatest, the machine was not installed and accessible. The mediator group applied different available methods and means to illustrate the knowledge they wanted to communicate, which had a positive effect on the learning environment.

But other conditions had, as mentioned earlier, negative effects on the learning environment. For instance, the equipment was installed during a period when several of the mediators were on vacation and thus unable to pick up information from the fitters as planned. And when the mediators were able to be present, the language barriers proved to be an obstacle for obtaining the necessary information.

The mediators certainly did not have favourable conditions for creating a rich learning room since several factors in the learning environment did not function optimally. In relation to equipment A, the organising of production and learning was not successful.

For several reasons the mediator group has not been able to couple production and learning during the individual development phases.

Learning and production in the start-up phase

Learning to operate the desk from looking at screen prints:

"...the screen was not installed before the machine was mounted. It would have facilitated learning had the screen been mounted... Learning was solely based on a number of screen prints placed on a board [in a certain sequence]..."

"...you learn more from hands-on... it was not possible to simulate the operation of the desk..."

Several have tried to operate the desk. One of the mediators said that he had not had the time to communicate the necessary information about the machine.

We were not appropriately equipped for communication knowledge to the production staff.

We were just thrown into it.

The necessary learning room was not created for the mediators in the start-up phase. One reason was probably the learning environment, where some of the mediators were transferred to another unit. Another reason presumably was that the new machines caused specific technical problems.

Several of the mediators worked in the spun bonded unit during the training process. This task had nothing to do with the production on the new machine. The training of mediators was not targeted at relevant persons. "...we are twenty people working in the spun bonded unit... so we have plenty of things to do..."

The machine continuously caused problems, implying that time to be spend on training was reduced to the minimal: ..."this meant that we didn't have much time to communicate our knowledge to others... The mediators on the line have done a tremendous job... but it is difficult to explain to people that everything is fine when the garbage piles up..."

"... one of the unpleasant things has been that the mediators had to manage the problems with the fitters... we were actually to blame for not knowing anything about it. The only information we received was that we should make the machine run... not until now are we beginning to learn when to lower the temperature and pressure... these are experiences that we are beginning to accumulate... not until now can we begin to pass on knowledge... now the atmosphere is no longer turbulent..."

"... during the same period, we had to move the old machines somewhere else in order to make room for the new ones."

"... Simultaneously with starting-up the new machines production continued on the old ones... It was chaotic... When we were unable to make the new machines run then we had to start-up the old ones... This was the situation day after day, day after day..."

"We were not given adequate time to train people".

What is production team A's experience of organising learning in combination with production?

The team consists of five people, one of whom is in charge of start-up, operating the desk, monitoring the line, updating information from the lab (fiber tests), and information via intranet.

Two of the five people are working in the bale press unit with surveillance, internal transportation, operating machines, etc. Internally the remaining three members of the team alternate between operating the desk and the bale press on the same shift thus allowing each of them to operate the desk every day: Person 1: three hours. Person 2: two and a half hours. Person 3: two and a half hours. This means that two of the persons operate the press for five hours and the desk for three hours every day. In this way them all gain experience in working on the line and especially in operating the desk.

The remaining two members of the team operate the old machine. Once a week, the team rotates in order to enable all members to get to know the new machine.

"...when problems occur, we try to find solutions ourselves. If we are unable to resolve the problem, we turn to the head of department... most of the time we find a solution... we have only stopped the machine once..."

The learning room of equipment A always consists of three of the five people on the team, and the internal job rotation schemes ensure optimal utilization of the learning room.

Conclusion: Establishing a Stable Learning Environment of Quality

Method: In the study the learning environment is defined through the participants' experience of learning processes and action room. The learning environment is delimited to comprise the participants' experiences of a concrete course and training in new production techniques in connection with the introduction of two new types of process technology. The study included a population of fifty.

We chose to work with the general concept of action room for learning (Ellström 1994). Here this concept refers to decision and action processes that are established by management and employees actively organising learning processes. In other words the learning of new requirements refers to decisions and actions that in general originate from the tasks, missions, methods and outcome of any organisation. Literature on the sociology of work defines *action room* as the possibility of workers to rotate among various functions and hence learning processes tied to these functions (Nielsen 1998). Based on this concept we defined five criteria for a good learning environment generally accepted within research on working life and learning which, we applied to the qualitative analysis of the specific learning environment. The study was conducted as a combined effect and process evaluation. For data collection we used both qualitative and quantitative methods.

Findings from the studies show that the most important conditions for the creations of a stable learning environment of quality can be summarised as:

The effect study demonstrates that the courses have contributed significantly to the creation of a learning environment that has motivated the participants for learning new requirements across occupational boundaries. The mediators, which represent a novelty within the organising of learning environments within industrial organisations, accepted positively the role as knowledge communicators, drawing on the teaching methods and technical English that they learned on the courses. Both the effect and the evaluation study show, however, the difficulties of creating a stable learning environment, especially in connection with acquiring the necessary knowledge and communicating "technical knowledge" to the production staff. The visits to the suppliers created the background for the emergence of a group culture around the communication task. In connection with the training program, the mediators had organised the jobs in teams. But the conditions for undertaking the training task were not stable. The culture was not adequately sustained and developed due to many of the mediators being transferred to other jobs in the organisation. The mediators were not, as assumed in the training model, integrated across occupational boundaries during the phase of learning the new technology and exchange knowledge and experience. Originally, the cross-boundary organising of the mediators' role was fundamental to the idea of the training program. It is our opinion that this situation affected the quality of knowledge communication negatively for both machines. The mediators were uncertain of which subjects to communicate to the production staff and when to do it.

The effect evaluation shows that the participants found the courses had been supportive in term of personal development, and they assessed the process to have helped create learning room in an - at times - unstable learning environment. The participants did not get the necessary "quiet" conditions for learning the new requirements in that production was given higher priority than learning. The courses functioned to support collaboration among the production staff when technical problems occurred. Learning of the technical requirements improved considerably during the "hands-on" period compared to the formal forms of learning. A few of the mediators became integrated successfully (as production workers) into the individual production teams, though under different conditions.

The group interviews demonstrate that despite the fact that the learning potential embedded in the individual functions was limited, the participants have found it challenging to generate knowledge about the new technology through group oriented learning processes.

It is our evaluation that the project has created action room and conditions for establishing qualitative learning within the individual production teams. Our findings show that the creation and development of independent action room and extensive and open communication among participants result in stable learning environments of quality.

We agree with following findings by exploring team learning in over 30 large companies across a range of industries: "Team processes are all but defined by pre-existing organisational processes. At one extreme, they are directive and driven. At another, they are dynamic and fluid and underlie a degree of self-managed activity. Team processes accordingly are potentially dynamic or rather basic depending on the level of structured or unstructured activity". (Murray & Moses 2005).

References

Projektbeskrivelse (1997): *Jobrotation på Fibertex A/S.*

Asmussen, Nils (1996): *Uddannelse, udvikling og evaluering*, Forlaget CUE, Århus.

Clematide, Bruno & Claus Agø Hansen (1996): *Et fælles begreb om kvalifikationer?* SUM beskrivelsesmetodik projektet - den teoretiske udredning. DTI, Arbejdsliv.

DTI Arbejdsliv: *Læring på arbejdspladsen* - Virksomhedsintern uddannelse og læring i teori og praksis, Maj 1997 (Udarbejdet for Landsorganisationen i Danmark).

Dylander, Benny & Kaj Olesen (1976): *Effekt af medarbejderuddannelse* - en sociologisk undersøgelse af kursuseffekt og implementeringsvanskelighed, Erhvervspædagogik, Teknologisk Institut.

Gibb, Stephen (2002): *Learning and Development* – Processes, Practices and Perspectives at Work, Palgrave Macmillan, London.

Ellström, Per-Erik (1994): *Kompetens, utbildning och lärande i arbetslivet*, Gotab, Stockholm.

Jørgensen, Christian Helms (1997): *Medarbejdere oplærer og underviser medarbejdere*, Evaluering af et uddannelsesprojekt på Fibertex, Projektrapport, Marts 1997.

Krogstrup, Hanne K. (1997): *Brugerinddragelse og organisatorisk læring i den sociale sektor*, Systime.

Lind, Jan-Inge & Per-Hugo Skärvad (1997): *Nya team i orgnisationernas värld*, Lund

Murray, P. & Maree Moses: The centrality of teams in the organisational learning process in: *Management Decision*, 2005, Vol. 43 Issue 9, Page: 1186 – 1202

Nielsen, Kjeld (1987): *Ny teknik, joborganisering og medarbejderkvalifikationer*, Aalborg Universitetscenter, Institut for Produktion 1987.

Nielsen, Kjeld (1995): *Kvalifikationsudvikling*, LEO Arbejdspapir nr. 6, oktober 1995.

Nielsen, Kjeld (1998): *Arbejdsorganisation, læring og kontrol.* Artikel in: Allan Christensen Den Lærende organisations begreber og praksis, Aalborg Universitetsforlag 1997 2. Udgave, 1. Oplag.

Nielsen, Kjeld & Ove Mølvadgaard (1999): *Kvalifikationsudvikling og læringsmiljø i procesindustrien* - En evalueringsundersøgelse af et efteruddannelsesprojekt på Fibertex A/S, Aalborg, LEO-serien nr. 22, LEO-gruppen ved Institut for Sociale Forhold og Organisation, Aalborg Universitet.

Rönnqvist, Dan & Per-Erik Ellström (1992): *Lärandehierarkin* - En studie av anställdas möligheter till kompetensutveckling inom sjukvården.

Scriven, Michael (1972): *Evaluation as a Paradigm for Educational Research*, The Journal of Educational Evaluation.

Vedung, Evert (1991): *Utvärdering i politik och förvaltning.* Lund.

Chapter 7

Learning Organisations in Practice

By Søren Voxted

Introduction

In the 1990s the mainstream in organisation theory was the learning organisation. First, as a theoretical model of how organisations can meet growing demands and challenges; second, as a method to manage organisational change. Management consultants who, drawing on the theories, offer to assist in developing private and public organisations into learning units often provide the latter.

But the learning organisation is only one of a series of new management technologies stipulating how organisations should be developed and structured in order to be in a position to meet the current challenges optimally. These concepts share the perception of human labour across hierarchies and functions as the most important resource for being able to tackle numerous and accelerating challenges.

Debates on the new management technologies have left the audience with the idea that the majority of business life has adopted the ideas. But nobody really knows whether this is the case. We only have limited knowledge about the dissemination of the new management technologies and of what characterises companies that have organised along these principles. Taking as our point of departure the concept of "the learning organisation"[34] we shall attempt to identify and characterise private sector Danish companies whose operations in practice work in keeping with the concept of the learning organisation.

Based on a survey study we shall first identify learning organisations and thus elucidate the dissemination of the concept. The second purpose of this chapter is to see what characterises the learning organisation compared to the remaining part of private business life in terms of the usage of human resources, the organising of work, and relations to the environment.

---

[34] In the following "learning organisations" and "learning companies" are used synonymously.

Third, drawing on our empirical findings we shall discuss to what extend company practice harmonises with the theoretical positions and models tied to Peter Senge's concept of "the learning organisation". Of the many divergent descriptions of the learning organisation, we have chosen that of Peter Senge because his idea of the learning organisations has gained a dominant position in the organisation theoretical discourse just as his book "The Fifth Discipline" strongly contributed to launch the concept in the 1990s.

The Learning Organisation as a Theoretical Concept

The impression of the need for companies to demonstrate greater flexibility and changeability, of growing competition both nationally and globally, and of the technological development have led to the development of new organisational principles and methods that, focusing on human resources, aim to strengthen the abilities of organisations for renewal and change. The idea is to change organisations from being traditional bureaucracies to becoming flexible units in which employees at all levels apart from demonstrating professionalism also demonstrate a high degree of responsibility, creativity, and actively contribute to problem solving.

The learning organisation is a common denominator for these principles and methods. The diverse definitions of the concept all include visions about the development potentials of organisations by making continuous learning and development of all parts of the organisations and for all members the most important cultural feature. Peter Senge defines the concept as:

> "Organisations where people continually expand their capacity to create the results they truly desire, where new and expansive patterns of thinking are nurtured, where collective aspiration is set free, and where people are continually learning how to learn together." (Senge, 1990:3)

Pedler, Burgoyne and Boydell's definition of the learning organisation emphasises that organisational development and learning include all parts of the organisation:

> "A learning company is an organisation that facilitates learning of all its members and continuously transforms itself." (Pedler et al., 1991:1)

Common to the theories of the learning organisation is: 1) the organisation as a whole and the individual is flexible and ready to question existing norms and routines; 2) the individual's engagement in and commitment to the goals of the organisation. This is conceptualised as creating a shared vision (Senge, 1990; Senge et al., 1999). According to the theories, however, the individual's accept of the shared visions is conditioned by his or her decisive autonomy in organising, planning, and developing own work, access to all relevant information, and opportunity for developing professionally and personally through the job.

That learning is imperative for the organisational development is evident from Peter Senge's model, which includes five *disciplines* forming the whole that he terms "the learning organisation" (Senge, 1990):

S*ystems thinking* is the "fifth discipline" and the most important one, and it is also the title of the book in which Senge presents the model. Organisations consist of a number of partly independent systems. In effect the task is to make sub-systems work optimally toward meeting the goals and visions of the organisation. Of the five disciplines systems thinking is the one that glues together the organisation, which makes it the cornerstone of the theory. At the same time systems thinking settles with the idea that expertise and specialisation necessarily leads to segmentation. But the answer is indeed not that all members must have all information or all is capable of performing all processes in the organisation. It is taken for granted that organisational members possess different knowledge and expertise according to which functions they have been hired to perform. The entire sum of organisational demands, and demands on the individual, is much too specific, and the development and the challenges much too complex for the individual to grasp. It is not the ideal of systems thinking that all members know everything, but that individuals of different knowledge and functions are capable of working in close interaction.

Personal mastery is the individual's proficiency in and will to master his or her field of work and responsibility, and ability and will to communicate and initiate learning processes based on his or her field of responsibility. It implies the ability to distinguish between information that is relevant for other parts of the organisation and which is not. Senge stresses that personal mastery must include commitment to and ambitions for one's own job, but at the same time he maintains that the employee has the legitimate right to criticise and to demand that work offers professional and personal challenges and development. Personal mastery is not only about meeting the demands, but also about the right to back out and set limits.

Mental models are the ability of individuals and the organisation as a whole to adapt to new thoughts, norms, and attitudes. The individual will typically have certain ideas about what is possible, and especially what is not possible, just as embedded in the organisational culture are norms and ideas about "the right way of doing things". Mental models break with thinking in grooves, such as "we have tried that", "are you sure", or "why that?". The organisation's ability to currently adapting and developing will lead to the necessity to reject previous assumptions and create routines that fit into new ways of thinking and doing things.

Shared vision refers to the organisation being subject to common goals and interests. The shared vision is built through a shared image of the organisation, its mission, and where it is heading by coordinating the visions of individual members into a shared vision. It goes without saying that this process cannot be managed top-down nor is it predictable. The shared vision must emerge though the process of open dialogue. It is vital to the process that all parts of the organisation recognise that proposed solution might point in different directions as all members legitimately can contribute with viewpoints and proposals. Contrary to other versions of the learning organisation, Peter Senge does not attempt to communicate the idea of the conflict free organisation, although his proposition for how to built a community of interests in the shape of a shared vision is somewhat simplified and deficient.

Team learning is the model's concept of learning. Peter Senge views the work community as the primary space of learning. The best way of acquiring new skills is through the daily practice when one, together with colleagues, is facing "real" problems and constructing the solutions in the same process as they are being tested. The advantage of problem solutions originating from teams rather than from individuals is that they are based on dialogue and are thus dynamic. In consequence the solutions are challenging and go beyond individual mental barriers. But this requires openness, understanding, and tolerance of the current learning process, leaving room for contributions from all members of the team.

The decisive precondition in the theories of learning organisations is the ability and will among organisational members to learn. To fully understand the role of learning in the theories, one must be conscious of whether learning goes beyond the traditional sense of acquiring knowledge and qualifications. Learning should at least to the same extent reflect openness and understanding of change, and the will to actively contribute to processes that create change.

There are three key elements in learning that the various theories of the learning organisation share:

1. The ability to explore and work out solutions that transcend existing norms, assumptions and premises in organisations (Argyris & Schön, 1978; Senge, 1990 & 1999).
2. To see knowledge and qualification as a collective resource in the organisation, where the decisive precondition is the will of the individual to communicate, pass on and openly employ his or her knowledge in teams (Starkey, Tempest & McKinlay (ed.), 2004).
3. The space of learning is directly coupled to the field of practice. Without being formulated explicitly as theories of learning organisations, the concepts of situated learning (Lave & Wenger 1992; Wenger, 1998) and action learning (Revans, 1982) is illustrative of this practice.

Lave and Wenger's approach differs from that of Senge in that they point out that communities of work (teams) are subject to social norms and practices as opposed to Senge, who claims that teams act and organise on the basis of conscious and explicitly formulated goals and visions. Senge has often been criticised for this idealised approach. He neglects that not all organisational members concede to the goals of learning.

Approach and Methodological Considerations

Operationalising the concept of the learning organisation in the way we do in this chapter is certainly not unproblematic. Several arguments could be put forward against this endeavour being possible. There are not only one, but several ideas about what creates the learning organisation. Likewise theories of learning organisations are ideal models not to be imitated but rather inspire and direct development in organisations (Darwin et al, 2001). But even if we take as our point of departure the idea that it is possible in practice to build learning organisations, it is hard to imagine that organisations are fully capable at fulfilling the theoretical instructions (Argyris & Schön, 1996).

Bearing this in mind I shall nevertheless start from a population of companies that I characterise as "learning companies" with the proviso that we cannot equate the theoretical ideal types with the companies identified.

The operationalisation is based on a method where the elements of identification are explicitly and centrally formulated theoretical dimensions that in approximated form are capturable empirically via surveys.

The data are findings from the DISCO project (the Danish Innovation System: Comparative analysis of challenges, strengths, and bottlenecks). The Industry and Trade Development Council initiate the DISCO project. The objective is to establish an overall picture of the conditions for renewal and change processes in Danish companies. The project is located at Aalborg University, Denmark.

In 1996 the DISCO project conducted a questionnaire survey. The questionnaire was mailed to 3,993 companies of which 1,316 were within the manufacturing sector and had at least twenty employees, and 2,684 were service and construction/engineering companies of at least ten employees. The total numbers of responding companies were 1,900 of which 684 were manufacturing companies and 1,216 were service and construction/engineering companies (Lundvall, 2002).[35]

Identification of Learning Companies

Learning companies are identified on the basis of affirmative responses to a series of questions in the DISCO survey:

1. The companies have implemented organisational changes and technological innovations in the period 1993-1995.
2. More than fifty percent of the employees have been allocated greater responsibility.
3. More than fifty percent of the employees have participated in internal or external training activities.
4. The companies give high or medium priority to long-term training plans in order to secure that employees possess the desired competencies.

---

[35] The study is described in detail in Allan Næs Gjerding (ed.) (see references) "Den fleksible virksomhed" or see www.business.auc.dk/DISCO

Based on the four issues, learning companies are defined as organisations that continuously are subject to change (1), in which management delegates responsibility to all or a majority of employees (2), in which the competencies of all or a majority of employees are currently up-dated (3), and in which the purpose of competence and personal development is strategic (4).

Again, it should be born in mind that the method, leaves us with a series of problems and limitations.

First, the uncertainty involved in identifying complex models and relations, such as those embedded in the theories of learning organisations based on selected questions from a survey study.

Second, one could argue against the four dimensions used to identify learning organisations. Above we have argued for the choice of the four dimensions, but other dimensions might also prove relevant. The questionnaire survey also includes team learning, and it would have been obvious to include this dimension with a view to the theories. However, team learning does not serve the second purpose of this chapter: what characterises learning companies?

Finally, the four basic dimensions could be questioned. Especially dimension 3 and 4 can be interpreted as contrary to Senge's understanding of learning as a continuous process occasioned by individual and organisational needs. Nevertheless, I find the dimensions relevant because they in important ways indicate that management understands the importance of currently developing employee competencies.

The mentioned reservations and problems mean that it will only be possible to give an approximate picture of the scope of learning companies in the private business sector.

Based on the listed criteria, 138 of the 1,802[36] companies can be characterised as "learning" that is 7.7%. The number of companies is modest - less than 10% due to the fact that in order to be characterised as "learning" the companies must meet all four dimensions. However, a considerable number of companies meet one or more of the four dimensions:

---

[36] The total population was reduced to include only companies that had responded to all four indicative questions.

1. 43% of the companies have implemented both organisational and technological changes during 1993-1995.
2. 51% of the companies find long-term training plans very or fairly important.
3. 39.5% have delegated responsibility to more than 50% of the staff.
4. In 39.5% of the companies more than 50% of the employees have participated in internal or external courses or training activities.

Table 7.1 shows the distribution of identified learning companies classified according to number of employees.

Table 7.1: Distribution of learning companies according to number of employees

Number of employees	Learning companies
10-19	6.3
20-49	5.6
50-250	9.6
More than 250	11.6

Table 7.1 demonstrates that the number of learning companies increases with company size. The predominance of larger companies among learning companies is also reflected by the fact that 7.7% of the companies employed 18.4% of the labour force in 1994.

An exception to this pattern is that more companies of less than 20 employees are learning than companies of 20-49 employees. The reason is that a relatively large share of small service firms are learning, and it is within the service sector that we find the largest share of learning companies.

Table 7.2: Distribution of the total population of companies on sectors (%)

Number of employees	Learning companies
Manufacturing	7.4
Construction/Engineering	3.0
Service	9.2

N= 1,802

The limited distribution of learning companies does not reflect that Danish business life in general is stagnant. Findings from the DISCO study show that in the period 1993-1995, 43% of the companies have implemented both organisational and technological changes. Only one of four companies in the study can be characterised as stagnant as they have neither implemented organisational changes nor introduced new technology.

One possible explanation of the large number of companies that have implemented organisational and technological changes is the scope of changes. However, when the companies have responded in the affirmative to having implemented organisational and technological changes, the scope of these changes might be limited. In order to elucidate the scope of the changes, we shall apply a different approach to determine to what extent the companies are using new management technologies drawing on the findings from the DISCO study. For the identification of companies dealing with the challenge of change Gjerding and Lund have developed an index of "Frequency of flexibility" (Gjerding & Lund 1996). The flexibility index is based on a series of questions in the DISCO survey – 14 questions of which ten function as indicators of organisational flexibility and 4 as indicators of market and product technological flexibility. Based on this model 25% of the companies are characterised as "dynamic" due to high flexibility in the organisation, the market and product technology. The figure covers companies that have responded positively to six of the ten questions that are indicators of organisational flexibility and two or more of the questions that reflect market and product technological flexibility. According to this index, primarily the large companies and companies within manufacturing and service are dynamic.

A majority of the companies, who state having implemented organisational and technological changes, have implemented fairly radical changes and not only minor adjustments. Other things being equal this sets the relatively modest number of "learning" companies off. The "dynamic" and the "learning" companies have not been merged. But based on the definitions of the two types of companies, most "learning" companies' are also "dynamic". In consequence more than two-thirds of the "dynamic" companies cannot be characterised as learning in view of the criteria used here.

In effect characterising the Danish economy as a knowledge economy becomes somewhat dubious. These results show that in the majority of the companies only a part of the employees participate in the knowledge-creating functions.

Within the manufacturing sector we find a large number of learning companies (14.3%) within chemical-, oil-, and plastics industry, whereas the food industry and the iron & metal industries each count for about 7%. Within the service sector we find more than 10% of the learning organisations in "business services", and "retailing and repairs". The latter category is interesting in that it is one of the areas characterised by little innovation and only a few companies introduce organisational and technological changes. Nevertheless one of three companies can be characterised as learning based on the stipulated criteria. On the other hand, other service industries have a very small share of learning companies. In the trade sector and the leisure sector less than 5% of the companies are learning.

Characterisation of learning companies

The second purpose of this chapter is to characterise learning companies. The characterisation is based on:

1. The educational background of employees.
2. Areas within which the job contents has changed for the employees and the factors determining this change.
3. How the companies ensure that the human resources match the needs, including to what extent employees undergo further training.
4. Principles for organising work, including factors that have pushed and pulled organisational development.
5. The employees' attitude toward work.

Drawing on findings from the DISCO survey elucidates the five dimensions. In discussing what characterises learning companies comparisons will be made with 1) other companies that have implemented organisational and technological changes[37], and 2) the static parts of business life represented by companies that have implemented neither organisational nor technological changes.

The educational background of employees

Some people think that organisations employing relatively highly educated persons are most inclined to develop toward becoming learning. This perception is not supported by the criteria for being a learning organisation as defined in our study, quite the contrary:

---

[37] Companies, meeting the first of the four criteria, characterising learning companies, but not one or more of the subsequent ones.

Table 7.3: Composition of employees based on basic education

	Firms that did not carry out changes	Firms that carried out organisational and technological changes	Learning companies
Employees with graduate or postgraduate degrees	1.6	3.2	4.0
Employees with further education	6.3	12.2	14.1
Vocational training	45.5	44.2	42.0
Unskilled	45.6	40.4	39.9

Source: DISCO survey

Even though the share of employees with graduate or postgraduate degrees is higher in learning companies, it is only marginally compared with companies that have implemented organisational and technological changes. Furthermore, the average share of employees from the two top categories in the table makes up less than 20% in learning companies. Learning companies have the lowest share of unskilled employees and companies that have not implemented changes have the highest share. Rather surprisingly, learning companies and companies that have implemented changes prove to be employing the same share of unskilled labour – 40%, which is only 5% less than companies not having implemented changes.

Thus graduated people do not dominate learning companies. Companies that opt for a human resource strategy based on the delegation of responsibility and continuous training activities for a majority of the staff are dominated by skilled and unskilled labour to the same extent as the business life in general.

There is, however, one important element of which the figures tell nothing – development over time. In order to elucidate this element the figures in Table 7.3 from 1994 are compared with the composition of employees in the same companies in 1990.

It should be born in mind that learning companies have the highest growth in employment. From 1990 to 1994 employment in learning companies has grown by 2.9% compared with 1.8% in other types of companies. The reasons might be that 1) increased focus on human resources has resulted in a market position that has facilitated stronger growth or, 2) the companies have used training activities and delegation of responsibility to master increased growth. It is not possible from the data to say which of the two explanations has caused highest employment growth in learning companies.

For several years an increasing share of skilled labour has characterised the Danish labour market at the expense of unskilled labour (Udenrigsministeriet, 1998[38]). This trend is also reflected in the DISCO study regardless of whether or not the companies are learning. But underlying the general trend is a series of surprising differences in development between learning companies and other companies.

During the period 1990-1994 the share of graduated employees has grown by 17% in learning companies, while the figure is 23% in the other companies. However, the fact that the figures are based on a relatively modest population makes them somewhat uncertain. In total the 1,800 companies studied employed only 4,600 persons of higher education in 1994.

But the same tendency characterised employees with baccalaureate degrees that represent an important share of the private labour market. This group has grown by 11% in learning companies from 1990 to 1994 and with 14% in the other companies.

Quite the opposite characterises skilled labour. Here, the growth is highest in learning companies – 8% compared to 5% in other companies, while the share of unskilled has dropped by 5% in both categories.

Though the share of graduated employees is highest in learning companies, the growth is higher in the other companies. The opposite is the case with skilled workers. Learning companies have the highest growth in share of skilled workers, while other companies have the largest share.

---

[38] The Danish Ministry of Education

Changes in work contents and causes of these changes

Increasing demands on the companies in terms of stronger competition, introduction of new technology, current product development and collaborative capabilities are factors that have led to changes in work contents for the employees (see Table 7.4).

Table 7.4: Conditions that have strongly or to some degree led to changes in work contents for the employees

	Firms that did not carry out changes	Firms that carried out organisational and technological changes	Learning companies
a. Increased competition	46.6	83.0	84.1
b. Better possibilities for developing product and services	26.7	61.9	63.8
c. Introduction of new technology	31.5	81.6	85.5
d. Need for greater flexibility among employees	44.3	84.4	89.9
e. Need for better contact with customers	36.4	71.2	73.9
f. Need for better contact with sub-contractors	18.1	48.4	44.2
g. Better possibilities for stimulating the development of employee competencies	29.9	70.9	78.3
h. Employee demands and desires	27.4	64.3	68.1

Source: DISCO survey

The difference is conspicuous between static companies and the two categories that have implemented organisational and technological changes. On the other hand, the differences between learning companies and other companies that have implemented changes are marginal. Nothing seems to indicate that learning companies in particular are exposed to new and intensified demands.

Differences are most conspicuous between "better possibilities for stimulating the development of employee competencies" and "need for greater flexibility among employees". As to the former, differences can be explained as natural consequences of the way in which learning companies are identified. But combined with the demand for greater employee flexibility in several of the learning companies, one hypothesis could be that the reason for the difference between learning companies and other companies having implemented organisational and technological changes is the role ascribed to employees in order to master external and internal pressure on the organisation.

This hypothesis is supported by the differences in share of companies that have increased demands on employees:

Table 7.5: Share of companies that state work contents to have increased - thematically categorised

	Firms that did not carry out changes	Firms that carried out organisational and technological changes	Learning companies
a. Autonomy in work	27.8	74.4	79.7
b. Emphasis on professional qualifications	27.2	59.0	58.0
c. Specialisation	20.6	35.8	34.8
d. Routine work	7.9	4.4	5.1
e. Contact with customers	23.5	53.5	56.5
f. Contact with subcontractors	12.9	36.9	38.4
g. Contact with other companies	11.3	24.5	28.3
h. Collaboration with colleagues	19.5	60.2	63.8
i. Collaboration with management	19.9	67.5	65.2

Source: DISCO survey

Learning companies are more likely to demand autonomy in work from employees and the ability to collaborate internally with colleagues and externally with customers, sub-contractors and other companies in general. To the question "contact with sub-contractors", for instance, a smaller share of learning companies state this issue to have become more important compared to other companies that have implemented changes. But simultaneously a larger share of the learning companies state collaboration with sub-contractors to have resulted in intensified demands on employees.

How companies make sure that human resources tally with the needs

In order to make sure that the labour force possesses the desired competencies, companies can 1) recruit and dismiss employees, including adapt the labour force temporally to the task (numerical flexibility), 2) initiate training activities for current employees (functional flexibility), and 3) variation in salary scale (Financial flexibility) (Atkinsson 1984).

Table 7.6: Tools that companies find highly or fairly important for ensuring that the human resources tally with their needs

	Firms that did not carry out changes	Firms that carried out organisational and technological changes	Learning companies
a. Recruitment	77.8	94.0	93.5
b. Dismissal	38.7	53.3	50.7
c. Reshuffle	34.2	61.8	65.9
d. Regulation of working hours	37.3	79.7	51.4
e. Further training	37.8	70.8	92.8
f. Collaborating with or outsourcing work to other companies/or individuals	20.1	38.1	47.8
g. Other measures	3.6	10.1	13.8

Source: DISCO survey

The most conspicuous difference is in the use of functional flexibility. It is hardly surprising that almost all learning companies assesses functional flexibility as important and that 93% of these companies find further training to be highly or fairly important. The figure merely confirms that learning companies find competence development and long-term training plans significant tools for developing the organisation. Against this approximately 70% of the other companies those have implemented changes state further training to be highly or fairly important. Even though the figure might seem high, three of ten companies that have experienced organisational and technological changes find further training to be of little or almost no importance. Consequently, functional flexibility cannot automatically be equated with innovative behaviour.

Another element telling of functional flexibility is the share of employees that have participated in internal or external training activities. The definition of learning companies entails that more than 50% of the employees have participated in training activities over a three-year period. The corresponding figures for other companies that have implemented changes are 43% and for static companies only approximately 20%. The latter figures do not reflect that companies neglect training activities. Of other companies that have implemented changes, 95% state that employees have participated in training activities, and in the static companies this goes for three of four employees. But these companies choose only to offer further training to certain employees (Voxted 1998).

In terms of numerical flexibility the opposite seems to be the case. The difference between learning companies and other companies that have implemented organisational and technological changes is marginal, cf. Table 7.6. It is, however, noticeable that companies having implemented changes prefer dismissals at the same time as they ascribe significant import to recruitment. This seems to indicate that companies oriented toward development are more prone to replace the labour force in order to secure that employees possess the desired competencies. This also applies to learning companies.

There are also significant differences between learning companies and other companies concerning the use of reduced and extended working hours. 50% of the learning companies find regulation of working hours highly or fairly important, while this tool is much more important for other companies that have implemented organisational and technological changes.

On the other hand, learning companies are much more prone to out-source tasks and collaborate with other companies and individuals. Combined with other facts, this suggests that learning companies differ from the remaining population of companies in their use of networks for solving tasks and as sources of change and development.

In relation to financial flexibility, learning companies and firms who carry out organisational and technological changes are at the same level using "quality- and result wages (not piecework wages)" (note Table 7.8).

That learning companies prioritise functional flexibility is also reflected in the fact that they find the development of employee competencies important or fairly important:

Table 7.7: Elements that management ascribes great or somewhat important to secure the development of employee competencies

	Firms that did not carry out changes	Firms that carried out organisational and technological changes	Learning companies
a. Solving tasks	84.2	91.7	94.2
b. Scheduling time to sparring with management/other employees	58.4	82.9	89.1
c. Planned job rotation	18.8	37.3	42.8
d. Organised team work	38.9	69.0	80.4
e. Encouraging collaboration across departments and groups	35.1	71.7	83.3
f. Standard courses and training plans (e.g. vocational schools)	38.9	47.5	47.1
g. Training activities tailored to company needs	40.8	63.8	79.0
h. Long-term training plans	31.5	54.6	100.0[39]
i. Other measures	4.9	10.1	12.3

Source: DISCO survey

Team learning and collaborative abilities are key features of the theories of learning organisations. Team learning, for example, is one of Peter Senge's five disciplines. Table 7.7 shows that findings from the DISCO study strongly reflect this theoretical approach. Two of the issues concern team learning: "organised team work" and "encouraging collaboration across departments and groups". And on both issues learning companies differ significantly from other companies.

---

[39] This is included in the definition of "learning companies".

Learning companies also differ strongly from other companies in their use of tailored training activities. Only on one issue in Table 7.7 do learning companies not differ significantly from other companies, i.e. in their use of standard courses and training plans (e.g. vocational schools).

The other issue that distinguishes learning companies from the other companies is "long-term training plans". This difference is to a great extent caused by our definition of learning companies. On the other hand, the study shows surprisingly that only about half of the Danish companies having implemented organisational and technological change find long-term training plans to have great or some importance as a tool for making sure that employee competencies match company needs. The figure is almost frightening low.

Application of Changes in the Organising of Work

In the DISCO survey we also asked about the use of a series of methods for organising work and the share of employees included in various initiatives. We also asked about which initiatives that promote or restrict organisational development.

Looking at the use of the methods we asked about, learning companies do not differ significantly from other companies that have implemented changes, but the former differ significantly from companies that have not implemented changes. But the pattern is different when comparing the share of companies in which such initiatives include a majority of the employees:

Table 7.8: Share of companies that use the listed ways of organising work. Figures in parenthesis are companies in which more than 50% of the employees are included.

	Firms that did not carry out changes	Firms that carried out organisational and technological changes	Learning companies
a. Interdisciplinary teams	280.8 (5.0)	71.2 (10.4)	76.1 (20.3)
b. Quality circles/groups	15.2 (4.8)	53.6 (15.7)	56.5 (22.5)
c. Systems for gathering employee proposals (not quality circles)	25.8 (12.4)	67.9 (25.6)	58.0 (28.3)
d. Planned job rotation	20.8 (7.2)	59.0 (6.4)	52.2 (7.2)
e. Delegation of responsibility	69.5 (28.1)	92.0 (33.3)	100.0 (100.0)[40]
f. Integration of functions	32.6 (7.5)	69.3 (13.2)	78.3 (32.6)
g. Quality- and result wages (not piecework wages)	22.4 (8.6)	52.0 (21.1)	57.2 (18.1)

Source: DISCO survey

The figures clearly demonstrate that learning companies are more prone to organise interdisciplinary teams, quality circles, and integration of functions comprising more than 50% of the staff.

The same applies to delegation of responsibility. Here the figures of companies that have implemented changes and companies that have not implemented are differing significantly. Only one of three companies that are *not* defined as learning has delegated responsibility to a majority of the employees.

In terms of delegation of responsibility a relatively larger share of companies in the service sector, and in construction and engineering, have delegated responsibility to a majority of employees where as the figure is lower in the manufacturing sector. The reason for the latter is probably that traditionally trade

---

[40] The definition of learning companies includes delegation of responsibility to more than 50% of the employees.

manufacturers have delegated responsibility to the individual worker. The industry has increasing been subject to a development implying that co-ordination of work and performance is organised in separate job functions.

In view of what promote or restrict organisational changes, learning companies differ conspicuously from other companies on the last two issues in Table 7.9: "Access to knowledge about initiatives in other companies" and "collaboration with educational institutions".

Table 7.9: Conditions that add to push or pull organisational development

	Firms that carried out organisational and technological changes		Learning companies	
	Promote	Restrict	Promoter	Restrict
a. Attitude toward foremen and middle managers	57.5	23.7	60.0	23.2
b. Qualifications of foremen and middle managers	46.9	28.3	47.1	31.2
c. Attitude among employees of no managerial responsibility	51.3	23.0	63.8	20.3
d. Qualifications among employees of no managerial responsibility	44.3	18.1	53.6	20.3
e. Works committees	34.4	3.0	31.9	2.9
f. Shop stewards	32.5	+-5	29.0	5.1
g. Qualifications of consultants	30.3	2.5	39.1	2.2
h. Public subsidy schemes	13.8	1.4	13.0	2.2
i. Access to knowledge about initiatives in other companies	378.1	3.0	56.5	0
j. Collaboration with educational institutions	31.8	1.1	45.7	2.2

Source: DISCO survey

The differences within the two latter issues demonstrate that learning companies are drawing on networks, and they also, to a higher degree than the other companies, assess the qualifications of external consultants to have pushed organisational development.

The first four issues concerning the attitudes and qualifications of foremen and middle managers and of employees of no responsibility are also interesting. In the category foremen and middle managers variations are insignificant. But compared to the other companies, learning companies find attitudes and qualifications among employees without managerial responsibility to have been important for pushing organisational development.

Employee Attitudes Toward Work

One of the key issues of the theories of learning organisations is employee attitudes toward work and the organisation as a whole. The theories claim the shared vision to be the decisive condition for establishing learning organisations.

Elucidating this issue by drawing on findings from the DISCO survey is problematic in that it only covers management statements. Assessing attitudes toward work should, ideally, include employee statements, and at least an analysis of the interaction between management and employees. The lack of a "shared vision" may be caused by different perceptions among employees and management of the appropriateness of change processes and resulting effects. Therefore Table 7.10 must be understood as exclusively reflecting management assessments.

Table 7.10: The importance that employees, according to management, ascribe to a number of condition in learning companies (figures outside parenthesis) and in other companies that have implemented organisational and technological changes (figures in parenthesis)

	High	Some	Low	None	Irrelevant/ Don't know
a. More knowledge about management strategies and visions	49.3 (32.9)	39.1 (43.3)	8.0 (12.4)	0.7 (5.8)	2.9 (5.7)
b. More challenging work	51.5 (30.9)	42.8 (47.1)	2.9 (11.4)	0.7 (4.4)	2.2 (6.3)
c. Better wages	21.0 (31.4)	60.1 (49.0)	16.7 (12.3)	1.5 (2.3)	0.7 (5.1)
d. More flexible working hours	18.8 (14.0)	45.7 (35.3)	21.0 (28.4)	10.1 (13.9)	4.3 (8.3)
e. Greater influence on work plans	37.7 (21.1)	47.1 (46.2)	8.7 (19.5)	2.9 (7.4)	3.6 (5.8)
f. More time for training activities	12.3 (9.9)	58.7 (40.1)	21.0 (28.8)	4.4 (12.7)	3.6 (8.5)
g. Possibility of working at home	3.6 (2.0)	15.2 (8.1)	31.2 (17.7)	22.5 (26.8)	27.5 (45.4)

Source: DISCO survey

Learning companies are giving higher priority to meeting employee desires for "more knowledge about strategy and visions", "more challenging tasks", and "greater influence on work plans". This points toward learning companies being better at meeting the theoretical specifications of "personal mastery" and "shared visions", even though the statements only rest on management evaluations, and learning companies have to a higher degree been able to motivate and engage employees.

Conclusion

The first conclusion is that relatively few companies, 7.7% can be characterised as learning based on the defined criteria. This fact decisively questions the discourse according to which Danish business life is currently developing toward introducing new Management technologies (or production concepts) in which challenges correspond to personnel strategies implying that the qualifications of the majority of the labour force are up-graded currently and the majority of the labour forces is being allocated responsibility for own work. This has been the message for a number of years represented by concepts such as "the Learning Organisation", "the Developmental Work", "Human Resource Management", "Total Quality Management", etc.

Most of the results from applying these methods derive from case studies. The method is quite applicable for describing how organisations can implement management technologies, but it does not tell us anything about the diffusion of the concepts.

Findings from our study show that novel management technologies, which include a majority of employees have not spread notably. The dominant feature is that new and tighter demands and challenges are resolved through personnel strategies that currently up-grade the qualifications of key employees and secure qualified labour through numerical flexibility.

However, the following conclusions are subject to some uncertainty in that conditions other than the criteria defining learning companies may be decisive for the differences presented in the chapter. The Disco study, for instance, shows that industry affiliation and company size are decisive factors for using continuous training and for innovative behaviour. The share of companies implementing changes and continuous training of employees, increases with company size just as companies within manufacturing and service are predominant. However, learning companies are more in line with the total population of the DISCO study distribution on the basis of company size and major sectors.

Time is another decisive factor, which the study only touches on to a limited degree. The figures applied are from the mid-1990s. However, the concept of "the learning organisation" did not begin to gain ground until during the 1990s and the number of learning companies must be considerably higher today.

To my knowledge, no studies have elucidated the development after 1996. However, figures from the Institut for Konjunktur-Analyse (IFKA) (Institute for Business Cycle Analysis) clearly disconfirm the assumption of explosive growth. The figures show that over a three-year period 60% of the labour force have participated in further training (IFKA 1999), approx. 50% of the companies have implemented long-term training plans, and approx. 60% of the companies indicate to have implemented comprehensive restructuring of work processes (IFKA 1998). These findings are somewhat higher than those of the DISCO study, but the differences are so modest that it is impossible to render probable any significant growth in the number of learning organisations.

The limited diffusion of companies applying personnel strategies in keeping with the new management technologies and which include all or a majority of employees seems not only to be a Danish phenomenon. A Swedish study also points to the fact that only a few companies have adopted what could be characterised as "flexible manpower use" (Karlsson 1999). Flexible manpower use is defined by the same criteria as those used in this chapter to identify "learning companies". An additional question is whether the new management and production concepts are always solutions to current challenges. An American study demonstrates that this is far from the case. Activities such as "Business Process Reengineering" and "Total Quality Management" have not yielded the desired outcomes in two of three companies, and in certain organisations implementation of the concepts even intensified problems (Maira & Scott-Morgan 1996).

Another, perhaps surprising, finding from the studies is that the composition of employees in learning companies in terms of education is not very different from that in other companies. In learning organisation the share of graduated employees is somewhat higher, but on average they only represent less than a fifth of the total labour force, and 40% of employees in learning companies have no qualifying education.

A third conclusion is that learning companies are no more subject to demands such as growing competition, technological innovation, and productivity than other companies, which have implemented changes. Nevertheless most of the learning companies state to have tightened demands on their employees even though the differences are relatively modest. A pattern is emerging showing that learning organisations differ most significantly from other companies in their demands for greater independence and ability to collaborate horisontally. Therefore a company developing into a "learning organisation" to meet internal and external demands and challenges seems to be conditioned by management strategic choices which place human resources and the ability to act independently in the centre.

The forth conclusion is that learning companies interact with their environments through network creation and other types of close collaboration. Examples of this from the study are:

- learning companies are more prone to outsource tasks (Table 7.6)
- experiences from other companies have promoted organisational development in the majority of learning companies (Table 7.9)
- a larger share of learning companies states collaboration with educational institutions to have furthered organisational development (Table 7.9)
- employees in learning companies are to a higher degree involved in collaboration with external relations (tables 7.4 and 7.6)
- a larger share of learning companies is intensifying demands for the employees' abilities to collaborate horisontally (Table 7.5).

Based on the data we can discern the outlines of a "6th discipline" in terms of learning organisations managing external relations through networks. The purpose of these networks is dual in that they are used in relation to daily operations and in connection with organisational change and renewal.

None of Peter Senge's five disciplines deal with the way in which learning organisations manage external relations, but networking might be considered an independent "6th discipline". However, networking and using the experiences of external relations as inspirations for change is a natural extension of the way in which Peter Senge characterises learning organisations. Peter Senge actually discusses this potential sixth discipline taking as his point of departure a corporation that established close collaborative relations with external partners in connection with a series of complex development tasks (Senge 1990:363).

The fifth conclusion is that what makes an organisation learning and the actual behaviour of the companies identified in this chapter as learning seems identical. This first and foremost refers to Peter Senge's five disciplines.

Even though it is not immediately apparent from the data to what extent learning companies are applying systems thinking, certain indicators point toward this being the case. For example learning companies are placing greater demands on employees for being able to collaborate horisontally. Furthermore, the forth conclusion points toward systems thinking in that learning companies are significantly more prone to networking.

Theory and practice is most obviously related in relation to learning form and method. The theories point toward the team as the central room of learning which is reflected in the survey responses. The survey explicitly asks about team learning (Table 7.6), and a significantly larger share of learning companies find this method to be highly or to some extent important. And the same table reflects that a predominant number of learning companies find it important to encourage collaboration between functions. Furthermore a much larger share of learning companies (1) applies team organising in terms of cross-disciplinary work groups and quality circles and (2) includes a majority of the staff.

However, the study gives reason to make reservations about team learning as the only form of learning. This is evident form the fact that 90% of the companies find further training highly or somewhat important. The reason may, of course, be that learning organisations are applying and ascribing import to the informal forms of learning, something that I briefly mentioned in the section on the methodology of the study. But this explanation does not seem valid in that there is a clear correlation between the companies' application and assessment of further training (internal and external courses) and application and assessment of learning forms that integrate production, such as team learning and sparring with management or colleagues. The study shows that learning organisations apply team learning as well as further training. And the interplay of the two form of learning seems logical. The functioning of the team will be based on, and delimited by, the members' existing knowledge and qualifications. Consequently, the team will need input in the shape of further training to support it and impart new knowledge.

As to "personal mastery" and "shared vision" the weakness of the data is, as mentioned earlier, that it exclusively contains management evaluations. Therefore, the figures pointing toward learning companies being better able to make employees engage in organisational objectives should be taken with a grain of salt. This in view of the larger share of learning companies stating that employees are interested in strategic objectives and employees that ask for greater influence and more challenging work.

Based on the study, it is difficult to say whether learning companies are better at settling with existing mental assumptions. Nevertheless there is one, though significant, aspect that points toward the management of learning organisations being better at readjusting mentally. A third of other companies have chosen to delegate responsibility for daily tasks to more than 50% of the staff. When delegating responsibility, it is always an open question which tasks employees can undertake autonomously. Companies and hierarchical levels may interpret the issue differently. A study based on data from the Central Bureau of Statistics shows that 70% of skilled and unskilled workers find that they are involved in the planning of their work (Bonka 1997). Though it is not possible to compare the two studies, this figure seems much higher than responses to the DISCO survey indicate. Nevertheless, the DISCO survey figures are interesting in relation to uncovering changes in mental assumptions because they represent managers' attitudes toward and perceptions of delegating responsibility. Therefore the significant difference between learning companies and other companies is important in this context. For some companies delegating responsibility to the majority of employees is equivalent to settling with the dogma of the right to manage and distribute work. And only a minority of companies has been able to ignore the dogma mentally.

Most of the companies that state to have delegated responsibility to a majority of employees have a staff of less than 50 people and a considerable share is static companies. This point towards the delegation of responsibility is being just as often the result of culture and traditions as of the strategic choice of management.

Finally, but still very interesting, the question is whether learning companies do better than other companies. It is difficult to say, among other things because the question is multifaceted. However, three conditions in the study point toward learning companies having experienced a more positive development: 1) the growth in employment has been higher in learning companies; 2) they are more prone to engage in external cooperation which is currently viewed as decisive for being able to sustain market position; and 3) viewed from the management perspective employees are more motivated and the conditions for cooperation are rated to be good.

Based on this, it is surprising that a larger share of companies do not opt for a personnel strategy that turns the company into a learning company.

First of all, because the companies know too little about the issue, which does not mean that they are unaware of the possibilities inherent in the concept of the learning organisation. But they lack knowledge about the possible effects of such methods and tools which is why many refrain from implementing personnel strategies based on involving and up-grading the qualifications of the entire staff. It is very difficult to measure the effects of organisational development and further training and hence to convince managers of the long-term utility of this type of activities. This applies in particular to SMEs.

This leads to the barrier against change and further training being relatively resource demanding activities. Not only in terms of money, but also in view of the new and stronger demands that the learning organisation places on management and employees. Much management is simply incapable of initiating and implementing the necessary activities, and especially in SMEs that traditionally are strongly focused on operations and little concerned with strategic planning, the lack of knowledge about and understanding of these processes constitutes a barrier.

Finally, both management and employees may have good reasons for not wanting to engage in the learning organisation. The resistance may be rooted in deficient abilities or lacking willingness to become involved in change and learning. Both personnel development that includes further training and changes in who are responsible for planning, organising, and control of work may encounter rather massive mental barriers at all levels. In this context middle managers constitute a decisive factor. Their knowledge of and place in the organisation are often decisive for the successful implementation of change and new knowledge among employees. The fact that this is the group that is most responsive to change only makes their participation even more decisive.

References

Atkinson, John (1984): *Flexibility, Uncertainty and Manpower Management.* Brighton, 1984.

Argyris, Chris & Schön, Donald (1978): *Organisational Learning: A theory of Action Perspective.* Addison-Wesley, 1978.

Argyris, Chris & Schön, Donald (1996): *Organisational Learning II.* Reading, Massachusetts, 1996.

Bonke, Jens (red.) (1997): *Levevilkår i Danmark.* København, 1997.

Darwin, John, Johnson, Phil & McAuley, John (2001); *Developing Strategies for Change*, Prentice Hall, Harlow

IFKA (Institut for Konjunktur Analyse) (1998): *Kompetenceløft i Danmark.* København, 1998.

IFKA (1999): *Det danske kursusmarked.* København, 1999.

Karlsson, Jan C. (1999): *Flexible Work Organisations – an Empirical Test of a Rhetoric.* I Holmer, Jan m.fl. (red): "Making Working Life Work", Karlstad, 1999.

Lave, Jean & Wenger, Etienne (1991): *Situated learning – Legitimate peripheral participation.* Cambridge, 1991.

Lund, Reinhard & Gjerding, Allan Næs (1996): *The flexible company - Innovation, work organisation and human ressource management.* DRUID-paper no. 96-17, Aalborg, 1996.

Lundvall, Bengt_Åke (2002); *Innovation, Growth and Social Cohesion –The Danish Model*, Edward Elgar, Cheltenham

Maira, Arun N. & Scott-Morgan, Peter B. (1995): *Learning to Change and Changing to Learn-managing for the 21st Century.* I Prism, Third Quarter, 1995, p. 5-13.

Pedler, Mike, Burgoyne, John & Boydell, Tom (1991): *The learning Company.* London, 1991.

Revans, Reginal (1982): *The Origins and Growth of Action Learning.* Lund, 1982.

Senge, Peter (1990): *The fifth Discipline.* Doubleday, 1990.

Senge, Peter et al. (1999); *The Dance of Change*, Nicholas Brealey Publishing, London

Starkey, Ken, Tempest, Sue & McKinlay, Alan (ed.) (2004); *How Organisations learn*, Thomson Learning, London

Undervisningsministeriet (1998): *National kompetenceudvikling – Erhvervsudvikling gennem kvalifikationsudvikling.* København, 1998.

Voxted, Søren (1998): Efteruddannelsessystemets rolle og muligheder i det danske innovationssystem. København, 1998.

Wenger, Etienne (1998); *Communities of Practice – Learning, Meaning and Identity*, Cambridge University Press, Cambridge

Chapter 8

The Institution HOME and the Concept of the Learning Organisation

By Allan Christensen

Introduction

This chapter is about the change process, which employees and managers at the Danish residential institution HOME initiated. It is about a collaboration project on desired changes leading to improvements in core services to the residents, better working conditions and improvements in the institution as a whole. It is also about the institution's search for and achievement of understanding the theoretical foundation of the concept of the learning organisation. Finally we shall look at the preparatory measures leading to the implementation of the change process.

Working under the concept of the learning organisation is very demanding for any organisation. An institution for physically and mentally disabled, is subject to greater demands and limitations, which requires great courage, reflection and commitment of the employees and the managers. Therefore the change project at the residential institution HOME is unique.

When companies and institutions decide to work and develop under the concept of the learning organisation they soon reach an understanding of the key elements of the concept and grasp the idea of the concept as a whole. The difficult exercise is to transform the concept into practice.

There are at least two things that seriously can affect attempts of transforming the concept into practice. The first concerns the interpretation of the concept, that is, whether the concept is interpreted as a template for the development of management decisions and processes, or whether it is interpreted as a template for learning and organisational development including the entire staff. If the concept is perceived and applied exclusively as a managerial tool, management ideas about and desires for one or several development processes risk becoming predominant and in effect the project will be one-sided and involve little dialogue. Pushed to the extremes this may imply that the existent potential among employees in terms of knowledge, learning, and development will have a hard time and may never materialise.

The other thing concerns management's patience with and belief in the employees. If the management and the employees perceive working with the concept of the learning organisation as involving a high degree of complexity, uncertainty, and unpredictability, a manager can, from the best of motives, attempt to structure and order the process by exerting tight control and firm management. In effect of being subject to the regime of a set of rules, the development project may assume an inappropriate form which in the worst case will lead to problems similar to those characterising bureaucratic organisations in connection with the implementation of changes.

These are the extremes and there is, of course, also a gray zone within which the two issues discussed are less pronounced. It is, however, evident that the preconditions for working under the concept of the learning organisation are less favourable if approaches related to the two issues mentioned push the organisation into the extremes. Characteristics of the management of the residential institution were delegation, responsibility, respect, and reciprocity.

Brief Description of the Residential Institution HOME

The county of South Jutland, Denmark owns the institution. It is the residence of twenty-five severely physically and mentally disabled people. Their deficiencies range from being multi-handicapped to functional disabilities, which require the support and help that municipal residential institution, cannot offer. Several of the residents are undergoing psychiatric treatment, and all residents are suffering to a greater extent than the general population from visual and hearing impairments and other more or less serious infirmities. On the other hand, they rarely suffer from common colds, flues, etc. Their age ranges from twenty-five to sixty-six.

The managers and employees are extremely conscious of the necessity of taking into account the specific needs of the individual resident and the fact that the needs change over time as the residents grow older.

The institution employs thirty-two people, which includes educationists, welfare workers, salaried trainees and the technical/administrative staff. The institution cooperates with three sheltered workshops located in Haderslev, Vojens, and

Christiansfeld. In addition the institution cooperates with the families, the county and the municipality. The institution has occupied the current premises since 1984. Over the years the buildings have been changed and renovated, and the institution is currently opening a new wing, which will house six residents.

New Objectives

For a year the institution had been contemplating which organisational change strategies that would be appropriate for a number daily task. The liaison committee had attended several talks for inspiration, such as on Senge's learning disciplines as described in his book "The Fifth Discipline", on project work and development, and on chaos theory and learning. Furthermore, the liaison committee had worked out a proposal for decentral collaboration projects on personnel policy which had received support.

The overall objective of the project is to create an institution (organisation) in which the learning organisation is the guiding principle. The sub-objective is to implement already known elements from the current formal and/informal organisation in a new one. The project includes the entire staff and the expectation is that the positive experiences will be transformed into the work practices and external relations of the institution.

The background for the project is that institutions, just as counties and municipalities have been subject to economic pressure in recent years in terms of demands for efficiency, service and quality as well as demands for greater user influence and openness. In order to meet these demands the liaison committee is of the opinion that the residential institution must be reorganised, and move toward the contents of the concept of the learning organisation. The tool for this is, among other things, the developing staff policy.

Expectations of the project and result criteria are stated as:

a) Improvements of the institution's core services to the residents:
- increase the life quality of the residents
- increase the residents' possibilities for acquiring the competence to communicate
- increase the residents' possibilities for forming social relationships
- increase the residents' possibilities for acquiring competence to make choices
- increase the residents' possibilities for assuming responsibility

b) Improvements for the staff:
- improve the basis for job satisfaction and working environment
- improve the opportunities for personal development and development of individual resources
- improve the opportunities for competence, influence, and responsibility
- improve the development and utilization of experiences and skills

c) Improvements for the institution:
- greater engagement among employees
- strengthen the exchange of experiences
- strengthen the shared values
- strengthen the foundation for recruiting and retaining employees
- strengthen the possibilities for improving the core services of the institution

In the project description, the institution also states its wish to cooperate with other institutions, which have experiences with similar projects, and it is open to share its experiences through communication and collaboration.

In connection with a thematic one-day workshop, the institution invited me to give a lecture on the concept of the learning organisation. However, this led to more thematic workshops on related and supporting issues. So far there have been three thematic workshops.

The thematic workshops were structured as a mixture of lectures and group work. The first thematic workshop introduced the participants to the concept of the learning organisation. Background, definitions, and concepts. How the concept is related to social development, including pressure from the environment. The concept as a framework for organisational development and learning processes. On subsequent thematic workshops the participants were introduced to organisation theory and processes, enabling structures in relation to organisational processes, decision making processes, organisational culture, and communication.

The primary purpose of the group work during the thematic workshops was to offer the opportunity of debating ideas. The issues under discussion would be further discussed on a series of meetings in the work groups after the thematic workshops.

In connection with the thematic workshops, the employees and the management demonstrated a rarely seen strong engagement and enthusiasm, which facilitated cooperation and generated expectations of durable and profound changes and improvements. This was also the case when some of the workshop themes were difficult to cope with and of limited entertainment value.

The Concept of the Learning Organisation as a Springboard for Change with Several Objectives

Implementing radical organisational changes is highly demanding of managers and employees – changes that are transformed into daily work practices and meet the objectives and expectations of change processes. Objectives and expectations might concern improving the life quality of the residents, strengthen the employee participation based on new premises, and improve the organisation through new management ideas and ways of adapting to the environment.

If we to this add the desire for organisational change that would make managers and employees prone to find new solutions to future problems, then it is easy to understand the tension and uncertainty prevailing among all members of the organisation.

Finally, the specific organisational change is subsumed certain inflexible conditions concerning the residents of the institution. Changes must under no circumstances create anxiety and uncertainty in the lives of the residents.

These were the conditions of the managers and employees in the residential institution HOME for preparing, building up and implementing organisational change in the form of decentral personnel policy projects of cooperation.

The concept of the learning organisation was launched in the early 1990s with two very different publications, i.e. Peter Senge's *The Fifth Discipline. The Art and Practice of The Learning Organisation* (1990) and Pedler, Burgoyne and Boydell's *The Learning Company. A Strategy for Sustainable Development* (1991). Prior to launching the concept, several authors had to varying degrees dealt with key issues of what later became the concept of the learning organisation. This applies to e.g. Argyris & Schön 1978 and prior to this publication Argyris 1963; 1976a and 1976b, etc.; Pedler 1983; Revans 1980 and 1982; Kolb 1991; Hedberg 1981; Sveiby and Riesling 1986; Sveiby 1990. In the Scandinavian countries several authors have contributed to the discourse on the learning organisation, such as Riis and Fick 1991; Riis and Neergaard 1994 and 1995; Neergaard 1994; van Hauen, Strandgaard and Kastberg 1995; Neergaard, van Hauen and Kastberg 1997; Rohlin, Skärvad and Nilsson 1994; Hildebrandt 1997; Brandi and Hildebrandt 1997; Morsing 1995; Christensen et al. 1997. Finally Cook, Staniforth and Stewart (1997) should be mentioned because to my knowledge this publication is the only one on the learning organisation that exclusively focuses on the public sector.

The many publications on the issue have attracted the attention of both theorists and practitioners. Several of the publications more than hint at the concept of the learning organisation being *the* approach, if the organisation wants to be in a position to manage contemporary and future problems. It would facilitate working both theoretically and practically with the concept if the publications were based on balanced loyalty toward and criticism of the concept, and then posed the questions of

1. what is a learning organisation?
2. what is management in a learning organisation?
3. to what extent is an organisation learning?

We shall return to these questions in the following, though we are unable to offer exhaustive answers. We shall have to confine ourselves to touch upon them and take a stand.

The following is a presentation of the concepts of the learning organisations that were discussed and processed during the thematic workshops at the residential institution HOME.

Learning, Development and "The Learning Company"

One of the early publications related to the launching of the concept of the learning organisation was Pedler, Burgoyne and Boydell "The Learning Company. A Strategy for Sustainable Development" (1991). The authors define the learning organisation as

> "A Learning Company is an organisation that facilitates learning for all its members and continuously transforms itself." (Pedler, Burgoyne & Boydell 1991:1)

The definition emphasises learning and development. It is difficult to determine the focus. Is it individual learning and development or organisational learning and development? Or is it both? The definition implies a both-and. At the same time, the authors suggest how the dynamic relationship between the two levels can be perceived. We shall return to the dynamics.

The authors operate with several models or conceptual juxtapositions depending on which aspects of the organisation they are focusing on. However, all conceptual juxtapositions contain the same eleven elements or dimensions that the authors find characteristic of the development toward the learning organisation. The basic form is the so-called *blueprint*, which will be discussed in the following. The eleven dimensions of the development process of the learning organisation are exhibited as a jigsaw, which constitute "the learning company profile". The jigsaws are combined in various ways forming "the fishbone", "the fir tree" and "the fountain tree". These forms are expressions of particular approaches to organisational learning and development. Figure 8.1 illustrates the basic form – the blueprint.

The authors are not giving a satisfactory account of the relation between the elements or dimensions of the model. This also applies to the *blueprint*. It is not clear whether working under the concept of the learning organisation involves all dimensions or whether it is possible to select those of particular relevance for the organisation's learning, development, and problem solving. It becomes apparent that the authors are most inclined to support the latter. Nor is it clear how the dimensions "Learning Approach to Strategy" (1) and "Participative Policy Making" (2) are related and are relatable to the dimensions "Learning Climate" (10) and "Self-development Opportunities for All" (11). Nor is there any account of the relation between the dimensions "Enabling Structures" (7) and "Self-development Opportunities for All" (11). The closest to an answer to these questions is the authors proposal for the self-development process in the sections "Becoming a Learning Company" and "101 Glimpses of the Learning Company". Thus we must conclude that only by drawing on the mentioned sections can we arrive at a more specific definition of blueprint or by the organisation itself introducing this definition.

Exactly because the contents and the interrelationships of dimensions and the dynamic aspects of the conceptual juxtaposition are relatively unclear, it is left to the reader or the user to select or de-select dimensions and to state their contents. It is thus left to the management and employees in the residential institution to shape the model according to the current needs for learning and development, that is, the job areas in which the need for learning and development is greatest. Likewise it is left to the reader or the user to indicate when the process starts and ends, including the connection between the chosen dimensions.

In the conceptual juxtaposition the concept of structure is only mentioned in connection with the dimension enabling or facilitating structures and only with a view to enabling and developing the central processes in the organisation. It is the course of these processes that individually or combined can contribute to development under the concept of the learning organisation.

While structure involves norms, rules, routines, superior/subordinate relations, information and decision routes, then the processes involve various forms of behaviour that employees and management exhibit in their goal-oriented attempts of supplying the best possible services to the residents, intensifying the core services, strengthening the institution as a workplace and its foundation for future preparedness for development.

There is a particular problem related to the mentioned processes and various forms of behaviour unfolding during the process. How is individual behaviour coupled to integrated or collective behaviour? How are visions/ideas and actions tied together? In their model of the energy-flow of the organisation (Figure 8.2) the authors suggest the practical coupling of individual and collective behaviour and of visions and actions. The model can be interpreted as follows: Among the employees and managers in the residential institution HOME are internal entrepreneurs or "fiery souls". These entrepreneurs often reflect upon how the situation could be and how the institution could develop toward this end. Undoubtedly all employees and managers occasionally think of different conditions and the development toward these. It is adopting a critical stand and entering into dialogue that leads from the individual to the collective level and from thinking to acting.

Figure 8.1: Characteristics of the learning organisation (Blueprint)

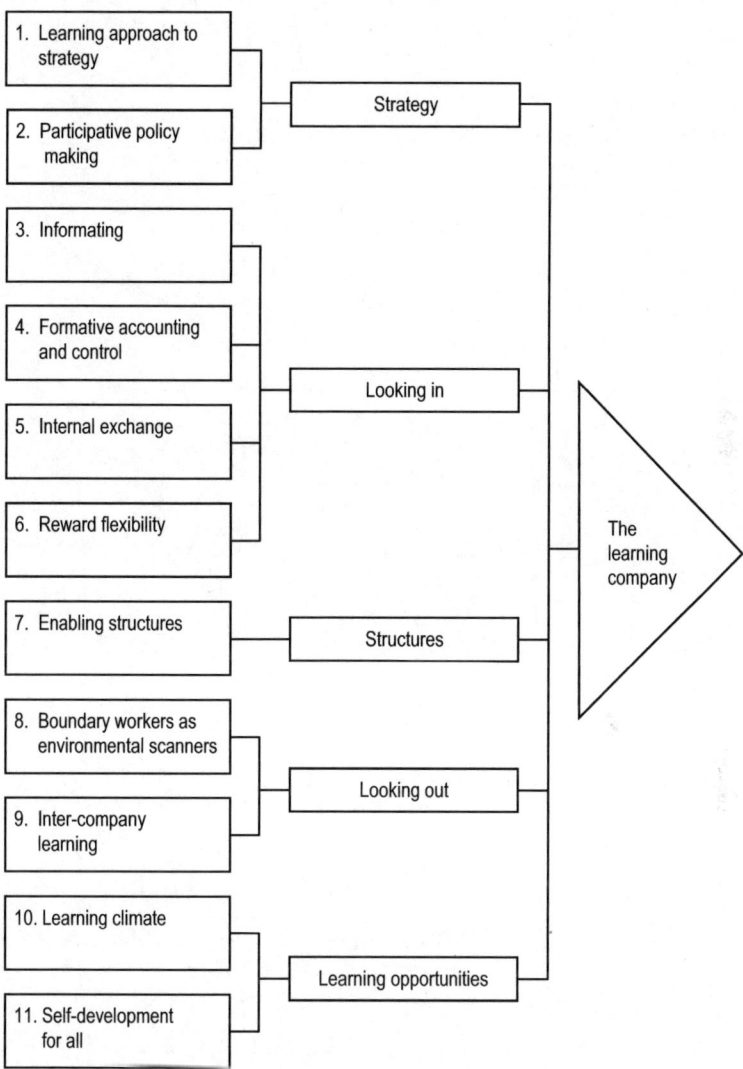

Source: Pedler, Burgoyne & Boydell 1991:25

Ideas about different conditions remain ideas until they are attempted transformed into action. It becomes easier for both employees and managers to relate to the vision/idea, if it is transformed into action. This is the start of transversal work and the beginning of making the idea collective and shaping it as a policy. When this development has started, the idea can further other persons' ideas about similar or different issues. The further process could be that the idea in a collective form (as policy) is communicated across institutions and gradually becomes part of the institution's service catalogue or new core services to the residents.

Figure 8.2: Model of the energy-flow of the learning organisation

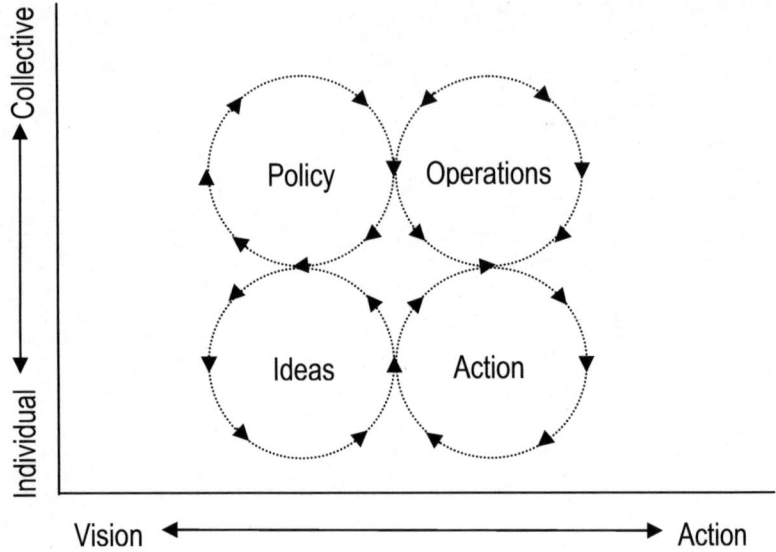

Source: Pedler, Burgoyne & Boydell 1991:32

Changes, Contexts and the Five Disciplines of Learning

In *The Five Disciplines of Learning* Peter Senge defines the learning organisation as:

> "organisations where people continually expand their capacity to create the results they truly desire, where new and expansive patterns of thinking are nurtured, where collective aspiration is set free, and where people are continually learning how to learn together." (Senge 1990:3)

The definition is not particularly clear and precise which is why there is good reason to include Senge's model and consider the appropriateness of the definition.

The model includes five elements or dimensions: *Personal Mastery, Mental Models, Shared Vision, Team Learning, and Systems Thinking.*

"Personal Mastery" is Senge's name for the discipline that concerns personal development and learning. Individual learning is the precondition for organisational learning. If individual learning is to lead to organisational learning, it is necessary to shift orientation from being reactive to being proactive and creative.

"Mental Models" is, in Senge's view, the most important discipline because it functions as a template for human and organisational action. Mental models are important parts of the foundation for interpreting existing situations and for managing behaviour in connection with this interpretation.

"Shared Visions" is the foundation for moving from "they-interpretations" to "we-interpretations". A shared vision is thus important when considering what to be learned and changed and through which process. A shared vision is based on the personal visions. The shared vision implies developing a higher degree of tolerance of new approaches, experiments, and of committing errors under new and complex conditions.

"Team Learning" takes as its point of departure personal visions and a shared vision. Team learning facilitates the common orientation that ensures common interpretations and goals. The orientation is the link between independent behaviour of the team members and behaviour that strives toward achieving the goals of the team and of the organisation. Through the dialogue and discussions of team learning, one's own assumptions and those of others are subject to debate. This might lead to a movement from the original mental models to new mental models and elements for the latter.

"Systems Thinking" is the discipline that enables efforts of seeing wholes in stead of parts. It is also the framework for reaching an understanding of contexts rather than of individual events and for seeing patterns of change rather than static snapshots. Two things are important in connection with systems thinking – feedback and systems archetypes. Reinforced feedback can be perceived as several processed being integrated or working together for the same end.

Reinforced feedback can be both positive and negative. The precondition for employees and managers being able to get an overview of the dynamics of the organisations is the creation of an overview of the nature of feedback processes, their way of functioning, connection and effect. The term "systems archetypes" refers to the building blocks that recur again and again. Therefore recognising the systems archetypes makes it possible to identify areas in the system where efforts would yield greater effect.

Both concepts have been presented and discussed on thematic workshops. However, Pedler, Burgoyne and Boydell's concept of the learning organisation soon proved to be the one preferred by the staff. This concept is clearly related to practice and the employees and managers were focusing on changes in the practices of the institution. The chosen concept is fairly void of – and at times unnecessarily – academic drill.

On making the Concept of the Learning Organisation Tangible and Applicable

The managers and employees at the residential institution have, as mentioned earlier, operated with several approaches to the design of the change process. One of the approaches has been the concept of the learning organisation as communicated through lectures and on thematic workshops. Below I shall briefly summarise the contents of the thematic workshops in relation to the concept of the learning organisation and to organisational models and concepts related to this concept.

The managers and the staff had already decided that the project – aside from understanding the concept of the learning organisation – must lead to practical results and renewal of the institution. The involved parties aim at change in terms of external adaptation and internal integration through self-reflection, learning, identity creation and reinterpretation. The foundation for change is thus more practical such as reflected in this definition:

> "Underlying any theory of change – and the specific change project of practitioners for that matter – is a strategy for changing organisations. By strategy I refer to the coherent approach, or the pattern, the combination of methods and techniques, applied in the attempt to push organisations in the desired direction. The strategy

is not necessary formulated as plans, but can be deduced from the actual patterns of action..." (Borum 1995:15).

In *Strategier for organisationsændring* [Strategies for Organisational Change] Borum (1995) discusses four major categories of change strategies:

- the technical-rational change strategy
- the humanistic change strategy including two variants: organisational development and cultural influence
- the political change strategy
- the explorative change strategy

The ideas and visions expressed by the institution's managers and staff seem primarily to fall within the humanistic and, to a certain extent, the explorative change strategies.

The humanistic change strategy is singled out due to its contents of solution method in principle. It concerns modification of interaction and communication processes, such as self-reflection, learning processes and the creation of new identity which are key elements of the change project. The technological change components of this strategy are also in keeping with the involved parties' perception of the elements of change (i.e. rooted in groups, based on consensus, focused on new forms of information, training, socialisation, and finally measured by behaviour as the expression of basic values). Likewise certain parts of the institution's change projects can be contained within Borum's explorative change strategy.

Understanding the concept of change and the concept of the learning organisation has required great efforts and much work from the staff. Therefore it is evident that their professional and perhaps also personal identities will be tied to these change processes and the outcomes. In effect of the concrete changes, the staff may be in the process of developing a "forerunner" institution and consequently an identity as innovator in the field of social work.

Let us return to the construction of understanding and preparing the specific change process.

The institution's staff expected prior to thematic workshops to gain a reasonable knowledge of the concept of the learning organisation, and to be able to focus on conditions related to the residents, the work groups and the institution in different ways. In effect they expected to be able to work with the implementation of specific innovation and change processes.

After the first thematic workshop in May 1998 at which various understandings of the concept of the learning organisation were introduced and discussed in the work groups, the liaison committee at the institution decided that the daily work groups should continue working with the understanding of the learning organisation as reflected in Pedler, Burgoyne and Boydell *The Learning Company. A Strategy for Sustainable Development* (1991). In the book, the concept is referred to as the *blueprint*, which includes eleven elements or dimensions.

Meetings were organised at which the four work groups (in the following referred to as the annex group, the ground floor group, the pavilion group and the first floor group) were to select five-seven of the elements/dimensions for continued processing. These meetings took place in August 1998.

The work groups ekspressed a desire for continuing to work with the following dimensions:

The annex group:
Participative policy making
Informating
Enabling structures
Boundary Workers as Environmental Scanners
Self-development opportunities for all

The ground floor group:
Participative policy making
Formative accounting and control
Enabling structures
Learning climate
Self-development opportunities for all

The pavilion group:
Informating
Enabling structures
Learning climate
Self-development opportunities for all

The first floor group:
Participative policy making
Formative accounting and control
Boundary workers as environmental scanners
Learning climate
Self-development opportunities for all

Prior to the next round of meetings (three) two project groups were formed. In order to facilitate transversal cooperation the project groups were formed as follows: Project group 1 consisted of the ground floor group and the first floor group, and project group 2 of the annex group and the pavilion group.

At the meetings after the first thematic workshop, the participants worked on interpreting the dimensions and give them contents. The groups related the dimensions to the everyday life at the institution by rewording the dimensions. In this context many concepts were clarified, problems identified and proposals for new approaches presented.

The thematic workshop in November 1998 was organised with presentations and group discussions of the theoretical foundation for the change project. It should include the following issues:

- organisation theory and organisational development
- structure and processes
- decision-making processes
- communication
- culture

This agenda was comprehensive for a one-day thematic workshop and the latter three items were discussed at a subsequent thematic workshop. Even though the workshop in November primarily dealt with concepts and models, it was nevertheless the occasion of a lively and serious debate on the relevance of these concepts and models for the daily work and the coming changes in the institution.

On the agenda for the thematic workshop in December 1998 were the last three items of the November agenda and discussions on organisational change. The latter should take place in work groups. First in mixed work groups, i.e. groups composed across the daily work groups, and later on in the daily work groups.

Based on the outcome of the previous thematic workshop, the groups were asked to present proposals for improvements of:

a) The everyday lives of the residents
b) Everyday innovations for the group (work group)
c) Innovations improving

- the everyday life of the individual employee
- the group's way of functioning
- the cohesion and strength of the institution

Four mixed groups were formed, that is, groups composed across the daily work groups. It is characteristic, though not surprising, that the groups' summaries almost exclusively focused on the residents. One of the employees says "It is difficult suddenly having to work with ourselves. We are used to giving priority to the residents." To the external observer there is no doubt that issues related to the residents are given high priority within the institution's organisational culture. Managers and employees are quite aware that core services to the residents must be of the highest quality. What are the proposals for improving the everyday lives of the residents? The proposal is legio and below there are a few examples:

- increased demands and responsibility – higher quality of life
- more time for the residents when they are at home, i.e. be prepared (have time) when the residents return from work
- flexibility toward the individual resident
- revise agreements currently
- we must be good at noticing what the residents want and are good at and give them responsibility
- new physical settings
- the residents must learn to choose. Can we fulfil the choices? How many choices are realistic?
- it is perhaps an idea to get "consultants" from other groups to participate in a discussion on the organising of one's group
- proposal: We can go shopping – also in the evening – with the residents.

When it comes to improvements for the individual employee, the work group or the institution, the responses are fewer though clear and central in relation to innovations in the institution. Some proposals for improvements concern working hours, functions, work processes and ways of functioning. Others concern the need for more collective activities, such as visits, vacations, breaks, and Christmas lunch. Yet others concern time for discussing expectations, norms, shared values, and – proposed by all the groups – regular collective thematic workshops.

The second round of group work on the thematic workshop was based on the daily work groups that were given the following task:

Present three scenarios for the development of the institution:

a) Scenario 1: few and limited innovations
b) Scenario 2: a moderate number and scope of innovations
c) Scenario 3: many and comprehensive innovations

Use key words related to the residents, the employees, the group, the management, and the institution.

Feedback from the various groups demonstrated that they had a clear sense of which development processes the various scenarios would involve. Their comments were actually quite impressive. One group presented the few and limited innovations in scenario 1 as a "vicious circle", innovations in scenario 2 as necessary innovations if the institutions should be able to manage recognised problems, and innovations in scenario 3 as preconditions for constructing a "forerunner" institution.

After the third thematic workshop the work groups (pavilion, annex, ground floor and summerhouse (previously first floor)) were asked to choose five subjects/areas that they found most important to change and with which they would like to continue to work. The five subjects should be chosen among proposals that were the outcomes of group work 1 on the third thematic workshop (December 1998). This resulted in nineteen proposals. The pedagogical committee in the institution was subsequently asked to read the nineteen proposals and work out a list of subjects for further processing. The committee produced seven subjects (listed below) and each employee was asked to single out in order of priority three subject groups that s/he would like to work with. Five subject groups are established of each four and at the most six employees. The aim is that at least two work groups are represented in each of the subject groups.

Subject 1: Staff care   Choose A, B, C:
Café – exercise – solarium – massage
Possibility for coffee/tea, soft drinks – refrigerator
External masseur once a month
Solarium paid individually
Minor library with technical books
Place – kitchen/pause, first floor and one of the vacant rooms

Staff care
The break could be scheduled differently
Courses (one from each group participates jointly if
both are interested in the subject)
Embellishment of the surroundings – colours, art
A collective health day with/without the residents

Staff care activities
Attractive rooms for the staff (computer games, books, journals)
Better utilization of space (common rooms)
Internal/external events (tours, concerts, cinema, etc.)
Staff club

Subject 2: External partners of collaboration/consultants
What can we expect of each other and how closely is it relevant to cooperate to give the residents optimal conditions?
Cooperation implies, for instance, workshop, psychiatry, special counselling, a mutual forum for ideas.

Cooperation with the workshop:
- courses
- thematic days
- understanding each other's work
- senior policy (know-how about cooperation can later on be marketed)

Subject 3: The residents' fields of responsibility:
To what extent can we make the residents responsible for themselves?
Are we permitted to interfere with the behaviour of other groups?
The above is a proposal for a collective theme day.

Communicating experiences:
From group to group, communication of special knowledge/skills (possible from institution to institution)
Projects on collective theme days.

Restructuring of work processes:
Is it possible to restructure the practical tasks leaving us with more time for educational work (e.g. by hiring external cleaners)?

Subject 4: **Cross-group activities:**
- Holiday excursions
- Day/evening activities
- Café
- Room for physical exercise
- Massage
- The single groups are responsible for a given activity.

Hobby room:
Workshop. Suggestion: A room is organised in continuation of the garage, possibly on the loft. Materials are fetched from the recycling centre.
Each has his/her own tool box.
Workbench in the loft. Free space for the residents – community workshop.
Everybody interested can use the room. Tidying-up twice a year.

Leisure time activity:
Proposal for evening classes on e.g. new activities
Collective arrangements across groups
More activities out of the house.

Subject 5 **Enabling structures:**
Staff <-> staff. Staff <-> **management**
Are we sufficiently good at using the sources of information we have?
Day-to-day, week-to-week, newsletters, annual plan, etc.
It is important to be able to benefit from a positive dialogue in which we draw on our experiences.
We should be open and attentive to "gray zones" making it possible to describe these and render them visible.

Give and receive positive and negative criticism – can we do that?

Meeting structure:
- Agenda
- Follow-up on decisions
- Chairing the meetings
- Change of meeting fora
- Change of "structure" – duration, contents
- Inspiration across groups

Subject 6: **Communication – Staff <-> residents**
Better understanding of the single resident's communicative skills – signals,
including greater co-determination, genuine choices.
Will better communication make the everyday life less conflictual?
Do we address the residents with dignity?
How can we improve/change these things in the everyday life?
Do we use the possibilities at our disposal at e.g. meetings with the residents, etc.?

Communication: Resident <-> resident
We wish the residents to demonstrate greater respect, responsibility and care of each other. Which are the strongest types of communication (signals) among the residents?
How great responsibilities in relation to conflicts are the residents capable of assuming?
"Educationist-free zone" – do we have that?

Subject 7: **What is the core of the profession?**
Make a description of the everyday life of Ms. Smith viewed in relation to a description of the everyday life of one of the residents.
What does it take to make it a good day for the resident?
It required resources, structure (educational), attitudes, respect and psychology in order for the resident to acquire the confidence and
feeling of security that makes "his or her everyday life optimal".

Self-development
- The group will work with the framework for the individual self-development
- Framework for personal development interviews
- Framework for course policies (e.g. minimum two participants per course)
- Summary of courses one has participated in
- Courses of dual purposes – professional and personal

Educational café
- Inspiration
- Presentation of literature
- Film
- Discussions on educational subjects

Name: _____

All employees, with the exception of members of the liaison committee, have prioritised subject with which the wish to continue to work. The prioritisation resulted in the establishment of work groups on the following subjects:

Communication (the dimension Informating). Weigh on communication among the staff and among the residents.

Enabling Structures. Weight on structures enabling processes of importance for the interpersonnel relations, relations between personnel and management, and in relation to the meeting structure.

Staff care and staff activities. (Reward Flexibility). Weight on conditions that can contribute to the creation of a good working environment for the employees.

External partners of collaboration/consultants and collaboration with workshop(s). (Boundary Workers as Environmental Scanners). Weight on securing the best possible information on contacts of importance for the everyday lives of the residents in and outside the institution.

The prioritisation also entailed the de-selection of subjects, such as subjects related to the key dimensions learning opportunities and strategy. It is not my impression that the staff found these subject uninteresting, but rather that strategy is perceived in part as the foundation of the already establish collaboration project on personnel development, and in part as contained in the conditions subject to negotiation between the county's administration/political level and the institution. Finally, most of the staff probably found the gap between strategy formulation and the everyday practice too wide.

The reasons for de-selecting subjects under the key dimension learning opportunities is probably that this dimension has been given great attention and has been discussed during the entire project in relation to the concept of the learning organisation. On the other hand, the prioritised subjects demonstrate that the employees want changes in a number of areas where these can be put into effect immediately and the leverage effect will be high.

Evaluation of the Institution's Work Under the Concept of the Learning Organisation

In the previous section we compared the institution's objectives for the change project with the results of the preliminary work focusing on the implementation of particular prioritised change processes. In the following we shall examine to what extent the institution's efforts under the concept of the learning organisation tally with a number of criteria presented in publications on the field.

In *Viden i virksomheden* (1987), [Knowledge in the company] Sveiby and Risling term these criteria success factors. These factors are the common features for successful professional organisations and comprise:

1. Management taking part in the daily work.
2. Quality and quality control.
3. Respect of knowledge.
4. Combination of professional competence and operations competence.
5. A strong and clearly defined culture.
6. Focus on one field of knowledge.
7. Systems for preserving knowledge
8. To stake on developing the employees.
9. Program for personnel turnover.
10. Fixed structures.

The management of the institution performs the strategic, financial, and administrative functions, but also takes part in the daily work.

The management and the staff are seriously reflecting on quality and quality control. This includes the life quality of the residents, the institution as a workplace for employees and management, and the institution's ability to develop it self and meet the growing external demands for quality.

Employees and management agree on the necessity for continuously increasing professional knowledge and for transforming professional competence into the best possible quality of life for the residents. They hold the same understanding of the change project, that is, they insist on that the change process must lead to both process development and visible changes in the everyday life of the institution.

The culture of the institution must be characterised as strong. It is rooted in the professionalism of social welfare workers, in responsibility, in participation, and in reflection.

The institution has no system for gathering and keeping up knowledge. The basic attitude is that employees and managers can achieve new knowledge through contact with others, and other interested in the institution's knowledge and experience must have access to it.

The institution stakes on developing the employees. The change project is an expression of this attitude.

The institution has no distinct program for replacement of key members of the staff, they are highly aware of the need for flexibility now and in the future. This awareness is reflected in their work with the organisation structure, which will probably centre on coherence in various functions and processes.

The institution's culture is relatively flat. A county institution must necessarily operate with the division of work into positions/functions, but the residential institution is not hierarchical. In connection with the implementation of the change project, the organising principle has been change to that of a project organisation. The organising comprises four project groups whose members come from different work groups, and a steering group consisting of the liaison committee. The educational committee supports the steering group.

Comparing the success factors with the institution's general characteristics and practices in working under the concept of the learning organisation shows that they are consistent and hence that the institution is strong and development oriented.

In *Signalement af den lærende organisation – billeder og perspectiver* (1997) [Description of the learning organisation – images and perspectives] Brandi and Hildebrandt give a solid presentation of the central contributions to the concept of the learning organisation. Furthermore, the authors conclude by asking three fundamental questions to the concept:

1. What is a learning organisation?
   We need more plausible and empirically justified definitions of what characterises the learning organisation, including more precise formulations of how to work in practice with the implementation of the learning organisation.

2. What is management in the learning organisation?
   We need more exact directions on what management is and how it is practiced in learning organisations.

3. To what extent is an organisation learning?
   The great question is measurement: We need to be able to assess to what extent the organisation has developed within a given period and the speed of learning at a given point in time.

In working under the concept of the learning organisation, the institution started from Pedler et al.'s (1991) eleven dimensions (the *blueprint*). The staff deselected Senge's (1990) five disciplines because it would be too time-consuming to make the disciplines concrete and because they were uncertain of how to relate the institution's tasks to the disciplines. However, the staff was well aware of the fact that working under the concept of the learning organisation based on Pedler et al.'s eleven dimensions would also be time consuming. Several of the dimensions were immediately seen as more concrete, that is, they would be easier to relate to the practice of the institution and make the framework for the change and learning processes on which to base new tasks. The new tasks were meant to be the outcome of the overall project. With the aim of improving the life quality the residents and their opportunities of choice, improving the institution as a workplace, and the institution's preparedness for change, the staff and the managers prioritised four dimensions as the starting points of the change and learning process.

Informating was given priority in that the total amount of information was to be the core of change and learning in relation to communication both between staff and residents and among the residents.

Enabling Structures were probably given priority as a platform for existing as well as new processes related to the implementation of the project. Emphasis was given to the types of enabling structures concerning the relationship between staff units, between staff and management, and the meeting structure.

Reward Flexibility was prioritised in a somewhat surprising variant, that is, as personnel care and personnel activities. However, it is easy to understand the purpose of this prioritisation. Improvements of the physical and mental working climate are meant to be "gatekeepers" for the objectives of the overall project.

Finally priority was given to the dimension *Boundary Workers as Environmental Scanners*. This concerns gathering information through contact with external partners of cooperation and consultants and by cooperating with workshop(s). The change and learning involved aim at gathering information, which again can be turned into change and learning.

The institution's management form in general and in relation to the project is characterised by participation, responsibility, quality, and self-development. The organisation structure is flat. In connection with the project the management process and the work groups are organised along the principles for project organisation. The management makes great efforts to enable to development of the work groups and the implementation of the project. The management follows up conscientiously on the current preparatory phase and proposals for the implementation of the various changes and learning processes.

In order to answer the question of "to what extent is organisation learning" a questionnaire was prepared covering several aspects of the change and learning project. The data show that in the last year the institution has continuously confronted itself with new aspects of its operations and development. In effect the employees and the managers have experienced new opportunities for self-development at the individual level, at group level, and at the level of the institution. At this point in time it is difficult to state exact measures for learning and speed of learning. But having visited and made observations in the institution I am convinced that new aspects of change and learning have been put on the agenda and that the intentions of the overall project have been strengthened.

In the final publications that I shall include in this premature evaluation, the criteria are more unclear and comprehensive. These publications give examples of the practical application of the concept of the learning organisation. They are: Neergaard, van Hauen and Kastberg *Den lærende organisation i praksis* (1998 [The learning organisation in practice] and Cook, Staniforth and Stewart *The Learning Organisation in the Public Services* (1997). For reasons of space it is not possible to go through all the examples. The immediate impression is that the cases take as their starting point specific problems but limited flexibility and freedom characterise the processes for the participants.

As to the present project we can only deal with the most important phases of the project. The first phase concerned attempts to arrive at an applicable understanding of the concept of the learning organisation and other relevant organisational issues. The second phase concerned coupling desired changes for the residents, the employees and the institution to the framework for change in the form of the concept of the learning organisation. The third phase concerned the work groups preparing the actual change process in terms of informating, enabling structures, personnel care/activities and finally information on partners of cooperation. The coming forth phase concerns the actual implementation of the changes.

The immediate impression of the effects of the institution's work under the concept of the learning organisation is that it has facilitated interpretations and attitudes in relation to the residents, the institution as a workplace, and the institution's change opportunities. In addition the institution is also opening up toward transversal dialogue and cooperation. In a higher degree than the publications mentioned above, flexibility and personal freedom characterise the change project of the residential institution.

The institution has all the elements of change preparedness in place. By implementing the actual change process it is highly probable that it will become a good example of how to transform the concept of the learning organisation into practice. Compared to the cases discussed in the above-mentioned publications, the institution is doing well.

Prior to the start of the change project, the institution much resembled other institution in the country for people of serious physical and mental handicaps. Rules, routines, hierarchy and very few changes characterised the everyday life. An entirely traditional organisation. Nevertheless, the management recognised that even though daily operations were/are governed by rules and regulations there is room for change. This combined with the management and the staff clarifying opportunities and limitations created the platform for initiating changes under the concept of the learning organisation. And they want the change project to be expressed in everyday language and to include everybody in the residential institution.

Tentative Evaluations of the Project Process

In connection with the thematic workshops and the work group activities, consultant Anja Amdisen, Special Counselling, South Jutland County, conducted a questionnaire survey among the managers and the employees. (Anja Amdisen is also a member of the steering committee). This survey was to constitute the basis for an evaluation of the process and for proposing future focus areas (see Pedersen 1999).

Findings from the survey show that more than three-thirds of the respondents expect the process of the learning organisation to lead to changes for both employees and residents. More than nine-tenths of the respondents state that they can use what they have learned about the learning organisation in their work. On the other hand, only fifty percent of the respondents expect the process of the learning organisation to have continuous effects. One interpretation is that even though the work has involved future focus areas then half of the respondents do not know what to expect of the continuous process. The reason could be that future focus areas are not yet clarified or that the objectives for the areas are unclear and hence the expectations also unclear or non-existent.

However, the respondents are much clearer about the prioritised areas that are informating, enabling structures, personnel care/activities and external partners of cooperation – areas that the work groups have been discussing. The communication functions though greater awareness of contents, scale and forms need to be developed. This must be related to the social cohesion and the daily work. There are few comments on enabling structures, but several respondents stress transversal and new forms of cooperation. In addition, several respondents point to that during the process they have started to think about other relations of cooperation, about opportunities and limitations, and about different approaches to solving problems. In terms of personnel care, several respondents state that closer cooperation among the units and more collective activities will imply that the employees become stronger affiliated with the institution. To the questions about external partners of cooperation several respondents find that there is a need for alternating much more between the institution and the workshops which would lead to better understanding and fewer negative expectations among the partners. However, within the same areas many respondents are still confused or holding back. This is only natural. The clear understandings and critical attitudes toward specific areas for further development emerge from the group work.

A Tentative Conclusion

If I had to answer the question "Does the institution harbour no sceptics?" at this point in time the answer would be no. There will always be employees who believe stronger in the project than others or who are more committed, but no one in the institution doubts that changes will be sustainable and comprehensive. There is no doubt about the objectives that the changes must fulfil.

What has been successful and what has failed? Both employees and managers have put great efforts into the development of the project. While working under the concept of the learning organisation they have continuously been open to new perspectives. Is there nothing that can stop "the wild thought" and the motivation for change? Yes, there are several things. Therefore it is important to clarify what to emphasis in order to secure motivation and the fascination of "wild thoughts".

The following proposals for future efforts are general in that potential proposals directed toward a specific level would be too numerous and too comprehensive in the early phase of the change processes. The work groups will work out proposals for this level.

If the various proposals for changes are allowed to live their own lives, that is, if they are not integrated into the common goals and perspectives of the institution, they will take the shape of isolated changes. Such isolated changes will represent a threat to the work under the concept of the learning organisation. In turn the continuous and accelerating changes will be subject to limitations due to the lack of a frame of reference. So far nothing seems to indicate that the groups will cease to share interests or that they will lose interest in communicating experiences.

What will be going on at the institution in the future? Managers and employees must see to that the continuous and accelerating changes under collective goals and perspectives are given collective prioritisation, that is, that the stroke of initiated changes is compared to the realistic possibilities. Few and minor changes in accordance with collective goals and perspectives and the participants' opportunities are preferable to huge empire-like changes that might become challenges for even super-motivated work groups.

References

Argyris, C. (1962): *Interpersonal Competence and Organisational Effectiveness.* Dorsey Press, Homewood 1962.

Argyris, C. (1976a): *Theories of Action That Inhibit Individual Learning.* American Psychologist 39; 638-654.

Argyris, C. (1976b): *Single-Loop and Double-Loop Models in Research in Decision Making.* Administrative Science Quarterly 21; 363-375.

Argyris, C. & D.Schön (1978): *Organisational Learning: A Theory of Action Perspective.* Addison-Wesley, Reading 1978.

Brandi, B. & S.Hildebrandt (1997): *Et signalement af den lærende organisation. - Billeder og perspektiver.* Ledelse i Dag nr.28/1997, p.320-332.

Borum, F. (1995): *Strategier for organisationsændring.* Handelshøjskolens Forlag, København, 1995.

Christensen, A. (red.) (1997): *Den lærende organisations begreber og praksis. Læring - Refleksion - Ændring.* Aalborg Universitetsforlag, Aalborg, 1997.

Cook, J., D. Staniforth & J. Stewart (ed.) (1997): *The Learning Organisation in the Public Services.* Gower, Hampshire, 1997.

Hedberg, B. (1981): *How Organisations Learn and Unlearn?* In Nyström & Starbuch (eds.) Handbook of Organisatonal Design, p.8-27, Oxford University Press, 1981.

Hildebrandt, S. (1997): *Træk af den lærende organisation.* I "Ledelse 97", Børsens Forlag, København 1997.

Kanter. R.M. (1983): *The Change Masters. Corporate Entrepreneurs at Work.* Routledge, London & New York 1983.

Kolb, D. (1991): *Organisational Psychology. An Experiential Approach.* Prentice-Hall, Englewood Cliffs, N.J.1991.

Morgan, G. (1986): *Images of Organisation.* Sage Publications, London, 1986.

Morsing, M. (1995): *Omstigning til paradis? Oticon i processen fra Hierarki til spaghetti.* Handelshøjskolens Forlag, København 1995.

Neergaard, C. (1994): *Creating a Learning Organisation. A Comprehensive Framework.* Ph.D. Thesis. Department of Production, Aalborg University, Denmark, October 1994.

Neergaard, C., F. Van Hauen & B. Kastberg (1997): *Den lærende organisation i praksis.* Industriens Forlag, København, 1997.

Pedersen, J.D. (1999): *- af mennesker, - for mennesker, - med mennesker, - inspireres vi til nu'et og fremtiden.* Sønderjyllands Amt, Vilstrupvej 120, 1999.

Pedler, M. (ed.) (1983): *Action Learning in Practice.* Gower, Aldershot 1983.

Pedler, M., J. Burgoyne & T. Boydell (1991): *The Learning Company. A Stragegy for Sustainable Development.* McGraw-Hill, Maidenhead, 1991.

Revans, R.W. (1980): *Action Learning.* Blond & Briggs, 1980.

Revans, R.W. (1982): *The Origins and Growth of Action Learning.* Studentlitteratur, 1982.

Rohlin, L., P. TH. Skärvad & S. Å. Nilsson (1994): *Strategiskt Lederskap i Lärsamhället.* MiL Publishers, Vasbyholm, 1994.

Riis, J.O. & J.Frick (1991): *Organisational Learning: A Neglected Dimension of Production.* Management Systems Design Proceedings on the APMS 90 conference in Finland, Edited by Eero Elorante, North Holland, 1991.

Riis, J.O. & C.Neergaard (1994): *The Learning Company: A New Manufacturing digm.* A Paper Presented at The Annual CIM Europe In Copenhagen, Oct.1994.

Senge, P. (1990): *The Fifth Discipline. The Art and Pratice of the learning Organisation.* Century Business, London, 1990.

Sveiby, K.E. & A. Riesling (1986): *Kunskabsföretaget.* Liber, 1986.

Sveiby, K.E. (1990): *Kundskabsledning.* Affärsvärlden, 1990.

Van Hauen, F., V. Strandgaard & B. Kastberg (1995): *Den lærende organisation. - Om evnen til at skabe kollektiv forandring.* Industriens Forlag, København, 1995.

Conclusion

The learning perspective

It has become common practice for employees and managers in many organisations to add a learning perspective to their everyday activities. Many of these activities are routine, but instead of just getting on with them as routine work, it is possible to learn new things in connection with them. The point of departure for adding this learning perspective is to "see" the activity beyond the routine. In other words, the point of departure should be reflection on the strength of problem- solving in relation to existing activities and on possible problem-solutions in relation to new patterns of activities.

As employees and managers, we can learn new things from or in relation to the process of production or performance. We can learn new things through our participation in the construction of the organisational processes concerning strategy, policies, management, decision-making, information sharing etc. In connection with these processes, it is important that the preconditions for participation are present and that they are real. Participation demands a foundation and well-defined goal. These processes can be developed and shaped internally in the organisation.

We can learn through our contacts, both internal in our organisation, and external contacts. Through such contacts, employees and managers develop internal and external networks, which in turn can create the foundation for organisational learning and change.

Through their examples, the authors of this book have shown that working according to the concept *the learning organisation* or using organisational learning as a theoretical frame, requires commitment and preparation. The examples also demonstrate that the approach to this task can vary a good deal. Furthermore, their examples tend to single out the most complicated stage of the task. That is, the stage when the diagnosis and preparations have been completed and the central areas for further work mapped out. At this stage, the employees and managers should be fully informed about the application of their experience and knowledge in the learning organisation and organisational learning. They probably have some expectations in relation to the further work involving the concept of the learning organisation, but their understanding of the overall goals for this further work may still be uncertain. In their examples, the authors seem to point out diagnosis, preparation and mapping-out of central areas as the crucial stage for presenting the potentials of the process and an opportunity for expanding the frontiers of those possibilities. If the understanding of the overall goals for the further work remains unclear, the explanation may be found in the initial considerations of realism in the main outlines of central areas for learning processes and organisational changes. It may be a question of handling uncertainty about how the results of certain processes and changes will function in everyday life.

It is beyond doubt that working under the concept *the learning organisation* or using organisational learning as a theoretical frame creates uncertainty for some employees and managers. But on the other hand, working in such an organisation also offers great opportunities and challenges to many more employees and managers.

Once employees and managers in most organisations have tried working under the concept *the learning organisation* or using organisational learning as theoretical frame, they will most likely not be willing to go back to a more traditional form. In spite of all uncertainties, the advantages of learning processes and organisational changes will probably be too large. In none of the authors examples appear statements from employees and managers that can be interpreted as a wish to return to the previous form for working.

Authors:

Allan Christensen, born 1943, Cand. Scient.Soc. from University of Copenhagen 1974.
Employed by Aalborg University, Department of Sociology, Social Work and Organisation as an ass. Professor.

Søren Keldorff, born 1945, Cand. Psych. from University of Århus 1975.
Employed by Aalborg University, Department of Sociology, Social Work and Organisation as an ass. Professor.

Erik Laursen, born 1947, Mag.Scient.Soc. from University of Copenhagen 1974.
Employed by Aalborg University, Department of Learning as a Professor.

Jens Lind, born 1948, Cand.Rer.Soc. from Odense University 1978 (Now University of Southern Denmark) and Ph.D. from Aalborg University 1985.
Employed by Aalborg University, Department of Sociology, Social Work and Organisation as an ass. Professor.

Ove Mølvadgaard, born 1944, Cand Phil. and Scient. from University of Århus.
Earlier employed by Aalborg University, Department of Sociology, Social Work and Organisation as an ass. Professor.

Kjeld Nielsen, born 1949, Cand.Rer.Soc. from Odense University 1977 (now University of Southern Denmark).
Employed by Aalborg University, Department of Sociology, Social Work and Organisation as an ass. Professor.

Jan Brødslev Olsen, born 1958, Cand. Mag. and Ph.D. from Aalborg University 1993. Employed by Aalborg University, Department of Sociology, Social Work and Organisation as an ass. Professor.

Søren Voxted, born 1961, Cand.Merc. from Aalborg University 1991 and Ph.D. from Aalborg University 2005.